FOOD SOVEREIGNTY IN CANADA

Creating Just and Sustainable Food Systems

edited by
Hannah Wittman
Annette Aurélie Desmarais
& **Nettie Wiebe**

Fernwood Publishing • Halifax & Winnipeg

Editing: Eileen Young
Cover Design: John van der Woude
Printed and bound in Canada by Hignell Book Printing

Published in Canada by Fernwood Publishing
32 Oceanvista Lane
Black Point, Nova Scotia, B0J 1B0
and 748 Broadway Avenue, Winnipeg, Manitoba, R3G 0X3
www.fernwoodpublishing.ca

Fernwood Publishing Company Limited gratefully acknowledges the financial support of the Government of Canada through the Canada Book Fund, the Canada Council for the Arts, the Nova Scotia Department of Tourism and Culture, the Manitoba Department of Culture, Heritage and Tourism under the Manitoba Publishers Marketing Assistance Program and the Province of Manitoba, through the Book Publishing Tax Credit, for our publishing program.

Library and Archives Canada Cataloguing in Publication

Food sovereignty in Canada : creating just and sustainable food systems / edited by Hannah Wittman, Annette Desmarais, Nettie Wiebe.

Includes bibliographical references and index.
ISBN 978-1-55266-443-8

1. Food sovereignty--Canada. 2. Sustainable agriculture--Canada. 3. Alternative agriculture--Canada. I. Wittman, Hannah, 1973- II. Desmarais, Annette Aurélie III. Wiebe, Nettie

HD9000.5.F737 2011 338.10971 C2011-903224-4

CONTENTS

ABOUT THE AUTHORS

Herb Barbolet is an Associate with both the Centre for Sustainable Community Development and the Dialogue Centre at Simon Fraser University. Herb helped found and works with Local Food First, a consortium of organizations developing a business approach to re-localizing our food supply. He is also a member of the Vancouver Food Policy Council and Vancouver Peak Oil Executive, as well as Research Associate with the Canadian Centre for Policy Alternatives, where he co-authored *Every Bite Counts.*

Naomi Beingessner is a Master's student in Justice Studies at the University of Regina. Her research focuses on food sovereignty and alternative land tenure in Saskatchewan.

Terry Boehm is a grain farmer in Saskatchewan. He is president of the National Farmers Union of Canada. He has worked for many years on issues concerning seeds and intellectual property, as well as transport, orderly marketing and supply management.

Annette Aurélie Desmarais was a farmer in Canada for fourteen years. She is Associate Professor of International Studies at the University of Regina. She worked as a technical support person with La Vía Campesina for over a decade, recently published *La Vía Campesina* (2007) and co-edited *Food Sovereignty: Reconnecting Food, Nature and Community* (2010). Her research focuses on rural movements, food sovereignty, gender and rural development.

Rachel Engler-Stringer is an Assistant Professor in the Department of Community Health and Epidemiology at the University of Saskatchewan. She has worked on food sovereignty in Canada for Heifer International and the Community-University Institute for Social Research.

Harriet Friedmann is Professor of Sociology and Fellow of the Centre for International Studies at the University of Toronto. She is a past Chair of the Toronto Food Policy Council and a present member, as well as a "facilitator of reflection" in "Community of Food Practice," which works towards justice and sustainability through food system renewal. Her research focuses on the history of food regimes, international trade, politics of global and local certification and standards and how societies can achieve sustainable, socially just agriculture.

Yolanda Hansen is the Coordinator of the Community Research Unit at the University of Regina. She studied community gardens and food sovereignty in Saskatchewan for her MA in Justice Studies.

Cathleen Kneen has been Chair of the Steering Committee of Food Secure Canada since 2006, and serves on the Management Team for the People's Food Policy Project, a pan-Canadian initiative to create a grassroots-based food policy for Canada rooted in the principles of food sovereignty. She is also the Canadian "focal point" for the IPC (International Planning Committee on Food Sovereignty). Since the 1970s she has been involved in community organizing, writing and speaking about food and farming, and, with her husband Brewster, produces a monthly newsletter of food system analysis, *The Ram's Horn*.

André Magnan is Assistant Professor in the Department of Sociology and Social Studies at the University of Regina. His principle research interest is the political economy of prairie agriculture, with a focus on the politics of collective marketing and new relations linking farmers, corporations and the Canadian Wheat Board.

Diane Martz is Director of the Research Ethics Office in the Office of the VP Research at the University of Saskatchewan and a research faculty member with the Saskatchewan Population Health and Evaluation Research Unit (SPHERU). She has extensive experience working in community-based research, focusing on the social, economic and cultural dimensions of rural health and well-being.

Hilary Moore has been farming full time since graduating from university thirteen years ago. Since she started farming, she has taught, supported and encouraged many people who are interested in farming, growing community gardens or simply gardening for themselves. She has also spent time promoting and implementing schoolyard gardens as outdoor classrooms. She is in her third year as President of National Farmers Union (NFU), Local 310. She is also the Ontario Representative on the International Planning Committee within the NFU.

Dawn Morrison works as a Community Self-Development Facilitator in *Secwepemc* territory — her ancestral home — where she combines her educational and professional background in the areas of horticulture, ethno-botany, adult instruction and business management with principles of Indigenous food sovereignty and eco-cultural restoration. She is the Coordinator/Director of the B.C. Food Systems Network Working Group on Indigenous Food Sovereignty and Community Facilitator of the Around the Kitchen Table Project Aboriginal Women's Group working on HIV/AIDS Awareness and Prevention.

Darrin Qualman lives near Dundurn, Saskatchewan, where he farmed in the 1980s and 1990s. He served as the Executive Secretary and Director of Research for Canada's National Farmers Union from 1996 to 2010. His publications include

The Farm Crisis, Bigger Farms, and the Myths of "Competition" and "Efficiency" (2003); *The Farm Crisis and Corporate Profits* (2005); and *The Farm Crisis and the Cattle Sector* (2008). He is currently working on a book about energy flows in civilizations.

Carla Roppel is Communications Specialist with the University of Saskatchewan. Recently, she has worked in communications with Saskatchewan health regions, and as a researcher, writer and editor for the National Farmers Union. In various capacities, Carla has coordinated and facilitated a number of international farmer-to-farmer linkages, exchanges and workshops for the National Farmers Union.

Nettie Wiebe is an organic farmer and Professor of Ethics at St. Andrew's College, University of Saskatchewan. She was Women's President of the National Farmers Union, and then served four years as the president of the NFU — the first and only woman to have led a national farmers' organization in Canada. She also served as a member of La Vía Campesina's International Coordinating Commission (ICC). She is actively involved in local and national politics in Canada. Co-editor of *Food Sovereignty: Reconnecting Food, Nature and Community* (2010), her research focuses on agrarian feminism and the intersection of environmental, agricultural and women's issues in rural communities.

Kevin Wipf is Executive Director of the National Farmers Union. He is also completing his PhD in Political Science at the University of Alberta. He has spent his academic and professional career examining agriculture and food policy, and is very interested in exploring alternatives to our current industrial agri-food model.

Hannah Wittman is Assistant Professor of Sociology and Latin American Studies at Simon Fraser University. She conducts collaborative research on local food systems, farmer networks and agrarian citizenship in British Columbia, and in Latin America with Brazil's Landless Rural Workers Movement (MST) and La Vía Campesina. She co-edited *Food Sovereignty: Reconnecting Food, Nature and Community* (2010); her research interests are in environmental sociology, agrarian citizenship and agrarian social movements.

LIST OF TABLES, BOXES, FIGURES

LIST OF ACRONYMS

AAFC	Agriculture and Agri-Food Canada
AIDA	Agricultural Income Disaster Assistance
ALR	Agricultural Land Reserve
ALUS	Alternative Land Use Services
APF	Agriculture Policy Framework
APHA	American Public Health Association
ASRA	*L'assurance stabilisation des revenus agricoles*
AWP	Alberta Wheat Pool
BCAFM	B.C. Association of Farmers' Markets
BCCDC	B.C. Centre for Disease Control
BCCMB	B.C. Chicken Marketing Board
BCFPA	B.C. Food Processor Association
BCFSN	B.C. Food Systems Network
BCHLA	B.C. Healthy Living Alliance
BCMAL	B.C. Ministry of Agriculture and Lands
BCPHSA	British Columbia Provincial Health Services Authority
BCSSPA	B.C. Small Scale Processors Association
BSE	Bovine Spongiform Encephalopathy
CAFS	Canadian Association for Food Studies
CAIS	Canadian Agricultural Income Stabilization
CAMC	Canadian Agri-Food Marketing Council
CBAN	Canadian Biotechnology Action Network
CBFO	Community-Based Food Organizations
CETA	Canada-EU Comprehensive Economic and Trade Agreement
CFIA	Canadian Food Inspection Agency
CGA	Canadian Grain Commission
CGC	Canadian Grain Commission
CHEP	Child Hunger and Education Program
CINE	Centre for Indigenous Peoples' Nutrition and Environment
CFA	Canadian Federation of Agriculture
CFIA	Canadian Food Inspection Agency
CFIP	Canadian Farm Income Program
CFS	Community Food Security
CLCN	Coastal Learning Communities Network
CPR	Canadian Pacific Railway
CRAFT	Collaborative Regional Alliance for Farmer Training
CSA	Community Supported Agriculture
CSFS	Centre for Studies in Food Security

CUSTA	Canada-United States Free Trade Agreement
CWB	Canadian Wheat Board
DFO	Department of Fisheries and Oceans
EEFC	East End Food Cooperative
EELC	Everdale Environmental Learning Centre
EFAO	Ecological Farmers Association of Ontario
EIT	Enterprise Infrastructure Traceability
FAO	Food and Agriculture Organization
FBAS	Farm Business Advisory Services
FCC	Farm Credit Canada
FCWB	Friends of the Canadian Wheat Board
FMNCP	Farmers' Market Nutrition and Coupon Project
FSC	Food Secure Canada
GATT	General Agreement on Tariffs and Trade
GENUP	*Groupe d'Études en Nutrition Publique*
GM	Genetically Modified
GMO	Genetically Modified Organism
GPS	Global Positioning System
GTA AAC	Greater Toronto Area Agricultural Action Committee
HMGA	Holland Marsh Growers' Association
IAASTD	International Assessment of Agricultural Knowledge, Science and Technology for Development
ICC	*La Vía Campesina's* International Coordinating Commission
IFSN	Indigenous Food Systems Network
IPC	International Planning Committee on Food Sovereignty
IPR	Intellectual Property Rights
IUNS	International Union of Nutritional Sciences
KAFN	*Kwicksutaineuk Ah-kwa-mish* First Nation
LMFC	Lower Mainland Food Coalition
LVC	La Vía Campesina
MicroFIT	Micro Feed-in Tariff
MIR	Meat Inspection Regulation
MPE	Manitoba Pool Elevators
MST	Brazil's Landless Rural Worker's Movement *(El Movimiento de los Trabajadores Rurales Sin Tierra de Brasil)*
NACC	North American Competitiveness Council
NAFTA	North American Free Trade Agreement
NCCAH	National Collaborating Centre for Aboriginal Health
NDP	New Democratic Party
NFFC	National Family Farm Coalition
NISA	Net Income Stabilization Account
NFU	National Farmers Union
NGO	Non-Governmental Organization
NSNC	Nova Scotia Nutrition Council

OCP	Official Community Plan
OCTA	Ontario Culinary Tourism Alliance
OMAA	Ontario Ministry of Aboriginal Affairs
OMAFRA	Ontario Ministry of Agriculture, Food and Rural Affairs
OPHA	Ontario Public Health Association
PFC	People's Food Commission
PFPP	People's Food Policy Project
PHSA	Provincial Health Services Authority
PNP	Peer Nutrition Program
PWGA	Palliser Wheat Growers Association
rBGH	Bovine Somatatropin
REACH	Regina Education and Action on Child Hunger
RR	Roundup Ready
RVFC	Real Voice for Choice
SOD	Saskatchewan Organic Directorate
SPHERU	Saskatchewan Population Health and Evaluation Research Unit
SPP	Security and Prosperity Partnership of North America
STE	State-Trading Enterprises
SWC	Status of Women Canada
SWP	Saskatchewan Wheat Pool
TILMA	Trade, Investment and Labour Mobility Agreement
TFA	Task Force on Agriculture
TFPC	Toronto Food Policy Council
TFS	Toronto Food Strategy
TRCA	Toronto and Region Conservation Authority Project
TRIPS	Trade-Related Aspects to Intellectual Property Rights
UAF	Urban Aboriginal Framework for Toronto
UGG	United Grain Growers
UPA	*Union des Producteurs Agricoles*
UPOV	International Union for the Protection of New Varieties of Plants
USDA	United States Department of Agriculture
VLGA	Vacant Lot Gardening Association
WFS	World Food Summit
WCWGA	Western Canadian Wheat Growers' Association
WGIFS	Working Group on Indigenous Food Sovereignty
WHPF	World Health Policy Forum
WTO	World Trade Organization

1. NURTURING FOOD SOVEREIGNTY IN CANADA

Nettie Wiebe and Kevin Wipf

The evening news coming into Canadian homes may carry stories of food riots in Mozambique, flooding of farmland in Pakistan or hunger in war-torn Sudan. But there are seldom any stories on domestic food shortages, food related street-riots or major problems with Canadian food supplies. We may occasionally come across news about how many Canadians are now lining up at food banks, but instead of being a story about hungry kids or anxious families suffering food insecurity, these stories are usually framed as economic hardships, rather than as failures in the food system.

The sporadic stories specifically about our food are usually about food safety issues or production problems caused by adverse weather or diseases. The former, such as the 2007 incident where listeriosis-tainted meat from a Maple Leaf plant caused twenty-two deaths, evoked a flurry of interest in that brand and that plant. It was handled with a recall of the contaminated meat, explanations of official regulatory protocols and reassuring publicity about the efficacy of those protocols. It didn't provoke widespread critical examination of the Canadian food system or even of the specific dangers posed by a highly concentrated meat-processing industry in Canada. Food production failures due to droughts, early frosts, too much rain, or diseases are not so much about food as about farm economic hardships, where it is clear that the lost production will be replaced from elsewhere and farmers will deal with their losses. The un-wary eater might well be lulled into believing that all is well in the current Canadian food system.

A more careful consideration reveals a much more complex and troubling story behind the headlines. While the glowing reports of massive and increasing food exports from Canada indicate that we are producing far more food than is needed here, the data from food banks and social agencies reveal that there are growing numbers of citizens who are experiencing food shortages and food insecurity. Food Banks Canada (2010) records an increase of ten percent in food bank use since 1999 with provinces such as Alberta experiencing a 61 percent increase in food bank use since 2008; almost 2.5 million Canadians are classified as food insecure (People's Food Policy Project 2011: 1).

There are other signs of a system in trouble as well: while agrologists, researchers and farmers proudly publicize increasing crop yields and production efficiencies, on-farm revenues continue to trail behind expenses so that the majority of Canadian farms rely on off-farm income to support the farm family and its food producing operation. Furthermore, although the supermarket shelves are loaded with a vast variety of products, the biological diversity of agricultural production is rapidly diminishing (ETCgroup 2009). Also troubling and a key characteristic of the current Canadian food system is the fact that much of what is actually eaten by Canadians comes from elsewhere in the world. Our dinner plates are loaded up from a global smorgasbord.

The global nature of our food system is illustrated in a practical and revealing way by an exercise that we invite you, the reader, to undertake. The assignment is simply to choose some item, or at most a few items, from your everyday diet and research information about its origins, travel, farm-gate pricing, production, processing and retail price. This may appear to be a small, easy task but it invariably turns out to be complex, time-consuming and indeed, almost impossible to complete. Most foods have travelled long and circuitous routes between field and plate; these routes are very difficult to trace. Grapes from Chile, frozen lamb from New Zealand or broccoli from Mexico have travelled thousands of kilometers, often making stops in various warehouses along the way, before arriving on a Canadian dinner table. Such a research project will yield many insights and a good deal of largely fragmented information; it will clearly demonstrate that our food system is complex, opaque and part of a global system.

Because large parts of the Canadian food system are thoroughly integrated into a global food system, the challenges and vulnerabilities of that global system are inescapably ours as well. The sudden spikes in food prices that provoke riots elsewhere create damaging price vicissitudes and real hardships for low-income families here. Although food costs represent less than 12 percent of the average Canadian family income (CFA 2011), food insecurity is a real and growing problem in Canada as food prices rise while incomes stagnate, jobs become less secure and even middle-class household financial security is threatened. In this context, increases in the grocery bills often force changes to food choices, affecting health and well-being.

Foreign commodity and currency speculation and trade disruptions can make or break whole sectors of our agriculture system, displacing food production, processing and farm families in their wake. For example, the increased value of the Canadian dollar compared to its U.S. counterpart, combined with an increase in feed grain costs and changes in country of origin labelling regulations in the United States, have contributed to the collapse and/or consolidation of much of the western Canadian hog industry. As elsewhere in the world, climate change threatens to affect weather and water in the food-growing areas of Canada. Meanwhile, shortages of oil are projected, which certainly cannot be ignored by production systems that rely as heavily on oil as Canadian agriculture does.

Many of the looming threats to human life on the planet are linked to and aggravated, if not generated, by the global food system. The most obvious is the suffering and death due to hunger, malnutrition and attendant diseases. The increased food production garnered from high-input, monocultural agricultural production systems and liberalized trade regimes is failing to resolve this human tragedy, with over one billion people in the world still suffering from hunger (FAO 2010). At the same time, industrialized, export-oriented agriculture, which characterizes much of the Canadian food system, is degrading soils, polluting water, denuding forested areas and undermining biodiversity in fundamental and life-threatening ways.

Our recent book *Food Sovereignty: Reconnecting Food, Nature and Community* describes and analyzes some of the key problems of the current global food system and explores the important alternative of food sovereignty (Wittman, Desmarais and Wiebe 2010). Food sovereignty offers a radical alternative to our current Canadian food system. In this second volume, like its predecessor, we invite citizens not only to better understand the complexities, dangers and challenges confronting Canadians at our own dinner tables but also to understand the potential for solutions. Our objective is to provoke everyone who eats not only to grapple with the destruction that our menus are visiting on our communities, our environments, Canadian farming families and our physical and cultural health, but also to actively engage in the exploration of food sovereignty as a viable and sustainable, life-giving alternative.

Initiating Food Sovereignty

The concept of food sovereignty evolved out of the experience and critical analysis of farming peoples. The inclusion of agriculture in the General Agreement on Tariffs and Trade (GATT) negotiations, articulated in the World Trade Organization (WTO), put official government stamps on decades of economic policies based on the globalization of a neoliberal, industrial, capital-intensive and corporate-led model of agriculture. This brought rural communities' widespread loss of control over food markets, environments, land and rural cultures into sharp relief. As an alternative to this neoliberal model, peasants, small-scale farmers, farm workers and Indigenous communities formed the transnational agrarian movement, La Vía Campesina (LVC). The National Farmers Union of Canada (NFU) was among the founding members of La Vía Campesina and remains active in the growing movement that now represents 148 organizations from sixty-nine countries.

The term "food sovereignty" was coined at the Second International Assembly of La Via Campesina in Tlaxcala, Mexico (1996a) to recognize the political and economic power dimensions inherent in the food and agriculture debate and to take a proactive stance by naming it. Food sovereignty, broadly defined as the right of nations and peoples to control their own food systems, including their own markets, production modes, food cultures and environments, has emerged as a critical alternative to the dominant neoliberal models for agriculture and trade. The commonly used food security language, which describes "a situation that exists when all people, at all times, have physical, social and economic access to sufficient, safe and nutritious food that meets their dietary needs and food preferences for an active and healthy life" (FAO 2001), ignores the defining power relations that determine production, distribution and consumption patterns within the food system. In order to ensure that sufficient quantities of food are available, the focus shifts to increasing food production and food imports. Not only does this emphasis serve to justify higher-input, more intensive production methods, it discounts who owns and controls (and profits from) those methods. For example, African governments that objected to shipments of genetically modified (GM) corn as food aid during famines in 2002, expressing concerns about contamination of their own seed varieties and about their food safety, were successfully pressured to accept them. Peasant concerns about corporate control over their future seeds, as well as self-sufficiency, affordability and the long-term viability of their Indigenous food production systems, were dismissed in favour of more immediate food security considerations (Manda 2003, Bhatia 2010, Mulvany 2004).

Governments (including Canada's) and agri-business corporations have pursued food security by promoting increased agricultural trade liberalization and the concentration of food production in the hands of fewer, and larger, agri-business corporations. As Qualman (Chapter 2) illustrates in his discussion of Canadian agriculture and trade policies and their outcomes, Canada has adopted the neoliberal, market-driven agenda for the food system with few modifications or exceptions. Excess production is exported, and often "dumped" — an international trade strategy that places food in targeted export markets at prices below the cost of production with government subsidies covering the producers' costs. Although Canada has largely opted to saddle farmers with the costs of selling food below the costs of production rather than subsidizing farm incomes, the outcomes in the international arena are the same: market prices are depressed and volatile, and domestic agricultural systems are devastated as farmers cannot compete with the influx of low-priced commodities saturating their local markets. Far from ensuring food security, these policies create widespread food insecurities and vulnerabilities.

These contemporary policies aimed at food security offer no real possibility for changing the existing, inequitable, social, political and economic structures that peasant movements believe are the very causes of food insecurity and the social and environmental destruction in the countryside in both the North and the South. To counter these structures and policies, La Vía Campesina (1996a) proposed a radical alternative, one "directly linked to democracy and justice," that put the control of productive resources (land, water, seeds and natural resources) in the hands of those who produce food. The Tlaxcala Conference defined eleven principles of food sovereignty, all of which were then integrated into La Vía Campesina's (1996b) Position on Food Sovereignty, presented at the World Food Summit in Rome in November 1996.

Subsequently, La Vía Campesina has worked with other organizations and civil society actors to further elaborate the food sovereignty framework. The concept continues to be broadened, deepened, refined and disseminated widely, as it provokes and shapes debates in important international civil society and international governing agency forums. Strategies and mechanisms for implementing food sovereignty are under ongoing and vigorous discussion. Canadian member organizations of La Via Campesina, the NFU and L'Union Paysanne in Québec, along with other non-governmental organizations (NGOs), civil society organizations and agencies, have participated in these international fora.

As the premise of food sovereignty is that sustainable food production and genuine food security are a function of community-based control over the food system, local, regional and national analysis and strategies are absolutely necessary. This is true for every region and locale around the world. No single global food sovereignty model can be designed and imposed from elsewhere. Indeed, it is the attempt to institute a global management system by transnational corporations, using economic and trade levers, along with the active collusion or imposed acquiescence of governments, that has provoked the urgent need for reorienting policies and reasserting local control, i.e. food sovereignty. Food sovereignty, by definition, must be "home-grown."

Food sovereignty in Canada requires developing appropriate strategies for change within our own array of unique political, cultural and ecological domains. The vast expanse of Canada entails a great variety of local growing conditions, cultures, political and economic circumstances. Farming and farm policies in Prince Edward Island vary a great deal from those of the Yukon, the Peace River region of Alberta, southern Québec or even its geographically closer region, the Annapolis Valley of Nova Scotia. It is impossible to describe all of this rich regional and local diversity as well as all of the many rapidly evolving and changing food projects in this one book. Instead, the writers and activists offer a sampling of food sovereignty initiatives that serve as a lens on Canada's diversity. Their thoughtful and vigorous discussions about food sovereignty, along with the diverse examples of practical initiatives currently underway in Canada, demonstrate the power and potential of a radical and transformative food sovereignty framework.

Food Sovereignty in Canada: Barriers and Pitfalls

The context for food sovereignty in Canada is particularly challenging on several counts. Firstly, unlike most other regions of the world, much of Canada does not have a long and deeply ensconced history of farming that predates export agriculture. Indigenous food systems were complex, ranging from intensive agriculture in some regions, to mixed farming, hunting and gathering, and intensive fishing in others. These systems were marginalized by the arrival of predominantly European immigrants, who built farming communities, introducing varieties of seeds and domesticated animals from Europe. The vast majority of these communities, with the exception of the very earliest settlements in eastern and central Canada, were created after agriculture was already oriented to providing a limited range of agricultural commodities for export. This history not only shapes what "traditional agriculture" means in our context but also informs the rate and processes of change. Because farming other than for export has relatively shallow roots in much of the country, the shifts to increasingly industrialized forms of production occurred very rapidly. There were fewer deeply rooted histories, traditions and methodologies to overcome.

Second, the rapid and continuing industrialization of agriculture in Canada has run parallel to an equally rapid displacement of farm families. Increased mechanization makes it possible to produce larger volumes of agricultural commodities and to work more land with less labour. Because this requires greater capital investment, the resultant debt loads have increased the financial vulnerability of farm operations. As well, a long-term decline in prices for some of the key grain, meat and horticultural commodities grown in Canada has created a serious cost/price squeeze for Canadian farm families,[1] resulting in a decline in farm numbers. Thus there are fewer and fewer people whose lives and livelihoods are committed to growing food; those who remain have to focus primarily on survival, leaving less time and energy and fewer resources for political participation or resistance. Because of their diminished numbers, farmers' electoral importance is also diminished and their political clout is thereby greatly reduced.

Third, the migration of people from the land, along with immigration from elsewhere into Canadian cities, has led to an overwhelming population balance in favour of urban Canadians. In 2006, 80 percent of Canada's population lived in an urban environment, as compared to 62 percent in 1951 (Statistics Canada 2010). This change means that the vast majority of Canadians is entirely reliant on store-bought food with little direct connection to the production of that food. This disconnection from the sources of their food, combined with the distances and complexity of processes which that food has undergone and reinforced through uninformative and sometimes misleading labelling, leaves grocery shoppers with an acute lack of knowledge about their food. In so far as knowledge is power, the preponderance of power in this food equation lies with the corporate players who process and market the items that line grocery store shelves.

A further impediment to Canadian food sovereignty is the dominant self-image that has been perpetuated about our food system. Because of our history of sending shiploads of grain, most notably high quality milling wheat from the prairies, into war-needy Britain or hungry nations elsewhere, we tend to view Canada as "the breadbasket of the world." Current agriculture export data support the view that Canada's food system is characterized by high productivity and efficiencies due to our cutting edge technologies (NFU 2003). Each innovation, from new technology such as Global Positioning Systems (GPS) for field operations to a new line of chemical inputs or new genetics such as genetically modified canola, is effectively marketed as a potential boost to productivity, with the suggestion, as an added incentive, that failure to adopt it will result in a loss of our competitive advantage in the global marketplace. The fact that the ownership of machinery, seed and chemicals is increasingly concentrated in the hands of fewer, consolidated companies is seldom even noted by proponents of these "advances," let alone critiqued (Qualman 2001).

This relentless pressure to adopt new technologies and increase production in order to protect Canada's "global leader" reputation is coupled with an equally virulent drive to protect and increase the Canadian agriculture trade advantage. The Canada-United States Free Trade Agreement (CUSTA) in 1989 led the way in demonstrating how liberalized agricultural trade could be inscribed into trade agreements designed to increase such trade. These prescriptions for opening borders and decreasing barriers to agricultural trade were extended when Mexico was included in NAFTA (NAFTA 1994) and when they were adopted globally as the blueprint for the WTO (1995). In recent years, a myriad of bilateral trade agreements have also been signed: another fifty such deals are currently under negotiation, including a major Canada-European Trade Agreement (Harris 2010). Key parts of our agriculture system, such as the beef-packing industry, are already out of our hands, while the struggle to hold onto other parts, such as the supply-managed poultry, egg and dairy industries and the marketing of wheat and barley exports, is intensifying. Recent investments in Canadian agricultural land by foreign interests presents another direct challenge to building food sovereignty here (NFU 2010). As foreign and corporate ownership becomes steadily more deeply embedded in all components of our food system, it becomes increasingly more difficult to even imagine taking back control over these resources, markets and policies.

Achieving food sovereignty in Canada hinges on making some fundamental changes in our domestic and trade policies, our diets, our "food cultures," our view of our place in the wider world, and many of our relationships to each other and our environments. The forces arraigned against Canadian food sovereignty are powerful and wide-ranging. However, as many of the writers in this book demonstrate, the possibilities and momentum for radical transformation are also powerful, and have the added strength of being connected to local, regional, national and global communities.

Food Sovereignty: Making New Meal Plans

Achieving food sovereignty in Canada must begin with a genuine appreciation of the sources, potential and limits of the living food systems which we inhabit. The Indigenous peoples in all regions of Canada have a deep knowledge of local climates and these living food systems, gleaned from thousands of years of living in these places. Despite being initially discounted and systematically destroyed by immigrants into Canada, the knowledge and practices of Indigenous food systems are crucial for the long-term sustainability of erstwhile abundant but now fragile and threatened ecosystems. As Dawn Morrison demonstrates in Chapter 6, Indigenous perspectives on the place of humans within ecosystems offer invaluable insights into the kinds of transformations in values, behaviours and worldviews that food sovereignty demands.

Furthermore, although the history of farming in Canada is relatively briefer than in many other parts of the world, we nevertheless have a rich experience of small-scale, ecologically appropriate farming in most regions of the country. Pioneering families have left a large legacy of information, experience, stories and wisdom about ways of living in the many unique contexts and climates that characterize Canada. Locally-produced and controlled food provisioning was the norm in most communities for most of our history. Many of the prescriptions of food sovereignty, from local control over markets, to sustainable production of culturally and seasonally appropriate food are rooted in the current and historical practices of many of Canada's agrarian communities.

It is obvious that population, and technological and cultural changes prohibit a wholesale return to earlier practices. However, traditional knowledge about seed varieties, growing patterns, appropriate and sustainable scale, waste management, cooperation and ways of living successfully in particular locations offers a rich trove of information and examples for current food sovereignty initiatives. While the dominant trend is pushing monocultures (growing a single crop over wide areas) and a decreasing variety of corporate patented seed, there is a countervailing interest in propagating farm and garden-saved seed varieties. Seed and plant exchanges, including so-called "Seedy Saturdays," where heritage and locally produced seed varieties are sold and exchanged, are expanding in many parts of the country (Wiebe 2003). As well, despite the overwhelming dominance of a few kinds of chickens, pigs and cows in the commercial markets, a variety of heritage breeds continue to be propagated on farms.

Food traditions open another vital avenue for food sovereignty, in Canada as elsewhere. In sharp contrast to the industrial model of food as a commodity, the food on the kitchen table within households often has complex, multi-layered meaning and associations. Beyond being necessary nutrition, food expresses cultural identity and evokes personal, familial and community memory. The frequently used advertisement of "home-cooked meals" to entice customers into restaurants, although clearly not quite credible, works because of positive memories and myths associated with that ascription. Most significant holidays, festivals and community events are demarcated by specific foods. From bannock at prairie pow-wows to the Thanksgiving turkey to the moon cakes at a mid-autumn Chinese festival, our cultures are rich with the variety and deep associations that foods evoke and signify. Culinary monocultures can be as threatening to our cultural resilience and community survival as agricultural monocultures are to biological diversity.

Despite the industrialization and attendant standardization of food, preparing food uniquely suited to occasions, tastes, cultural traditions and seasons remains a very important part of the quality of life for many Canadians. For most, living well and eating well are inextricably bound together in the same way as physical and psychological/spiritual health are linked, although these connections may not always be apparent or acknowledged. Although women continue to have primary responsibility for food in many households and hence play a large role in protecting and enhancing food cultures, there is a growing interest in food varieties and food cultures across genders and generations. Food movements, such as the Slow Food movement, the "hundred mile diet," farmers' markets, community shared agriculture projects, recipe exchanges and food tourism (built on the pleasures of experiencing local food customs), are all aspects of the growing interest in alternative sources, varieties and cultures involved in the cooking of food. This challenges the notion that food is just another standardized commodity where unit price determines customer choice. It represents a key alternative perspective on the meaning, role and importance of food.

The importance of changing perspectives on food should not be underestimated. While it is problematic that the number of family farms is falling, there is a growing coincidence of perspectives and values between those who engage in family farming and those who live in urban Canada but defend family farming on the grounds that it is linked to their own possibility of eating well and having access to sustainably produced food from a known source. Building relationships and understanding between farmers and urban eaters enhances power on both sides of this food equation. Furthermore, as the demand for more local, ecologically and culturally appropriate food grows stronger, the number of small-scale farms where that kind of production is feasible will also grow.

Another important positive trend in the struggle for Canadian food sovereignty is the growth of urban agriculture. As the chapters by Yolanda Hansen (Chapter 9), Harriet Friedman (Chapter 10), Hannah Wittman and Herb Barbolet (Chapter 11) attest, food-conscious urban Canadians are working to reintegrate food production into their cities and regions, as well as their own backyards and roof tops. These initiatives are not only significant in terms of decreasing reliance on food from far away, they also increase understanding of, and control over, food sources and systems. The upsurge of interest in food issues is translating into different research perspectives and priorities, as nutritionist Rachel Engler-Stringer explains in Chapter 8, and into more widespread engagement in food policy work, as Cathleen Kneen demonstrates in Chapter 5. Urban food charters, food coalitions and food policy councils are all positive signs of this trend.

The ongoing, well-funded media barrage touting the benefits and competitive advantages of new technologies in agriculture, combined with the economic pressure on farmers to produce more, has been effective on many fronts. For example, when Monsanto introduced its first commercial variety of GM canola into the Canadian prairies in 1996, the uptake was rapid. However, with experience and more information, resistance to the environmental impacts, costs and corporate control of genetically engineered seeds has grown. Monsanto's attempt to introduce rBGH (bovine somatatropin) into milk production met with strong broadly-based public opposition, which brought about its failure in 1998. The experience of having GM-contaminated Canadian flax rejected by European buyers has been costly for Canadian farmers. There is also mounting opposition to GM alfalfa and wheat from farmers, marketers and consumers. Meanwhile, the growing demand for organically-produced foods shows that more Canadians are seeking alternatives to chemical-dependent agricultural production. As progressive farm leaders Terry Boehm and Hilary Moore clearly articulate in interviews conducted by Naomi Beingessner (Chapter 3), alternative modes of production, less reliant on the transnational corporate giants, are a key part of the strategy to achieve food sovereignty.

Perhaps the most daunting concrete barrier to Canadian food sovereignty is the array of neoliberal trade agreements that dictate the terms for Canadian agricultural exports and food imports. However, there are signs that this trade regime is less robust than it once was. For example, resistance to the agriculture components in the WTO draft agreement has stalled the negotiations, making it unlikely that an agreement will be reached in the foreseeable future. As Andre Magnan describes in Chapter 7, farmers and farm organizations continue to fight for the protection of our remaining domestic marketing agencies such as the supply-managed industries and the Canadian Wheat Board (CWB). It is becoming clear to Canadians that the benefits of increased trade from these trade agreements have largely accrued to transnational agri-business corporations, bypassing farmers, rural communities and most Canadian citizens: growing awareness of this reality has strengthened citizen resistance politically. The increasing number of community-shared agriculture units and farmers' markets thriving in Canadian cities, towns and many smaller communities also provide evidence of effective grassroots forms of resistance to the trade-driven corporate-dominated food system of supermarkets.

The radical project of food sovereignty is sweeping in its breadth and complexity. An overview of some of the key impediments to its implementation illustrates the immensity of the problems we encounter in the struggle to wrest control over food back into the hands of citizens and their communities. However, as the foregoing also illustrates, public engagement, resistance and nurturing of alternatives are occurring everywhere. Most importantly, we have our own lively and growing discourse on food sovereignty here in Canada, including a People's Food Policy Project (PFPP) that involves over 3,500 Canadians discussing and debating the principles of food sovereignty (People's Food Policy Project 2011 and Chapter 5). National food policies, including some references to food sovereignty, figured in some of the party platforms of the May 2011 federal election campaign.

A Paradigm Shift in Agriculture and Food Policy

Are the conditions right for a policy paradigm shift in Canadian agriculture? Since the Second World War, Canadian agricultural policy has been anchored on two governing paradigms. A core premise of the state-assistance paradigm (early 1940s to late 1980s) is that, because agriculture is a unique sector due to its importance for national food security and economic development, it is therefore entitled to special attention by governments. Various regulatory and expenditure instruments were used in an attempt to both give farmers more market power and shield them from market forces. In contrast, the neoliberal paradigm (late 1980s to the present) holds that agriculture is an economic sector no different from any other, and farmers should therefore be reliant on the market alone for their incomes. Consequently, many regulatory and expenditure mechanisms that supported Canadian agriculture and food systems were either changed or terminated, and attempts have been made to eliminate others that still remain. For example, the Western Grain Transportation Act was terminated; some farm subsidies were changed from commodity-specific price supports to decoupled direct payments; and, in the area of food safety, there was a shift to "regulation for competition." Despite the prescriptions offered by each paradigm, both have failed to resolve problems that have plagued the Canadian agriculture sector since the 1930s.

Public policy is formulated within a framework of assumptions, values and power structures that broadly define the problems to be resolved, the goals to be achieved, who should be involved and what kinds of policy instruments are appropriate (Hall 1993: 279). The framework or paradigm eventually becomes embedded in governing institutions and societal discourse to the point where it is taken for granted and largely unexamined. However, paradigms can and do get challenged and changed. First, a paradigm change can occur in the event of crises caused by policy failure, where unanticipated developments contradict the paradigm's core assumptions and destabilize it. Such developments can arise from contradictions within the paradigm itself, structural change within the economy, or both. Adaptive reforms to the paradigm will be attempted, but, if they cannot be made or do not work, a window opens for a new paradigm to take hold — redefining the problems, objectives and instruments used to reach the new goals. Second, paradigm change depends on the existence of a persuasive rival paradigm that offers an alternative interpretation of policy problems and their solutions. The alternative interpretation must also correlate with evidence, experiences of the public and societal values; essentially, the viability of the alternative paradigm is determined by its political, economic and administrative practicality. Third, paradigm change requires either a change in the policy making process and/or a transition in political power where new actors with new ideas are involved in authoritative decision making. A final impetus for policy change is a function of the historical conjuncture created by the moment when an event takes place, the event's position in a particular sequence of events, and the context in which the event takes place. These accidents of history can determine whether an opening for policy change is created and what its impact on policy development may be (Thelen 1999: 388–92).

As Darrin Qualman clearly demonstrates in Chapter 2, farm incomes in the export-oriented agricultural sectors remain chronically low, and depopulation of rural areas continues at a rapid pace. Hunger persists for many Canadians, despite the production of an overabundance of food. Finally, environmental degradation continues as land, water systems and wildlife are stressed from the intensive conventional agricultural production process. The new rival paradigm, food sovereignty, is emerging in response to these crises. We argue, based on the challenges to food sovereignty outlined above, that the adoption of a food sovereignty paradigm in Canada requires the implementation of four important policy pillars: 1) the incorporation of agriculture policy into a broad and comprehensive national food policy; 2) an inclusive and bottom-up policy development process; 3) the constitutional entrenchment of the right to food; and 4) a new agriculture policy oriented toward local food systems and environmental sustainability.

A National Food Policy for Canada

The practical project of institutionalizing a food sovereignty paradigm in Canada will require sweeping changes to current agriculture policy. The first challenge is to develop a comprehensive national food policy, incorporating the presently disparate policy areas such as agriculture, health care, social welfare, the environment and justice. The only previous state-directed attempt to create a national food policy in Canada occurred in the late 1970s (Rideout et al. 2007: 570–71) when two federal departments, Agriculture Canada and Consumer and Corporate Affairs Canada, took the lead in its development. However, this initiative did not propose a significant departure from the status quo. The strategy remained oriented toward competitive export production and no meaningful measures were proposed to address issues related to consumption and nutrition, such as the promotion of healthy and local foods. It ultimately failed due to reluctance within Agriculture Canada and resistance from production, processing and distribution companies concerned about the imposition of new regulations (MacRae 1999: 184–85).

Alternatively, the food sovereignty paradigm views agriculture as part of an entire food system. Thus, agricultural and food policy must be a component of a broad, comprehensive national food policy that reflects the complex system of interdependencies that exist throughout this system (McRae 1999: 182–94). A national food policy requires horizontal integration across policy sectors and vertical integration encompassing all levels of government.

A Citizen-Driven Food Policy

A new national food policy also requires a significant departure from the current policy process in order to be both meaningful and successful. At present, Canadian policy making in agriculture is highly institutionalized and top-down in orientation. All final decisions at both the federal and provincial levels are taken by the political executives who are advised by their departments of agriculture. These bureaucracies are hierarchical in nature and are staffed by professional civil servants. Other important actors include the House of Commons and Senate Committees dealing with agriculture. These bodies, along with the rural caucuses of each political party conduct consultations and make recommendations to the minister of agriculture on certain policy issues. But there are some obvious participants in a food system missing from this process — eaters and farmers. This problem is being addressed by the People's Food Policy Project, Food Secure Canada (FSC) and other civil society organizations that are working to bring both urban and rural people to the policy table.

Under a food sovereignty paradigm, the policy process in agriculture is integrated within a comprehensive food policy making process, where citizens are active participants shaping policy via direct democracy (Pimbert

2009: 12–14). Processes for such direct participation would vary by location. Pimbert suggests citizen-based councils, consisting of delegates representing popular assemblies working in networks, so that the interdependence of local concerns in the wider context can be addressed. Finally, policy development is oriented toward fundamentally different objectives. For example, policies aim to achieve optimal nutrition of the population and a fair income for farmers and environmental sustainability, rather than improved international competitiveness, reliance on the market and the use of GMO (Genetically Modified Organism) technology. In summary, by integrating the entire food system, empowering all citizens in the policy development process and putting the needs of people and the environment first, food sovereignty achieves a very different approach to agriculture. A variety of kinds and levels of citizen involvement in changing food systems are described and analyzed in other chapters of this book.

Entrenching the Right to Food

A clear, public way of institutionalizing the food sovereignty paradigm in Canada would be to entrench food rights in the Canadian constitution and laws, as has been done in several other jurisdictions. Since the constitutional entrenchment of the *Charter of Rights and Freedoms* in 1982, Canadian citizens have won many court challenges that have effectively changed some long-standing public policies (Brooks 2009: 187–88); for instance, court challenges have changed family and marriage laws in Canada. There is good reason to believe that the constitutional entrenchment of the right to food can have the same effect.

Between 1999 and 2010, food sovereignty and the right to food was included in national legislation introduced by the governments of Venezuela, Mali, Bolivia, Ecuador, Brazil, Nepal and Senegal (Beauregard 2009). Going beyond protecting civil and political rights to include the guaranteed legal protection of food and other important social rights, forces governments to ensure that all legislation dealing with food and agriculture is consistent with the Constitution. It also creates justiciable food rights, allowing citizens to launch court challenges in their defence (Riches 1999: 207–08; Rideout et al. 2007: 568).

Without a doubt the legal recognition of food rights in Canada constitutes a fundamental reconceptualization and reshaping of our food system. Canada has recognized the right to food on the international stage, which implies a commitment to taking the necessary action to protect this right domestically (Rideout et al. 2007: 567). In an attempt to recognize the right to food at the domestic level, as a response to the World Food Summit Plan of Action, the federal government introduced Canada's Action Plan for Food Security in 1998. It included plans to achieve the right to food, resulted in the short-lived creation of the Food Security Bureau within Agriculture and Agri-Food Canada (AAFC). Missing in this experience is the protection of the right to food through fundamental and binding domestic law. Ultimately, the right to food in Canada can only be assured through its entrenchment in the Constitution.

Supporting Sustainable Local Food Systems

The shift to a food sovereignty paradigm requires measures to reorient agricultural production to domestic consumption, to ensure adequate incomes for farmers and to ensure environmental sustainability. Other sections of this book discuss the importance of controlling corporate power, protecting domestic markets and production, using supply management or other strategies, and supporting agro-ecological and small-scale farming. In addition, sustainable local food systems can be supported through the fair trade of surplus food production and the exchange of foods that cannot be grown in Canada, regulated to ensure that food production meets environmental and social standards and that farmers receive a fair price for their products. The adoption of a new trade policy for Canada would have to be a key part of concrete actions geared to create a new global trade regime, requiring as much international as domestic effort. Finally, a shift from the neoliberal paradigm must address the dramatic disinvestment in rural Canada that has already taken place. Physical infrastructure such as roads and railway branch lines have been closed or are deteriorating, and rural services, including schools and hospitals, have been lost. The shift to the food sovereignty paradigm is dependent on the re-establishment of measures geared to rebuilding and reinforcing rural infrastructure. Without this, the revival of rural communities and local food systems cannot succeed. The adoption of all of these measures demands political will and bold action of governments in Canada, in conjunction with strong civil society movements demanding change.

Weaving Food Webs and Loosening Food Chains

The language of food sovereignty was initially introduced by La Vía Campesina to express both the truth of power relations within the food domain and the hope for the democratic, widely dispersed, just distribution of those powers over food. This book names and examines the power structures within the industrial food system in Canada and sheds light on mechanisms and strategies that social movements and community organizations in various places across the country are using in the transformation to food sovereignty.

In order to transform the dominant forces, including those related to politics, economics, gender, the environment and social organization, we need to be able to imagine and articulate new relationships to food, community and ultimately the earth. A major shift in thinking is required. Instead of the current construct of farmers producing and individual consumers buying food, where both the access to and production of food are determined by the market, food sovereignty begins from the position of citizens engaged in decisions about providing life-sustaining good food. This process must be understood within an ecological, social and cultural context: growing, buying, preparing and eating food is embedded in social and ecological relationships, rather than primarily market relationships.

In the dominant conceptual frameworks and organizing principles of "food chains," the links of the chain are comprised of production inputs, commodity production, processing ("value adding"), packaging, transporting, marketing/retailing and, finally, consumption (Kaufman 2004). For food sovereignty to flourish, this conceptual construct must give way to a framework of "food webs" where people and other elements of living food systems are connected and interdependent in a multiplicity of complex ways. In short, the food system must be reconceived as dynamic, interlaced, living webs rather than linear chains.

Not only is the food chain construct linear but it reinforces unjust hierarchical economic and political valuations. For example, raw or farm-gate foodstuffs are commonly described as basic commodities that must undergo "value-adding" in order to be useful. The implication is that the natural product has little or no value before it has been transformed through industrial processing and packaging. In a capitalist economy such as Canada's, "value" and "price" tend to be conflated. Comparing grocery-shelf prices of foods with those paid for key raw ingredients in such foods illustrates the economic impact of the value-adding stance. For example, the farm-gate price for the primary ingredient in a loaf of bread — wheat — typically represents less than 10 percent of the price of the bread (Martz 2004). This price/value gap is reflected in the diminished financial profit position of farmers in Canada vis-à-vis other players in the food chain (NFU 2005). It also has an impact on the social standing of "raw product" producers, reducing them to the least valued, most easily displaced and replaced links in the chain. As Steven Blank bluntly puts it, farming is an entry-level, low-skill job, and it is industrialization that takes a society "up the Economic Food Chain" (Blank 1998: 190). "Just like unskilled individuals, national economies start in agriculture but stay only until they acquire the skills needed to move into a more profitable industry" (Blank 1998: 12).

In contrast, the language of food webs highlights the necessary and reciprocal interconnectedness of the actors in the food system, as well as acknowledging our ultimate dependence on nature's goods for sustenance and survival. The former grounds the call for recognition, respect, inclusion and equality among those human agents, who are ultimately the decision makers, within the web. These are the prescriptions of democracy, justice and balance that strengthen the human social fibers of the food web. Acknowledging our dependence of nature's goods speaks to the fundamental conceptual re-integration of humans into ecological contexts as part of, rather than dominant over, nature. Far from nature being a resource to be exploited, manipulated, consumed, trashed and discarded, seeing ourselves as part of a web changes our respect, valuation and care of those other living strands within the web that supports us.

The radical social and political transformations envisioned by this change of perspectives and articulated in the food sovereignty concept have implications particularly for women. Women play a key role in food production and procurement, food preparation, family food security and food culture. Food sovereignty requires a revaluation of this work and profound changes to unequal gender relations. It demands equality, respect and freedom from violence for women. Chapter 4 by Annette Desmarais, Carla Roppel and Diane Martz outlines some of the key solutions to the recurring crisis offered by women farmers. Although the official policy discourse often ignores and marginalizes farm women, their perspectives and insights into changing the system are vital. The neoliberal industrialized food system undervalues and underpays the food production and preparation work of women (Barndt 1999). But this denigration of food-related work, the deskilling that results from reducing food to standardized, processed, packaged commodities, and the loss of community and cultural relationships to food are not inevitable. As women continue to have primary responsibility for household and community food security and food traditions, they are in a strategic position to effect food system changes. Food can be a locus of women's struggle for power, equality and community rebuilding. It is clear from the work in this book that women are providing leadership and energy in many of the food sovereignty initiatives. Women here and elsewhere in the world are poised to re-orient, reintegrate and rejuvenate the food economy and culture in many different venues and ways.

Every Canadian who eats has a stake in the food system. As noted above, food sovereignty has to be home-grown, hence our focus on our home ground, Canada. Although this book focuses particularly on food sovereignty for Canada, it has global implications. Experiences and analyses from here will resonate with those who live in other highly industrialized "developed" economies, those who participate in the globalized food system, whether as food producers or eaters, and all those who care about the fate of the earth. The struggles and opportunities for achieving food sovereignty in Canada are both an example for and a part of the global struggles for food sovereignty.

There are urgent reasons for all of us to break free of the binding corporate food chains that are choking off social, ecological, economic and political life forces. Working for food sovereignty, in Canada and elsewhere, is the work of nurturing healthy, integrated, just and sustainable food webs.

Note

1. A cost-price squeeze occurs when production costs are higher than, and/or increase faster than the commodity prices received. Farmers do not receive prices for their commodities that cover their production costs and thus do not provide a return on investment.

References

Barndt, Deborah (ed.). 1999. *Women, Food, and Globalization: Women Working the NAFTA Food Chain.* Toronto: Sumach Press.

Beauregard, S. 2009. "Food Policy for People: Incorporating Food Sovereignty Principles into State Governance." Senior Comprehensive Report, Urban and Environmental Policy Institute, Occidental College, Los Angeles, April. <departments.oxy.edu/uepi/uep/index.htm>

Bhatia, Juhie. 2010. "Africa's Hunger Hardships Spur Biotech Debate." <pulitzercenter.org/blog/untold-stories/africas-hunger-hardships-spur-biotech-debate>

Blank, Steven C. 1998. *The End of Agriculture in the American Portfolio.* Westport, CT: Quorum Books.

Brooks, Stephen. 2009. *Canadian Democracy.* Sixth edition. Toronto: Oxford University Press.

CFA (Canadian Federation of Agriculture). 2011. "Canadian farmers look forward to Food Freedom Day" <http://www.cfa-fca.ca/programs-projects/food-freedom-day>

ETCgroup. 2009. "Who Will Feed Us? Questions for the Food and Climate Crises." <etcgroup.org/en/node/4921>

FAO (Food and Agriculture Organization of the United Nations). 2010. "Hunger." <fao.org/hunger/en>

_____. 2001. *The State of Food Insecurity in the World 2001.* Rome: Food and Agricultural Organization of the United Nations. <fao.org/docrep/003/Y1500E/y1500e06.htm#P0_0>

Food Banks Canada. 2010. "Hunger Facts 2009." <foodbankscanada.ca/main2.cfm?id=10718648-B6A7-8AA0-6A3C6F3CAC0124E1>

Hall, Peter A. 1993. "Policy Paradigms, Social Learning, and the State: The Case of Economic Policymaking in Britain." *Comparative Politics* 25, 3.

Harris, Kathleen. 2010. "Canada's Robust Bids for Trade Deals." *Ottawa Sun,* October 23.

Kaufman, Jerome L. 2004. "Introduction." *Journal of Planning Education and Research.* 23,4.

La Vía Campesina. 1996a "Proceedings from the II International Conference of La Vía Campesina." Brussels: NCOS Publications.

_____. 1996b. "The Right to Produce and Access to Land." Position paper of La Vía Campesina on food sovereignty presented at the World Food Summit, November 13–17, Rome, Italy.

MacRae Rod. 1999. "Policy Failure in the Canadian Food System." In M. Koc, R. MacRae, LJA. Mougeot and J. Welsh (eds.), *For Hungerproof Cities: Sustainable Urban Food Systems.* Ottawa, Ontario: International Development Research Centre and the Ryerson Centre for Studies in Food Security.

Manda, Olga. 2003. "Controversy Rages over 'GM' Food Aid." *Africa Renewal* 16, 4. <un.org/ecosocdev/geninfo/afrec/vol16no4/164food2.htm>

Martz, Diane J.F. 2004. "The Farmers' Share: Compare the Share 2004." Muenster, SK: The Centre for Rural Studies and Enrichment, St. Peter's College. <stpeterscollege.sk.ca/crse/crse/html>

Mulvany, Patrick. 2004. "The Dumping Ground: Africa and GM Food Aid." *Open Democracy*. <opendemocracy.net/ecology-africa_democracy/article_1876.jsp>

NFU (National Farmers Union). 2010. "Losing our Grip: How a Corporate Farmland Buy-up, Rising Farm Debt, and Agribusiness Financing of Inputs Threaten Family Farms and Food Sovereignty." June 7. <nfu.ca/press_releases/2010/06-07-losing_grip.pdf>

______. 2005. "The Farm Crisis: Its Causes and Solutions." <nfu.ca/briefs/2007/1988%20vs%202007%20FINAL%20bri.pdf>

______. 2003. "The Farm Crisis, Bigger Farms, and the Myths of Competition and Efficiency." November 20. Saskatoon: National Farmers Union.

People's Food Policy Project. 2011. "Resetting the Table: A People's Food Policy for Canada." <www.peoplesfoodpolicy.ca>

Pimbert, Michel. 2009. "Towards Food Sovereignty." *Gatekeeper* 141. London: International Institute for Environment and Development, Natural Resources Group.

Qualman, Darrin. 2001. *The Farm Crisis and Corporate Power*. Ottawa: Canadian Centre for Policy Alternatives.

Riches, Graham. 1999. "Advancing the Human Right to Food in Canada: Social Policy and the Politics of Hunger, Welfare, and Food Security." *Agriculture and Human Values* 16, 2.

Rideout, Karen, Graham Riches, Aleck Ostry, Don Buckingham and Rod MacRae. 2007. "Bringing Home the Right to Food in Canada: Challenges and Possibilities for Achieving Food Security." *Public Health Nutrition* 10, 6.

Statistics Canada, 2010. "Population, Urban and Rural, by Province and Territory." <40.statcan.ca/l01/cst01/demo62a-eng.htm>

Thelen, Kathleen. 1999. "Historical Institutionalism in Comparative Politics." *Annual Review of Political Science* 2.

Wiebe, Nettie. 2003. "The Subversive Gardener." *Western Producer* May 29.

Wittman, Hannah, Annette Aurélie Desmarais and Nettie Wiebe (eds.). 2010. *Food Sovereignty: Reconnecting Food, Nature and Community*. Halifax, NS: Fernwood Publishing.

2. ADVANCING AGRICULTURE BY DESTROYING FARMS?

The State of Agriculture in Canada

Darrin Qualman

Three-quarters of a trillion dollars — that's the total value of the grains and livestock and vegetables and other food products grown and raised by Canadian farmers since 1985. Here's another number: zero. That's the total of farmers' net income from the markets (farm support payments excluded) over that same period. Since 1985, chemical and seed companies, fertilizer makers and assorted agri-business corporations have captured 100 percent of the value of Canadian farm production — the whole three-quarters of a trillion dollars, leaving farm families to survive financially on off-farm income, taxpayer-funded support payments and loans. In these and similar numbers, detailed below, we find evidence that Canada has one of the most profoundly dysfunctional agricultural policies in the world, and we begin to see the critical need for alternative food, trade and agricultural policies based firmly upon food sovereignty.

Food sovereignty, as Nettie Wiebe and Kevin Wipf point out in Chapter 1, is many things depending on place, time, culture, needs and so on. As with many forward-looking ideas, it is difficult to predict exactly what food sovereignty will look like in practice — to provide an exact blueprint of food sovereignty is not only difficult but is also counter-productive. So it might be easier to define what it *isn't*. There is broad agreement that food sovereignty is not:

- a set of policies simplistically aimed at maximizing production and exports
- a disregard for the destruction of family farms and rural communities
- a push toward a high-input, high-cost, high-energy-use model of food production that generates chronic negative returns for the farm families who work the soil
- a concentration of land ownership into the hands of fewer and fewer owners, many of them non-farmers
- a corporate takeover of a growing number of agricultural sectors (e.g. hog production and cattle finishing)
- a push toward massive production units that concentrate potential pollutants

- the transfer of key food processing facilities to foreign companies, even to foreign lands
- economic policies that make foreign-based transnationals the primary beneficiaries of the wealth created by the farm families working our land
- a system that makes citizens ever more dependent on food supplied further and further from their homes.

In this chapter, I demonstrate that the preceding list summarizes the main objectives and/or outcomes of Canada's current food and agriculture policy model. This chapter also details how Canada's export-focused, high-input, opposite-of-food-sovereignty policies have been a financial, social and environmental disaster for Canadian farms, farm families, rural communities and landscapes. Thus, in the rubble of the Canadian agricultural sector we find the strongest possible case for food sovereignty-based policies.

The Aggressive Pursuit of Export Expansion

> Almost 45 per cent of [Canada's] domestic food and agricultural production... is exported either directly as primary products or indirectly as part of processed products. In 2008 we exported $42.8 billion (Cdn) worth of food and agriculture around the world! We were also the fourth largest exporter in the world! (AAFC 2010e)

> Trade figures tell a compelling story about the competitiveness of Canadian primary agriculture, given the importance of exports to the sector. (AAFC 2009: 5)

If Canadian food and agriculture policies have a cornerstone, it is this imperative: maximize exports. Over the past two decades, Canadian governments and transnational agri-business corporations have set aggressive food-export targets, which they have met — nearly quadrupling our agri-food exports in the twenty years spanning 1989 to 2009 (AAFC 2010d; AAFC 2010a).

At their July 1993 meeting in Prince Edward Island, Canada's federal, provincial and territorial ministers of agriculture set a target of $20 billion in agri-food exports by the year 2000. Essentially, the goal was to double the export levels of 1989. In 1996, the ministers — having reached their $20 billion goal ahead of schedule — committed themselves to the objective of redoubling exports by 2005, to nearly $40 billion. (More precisely, the stated target was 4 percent of global agri-food exports, a share approximately equal to $40 billion.) Though championed by our elected agriculture ministers, this 4 percent/$40 billion goal was actually put forward by the Canadian Agri-Food Marketing Council (CAMC), an industry group that included as members Maple Leaf Foods, Cargill, McCain's and other agri-food corporations.

Figure 2-1 highlights Canada's success in spurring export growth. This country, long an exporter of grains and other foods, dramatically increased the rate of export growth following the 1989 implementation of the Canada-U.S. Free Trade Agreement (CUSTA), the 1994 implementation of the North American Free Trade Agreement (NAFTA), the 1995 implementation of the World Trade Organization (WTO) Agreement on Agriculture, and the implementation of numerous other bilateral and multilateral investors' rights and trade agreements. AAFC states:

> The [agriculture and agri-food] system is becoming more internationally focussed.... Canada, as a major player in world agri-food trade has increased its share of world agriculture and agri-food trade in response to trade liberalization and changing market conditions over the past fifteen years. The North American Free Trade Agreement (NAFTA), in particular, has led to increasingly integrated agriculture and agri-food trade within the North American market as demonstrated by the quadrupling of exports to the U.S. and a ninefold increase in exports to Mexico since 1991. (AAFC 2007: xv, xviii)

Figure 2-1 Canadian Agri-Food Exports: 1970–2010

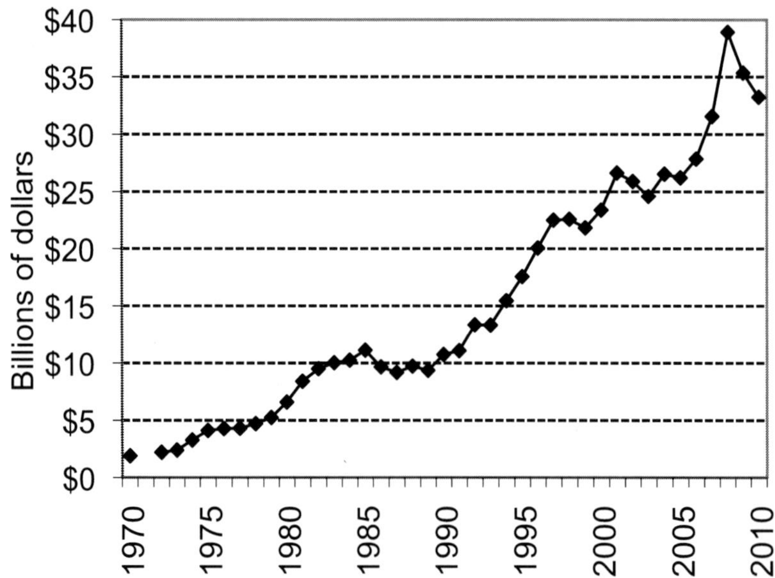

Sources: Data provided upon request from Agriculture and Agri-Food Canada; AAFC, Agri-Food Trade Service, <www.ats-sea.agr.gc.ca>; AAFC, *Medium Term Outlook for Canadian Agriculture: International and Domestic Markets*, January 2010.

Expanded Output

Exports are up, at least partly because Canadian production of grains and oilseeds, livestock and other farm products is up. In the twenty years between 1989 and 2009 Canada has increased its production of corn, wheat, barley, canola, soybeans and other major grains by 24 percent (see Figure 2-2). In a similar vein, production of beef cattle has increased by 28 percent over the same period (Statistics Canada CANSIM 003-0026), and production of hogs has doubled — these increases have all been slated for export markets (AAFC 2005; AAFC personal communication 2010). In dollar terms, Canadian farm production (not counting support program payments) has nearly doubled in two decades: $43.6 billion in 2009 vs. $22.8 billion in 1989 (Statistics Canada 2010a; AAFC 2010b).

Figure 2-2 Canadian Production of Major Grains: 1970–2009

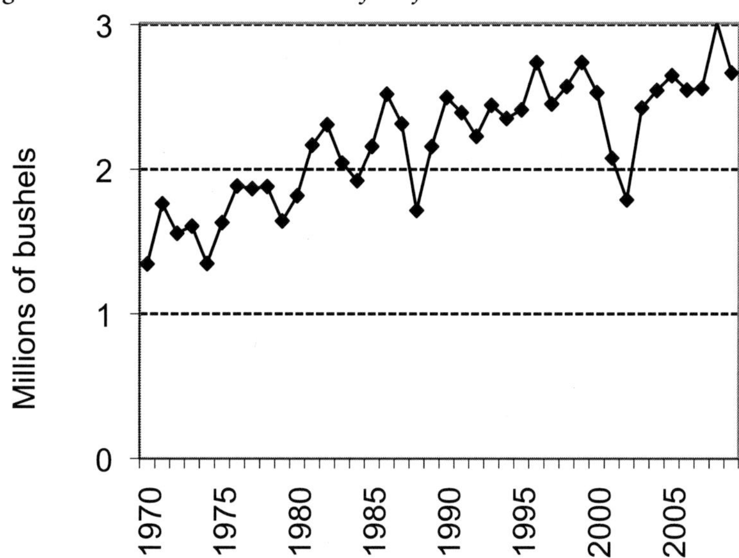

Source: Statistics Canada CANSIM table 001-0017.

Bigger, High-Tech, More Efficient Farms

> The sector has repeatedly shown its ability to compete though the adoption of new technologies, as well as management and organizational practices. This continuous adaptation has given rise to structural change, adjustments, and consolidation. As a result, Canada's agriculture sector looks substantially different today, with fewer, larger farms producing ever greater output. (Canadian Ministers of Agriculture 2010: 3)

> Innovation is the key to the agriculture and agri-food system's long-term prosperity. Innovation improves the manner in which capital and labour inputs are combined, resulting in more efficient and effective production. This contributes to increased productivity growth and enhanced competitiveness. (AAFC 2007: 47)

How has Canada managed to boost food production and nearly quadruple exports? Part of the answer is that, pushed by corporate and elected leaders, many farmers have adopted a food production model based on maximum use of technology, energy and purchased inputs. Many farmers are using genetically modified (GM) seeds (primarily canola, corn and soybeans), direct-seeding machinery, automatic steering ("GPS") systems for tractors, large and expensive sprayers, robotic milking machines, computerized feed ration mixers or other capital-intensive food production technologies.

Farms are larger. Canada has embraced a model of farm size maximization and, in some sectors, giantism. Grain and oilseed farms, especially in western Canada, routinely encompass thousands of acres, with some very large farms covering 10,000 or 20,000 acres, or more. One corporation, One Earth Farms, is attempting to farm more than 100,000 acres in Saskatchewan, and the company has repeatedly stated that it intends to grow to one million acres — more than 1,500 square miles (NFU 2010a: 6).

Livestock production units are similarly increasing in size. Whereas a large cow-calf operation might have had 100 cows a generation ago, today, 300-cow operations are not uncommon. Feedlots are even larger; several single-location feedlots in Canada and the U.S. boast throughput of hundreds of thousands of cattle per year.

Hog farms have shown the most rapid rise toward giantism. Whereas hundred-sow operations were common in Canada in the 1980s and thousand-sow operations were rare, today many of Canada's largest production units house 5,000 sows. Dairy operations have also increased in size, though less dramatically. So, too, have potato farms. As AAFC points out, "Million-dollar farms now account for 40 percent of gross farm receipts. Million-dollar farms doubled their share of gross revenue from 18 percent in 1986 to 40 percent in 2006" (AAFC 2009: 105). Those million-dollar-plus farms make up just 3 percent of farms overall (AAFC 2009: 105). Thus, approximately 7,500 production units produce 40 percent of Canadian food output.

In addition to becoming bigger, Canadian farms have become more "efficient." Per farm-, per farmer-, per hour-, per animal- and per acre-output rates have increased dramatically, and this is used by some as evidence of higher levels of efficiency. All data shows that, for more than fifty years, the Canadian farming sector has consistently led the rest of the economy in terms of productivity gains (Statistics Canada 2001: 19; Statistics Canada 2007; Statistics Canada CANSIM table 383-0022; NFU 2003: 22-23).

Net Farm Income

Measured by production volumes, exports, per-farm output and a range of other economic indicators, Canadian agriculture ranks as one of the most successful national food production sectors in the world. However, although Canadian farms are among the biggest, most productive, most export-prolific, most efficient and most high-tech in the world, all is not well. Since at least the mid-1980s, our farms have also been among the world's least profitable.

When the Great Depression ended, Canadian agriculture resumed producing a large positive net income, and did so, consistently, until the mid-1980s. Then, in 1985, for the first time in Canadian history, realized net farm income from the markets (with taxpayer-funded farm support payments factored out) fell almost to zero; it has remained near zero, and often below,

Figure 2-3 Realized Net Income from the Markets (Inflation Adjusted): 1926–2010

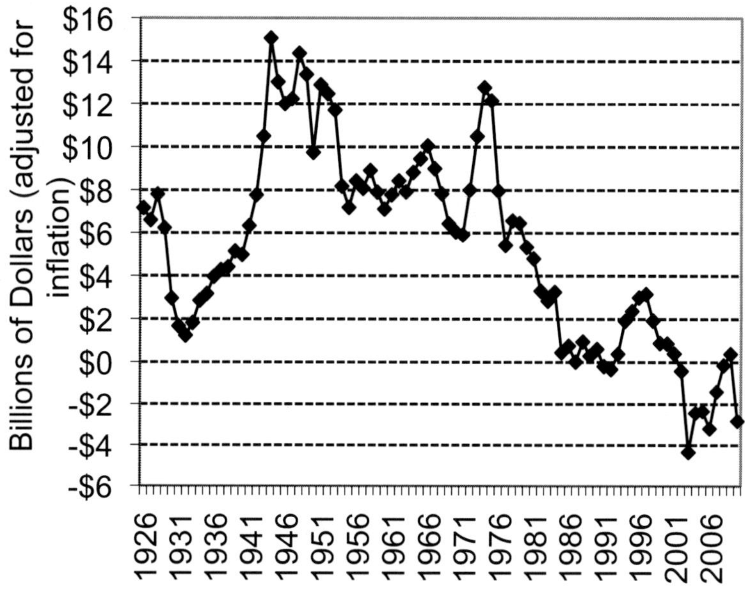

Sources: Statistics Canada, 2002, *Agricultural Economic Statistics*, Cat. No. 21-603-E, May, Ottawa: Statistics Canada; Statistics Canada, 2010c, *Net Farm Income–Agriculture Economic Statistics*, Cat. No. 21-010-X, May, Ottawa: Statistics Canada; and Statistics Canada, 2010d, Consumer Price Index. Cat. No. 62-001-XWE, vol. 89 no. 11, December, Ottawa: Statistics Canada.

for most of the ensuing twenty-six years. Figure 2-3 shows the ups and downs of Canadian net income from the markets for the past eighty-five years. It also shows that, since 1985, Canadian farmers have been grappling with the worst farm income disaster in Canadian history.

Why have net incomes remained so low for the past twenty-six years? The reason is not that Canadian farmers failed to produce and sell. To the contrary, Canadian farms produced record amounts — tens-of-billions of dollars worth of food products each year. As noted in the opening paragraph of this chapter, if we add up all farm production revenues from 1985 to 2010, we generate a figure of $795 billion dollars — more than three-quarters of a trillion dollars. However, if, over that period (1985 to 2010), if we add up net farm income, acquired from the markets, we generate a figure of negative $3.1 billion. Despite their work, innovation and production, farmers earned a net income of less than zero. What happened to that three-quarters of a trillion dollars? Chemical, fertilizer, machinery and petroleum companies, banks and others captured the entire amount.

Government ministers and senior Agriculture Canada managers have reacted to this farm income crisis —the worst in Canadian history — by denial or attempts to contort the truth. For example, the Ministry of Agriculture, commenting on these worse-than-Depression net incomes, stated: "The downward trend in real net cash income reflects lower production costs in an increasingly-efficient agricultural sector" (AAFC 2009: 103). Perhaps it doesn't need to be said, but economists and CEOs would be surprised if told that lower production costs and increased efficiency would actually lead to lower net income — most have confidence the opposite is true.

Not only does AAFC try to explain away farmers' zero net income, they actually try to deny it:

> The value that Canadian farm families produce through their work and focus on running successful businesses has translated into a healthy economic position overall, with rising farm family income, higher net worth compared to other Canadian families, and significant returns on assets. (Canadian Ministers of Agriculture 2010: 9)

In their attempt to support such a claim, AAFC includes farm support payments and wages from off-farm jobs in "farm family income" (quotations here from Ministers of Agriculture, above). With net farm income chronically negative, in most years farm support payments and off-farm income have made up 100 percent of that "farm family income" to which AAFC is referring. If farm family income is rising, that is only because farm families are working two or three jobs and receiving generous taxpayer support. AAFC also mentions "higher net worth compared to other families." But farm net worth cannot be counted as income, or even as savings — it cannot be liquidated or spent, because a large portion of the farm assets are in use for food production and are also being maintained to be passed to the next generation. Finally, AAFC mentions "significant return on assets." That assertion is simply false. Figure 2-3 shows that Canadian net farm income from the markets has been negative for most of the past two-and-a-half decades. Since net farm income is negative overall, return on assets will be negative as well, not "significant" as AAFC erroneously asserts.

AAFC strains to put a positive spin on a very negative situation One tactic is to pretend that, while overall net income may be negative, net incomes on big farms — "large business-focused" farms, according to AAFC's typology (AAFC 2002; Statistics Canada 2009) — are positive. Essentially, AAFC tries to give the impression that the big, efficient farms that really try to make profits do so; and that the money-losing farms are small, inefficient, and, in AAFC's words, "non-business-focused." Canada's Ministers of Agriculture actually say this: "Smaller farms are more likely to experience a consistent lack of profitability and negative net farm income" (Canadian Ministers of Agriculture 2010: 9). This attitude is echoed by AAFC: "The larger the farm, the more likely it is to be profitable" (AAFC 2010c: 5).

Sorting the truths from all the falsehoods about large-farm profitability would take up much space, but it is highly debatable that AAFC's assertions of healthy profits on large farms are accurate. First of all, large farms require billions of dollars in tax-funded farm program payments in order to remain solvent. Fifty-nine percent of program payments — about $2 billion dollars annually — go to farms with gross revenues of over $250,000 per year (AAFC 2009: 105). Many of these farms have revenues of millions of dollars per year. Second, grain and oilseed farms, as well as hog farms — the farm types that

Figure 2-4 Market Income and Program Payments on Farms with Revenues > $250,000: 1990–2005

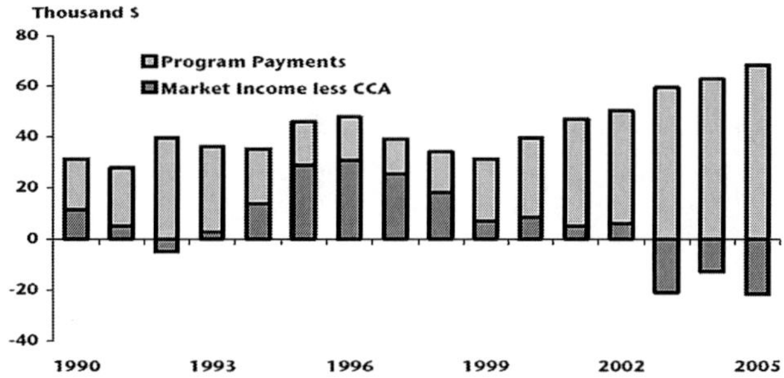

Note: CCA – Capital Cost Allowance (depreciation)

Sources: Agriculture and Agri-Food Canada, *An Overview of the Canadian Agriculture and Agri-Food System: 2007*, p. 108.

have been most aggressive in expansion and that now sport some of the largest operations — post some of the largest farm losses (Statistics Canada Canadian Farm Financial Database). Finally, AAFC's own data shows that in eleven of the sixteen years encompassing 1990 to 2005, inclusive, Canada's large and very large farms earned little or no net income from the markets, recording losses in several years (see Figure 2-4).[1] Moreover, over that sixteen-year period, farm support payments made up the bulk of net income on these large and very large farms. AAFC itself points out: "Program payments received by farm operators, with revenue of $250,000 or more, tripled between 1995 and 2005" (AAFC 2007: 108). Data for 2006 to 2010 continue the pattern shown in Figure 2-4 (Statistics Canada 2009; AAFC 2011). AAFC's own reports and data falsify its contention that net income shortfalls are phenomena confined to small farms.

Figure 2-5 Canadian Agri-Food Exports and Realized Net Income from the Markets: 1970–2010

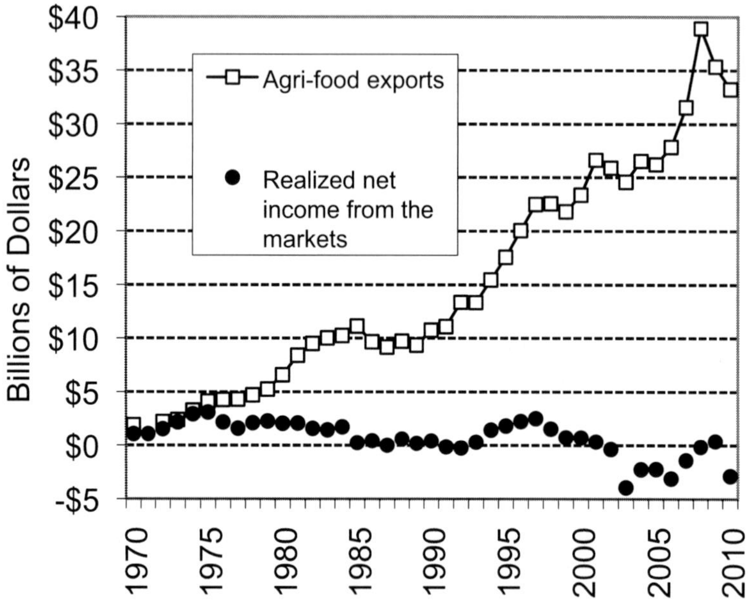

Sources: Export data provided upon request from Agriculture and Agri-Food Canada; AAFC, Agri-Food Trade Service <www.ats-sea.agr.gc.ca>; AAFC, *Medium Term Outlook for Canadian Agriculture: International and Domestic Markets*, January 2010. Income data from Statistics Canada, 2002, *Agricultural Economic Statistics*, Cat. No. 21-603-E May, Ottawa: Statistics Canada; Statistics Canada, 2010c, *Net Farm Income–Agriculture Economic Statistics*, Cat. No. 21-010-X, May, Ottawa: Statistics Canada.

Putting this data together paints a dismal picture (see Figure 2-5). The juxtaposition of sinking net income with soaring export sales graphically illustrates the failure of a Canadian agriculture policy built upon export maximization, productivism, technophilia and input maximization. Furthermore, in this evidence of the *failure* of Canada's agriculture and food policies, we see the logic of food sovereignty reaffirmed.

A Chronic Drain on Taxpayers

> Program payments help to cover low market incomes. Program payments are important for farmers' net market losses.... Program payments are helping to maintain the long term viability of the farm sector. (AAFC 2007: 100, 108)

As we have seen, the policies and strategies advanced by Ottawa, the provinces and the large agricultural corporations, such as Monsanto, are money-losers for Canadian farm families. In order to prevent collapse in the farm sector, taxpayers have been pressed to provide $3 billion to $4 billion per year through a range of farm support programs. Over the past decade-and-a-half, support programs have primarily taken five main forms:

1. *Crop Insurance:* Farmers can pay premiums into insurance programs that protect them from yield losses caused by weather, insects, plant diseases and other uncontrollable or hard-to-control events. Because program costs are split between farmers, the federal government and provincial governments over the medium term, most farmers receive more money than they pay in through premiums.
2. *Margin-based support programs:* Past programs such as AIDA (the Agricultural Income Disaster Assistance program), CFIP (the Canadian Farm Income Program) and CAIS (the Canadian Agricultural Income Stabilization program), and the current AgriStability all seek to protect farmers against large and sudden farm income contractions caused by price declines, weather disasters, disease outbreaks, border closures and other macro-events. In general, a farmer is paid if his or her farm margin (revenues minus selected expenses) falls below a set percentage (often 70 percent or 85 percent) of a multi-year average. Premium and fee formulas vary, but annual payouts, overall, significantly exceed premiums and fees. These programs are a significant conduit to deliver income support and stabilization dollars to farmers.
3. *Savings account programs:* The now-ended NISA (the Net Income Stabilization Account) program and the current AgriInvest program have allowed farmers to make deposits into savings accounts and to withdraw

those deposits when net farm incomes fall. A portion of a farmer's deposit is matched by a government contribution.

4. Ad hoc payments: Federal and provincial governments continue to make ad hoc payments to farmers to offset very large potential losses. A recent example of this was payments to cattle farmers and other producers in the wake of border closures triggered by the discovery of BSE (bovine spongiform encephalopathy) in a Canadian cow.
5. Québec's ASRA: Québec has operated a unique income stabilization program since 1979. Very briefly, the ASRA (L'assurance stabilisation des revenus agricoles) program is a multi-risk (weather, prices, disease, etc.) program that seeks to support and stabilize farm incomes in relation to production costs and in relation to incomes and wages outside of the farm sector.

Through these programs and others, federal, provincial and territorial governments have transferred approximately $67 billion of taxpayers money to the farm sector since the mid-1980s — about $8,000 per Canadian household. Because so much of our food output is exported, a large part of that $8,000 per family can be seen as a subsidy from Canadian households to the foreign buyers of our pork, soybeans, wheat and other farm products. Or seen another way, perhaps that $8,000 per Canadian family is a transfer from taxpayers to the world's dominant agri-business transnationals.

Who Is Profiting within the System?

> Monsanto realized record sales for a fifth consecutive year in fiscal 2008, delivering compound annual earnings growth of 20 percent-plus during that time.... It is very gratifying to repeat a message you have heard for what is now the past five fiscal years: We achieved new records in net sales and net income. (Monsanto Annual Report 2008: 1)

> High fertilizer prices help lift Agrium to record profits. —February 2011 headline in the *Toronto Star*

> Our earnings of more than $500 million, announced last week, were the highest ever for a first quarter and marked our third straight quarter of record results. According to our forecasts, the company is on track to earn record profits for the full year of 2011. — February 2011 speech by John Deere CEO Samuel Allen (John Deere 2011)

As farm families have watched their net incomes deteriorate, and as taxpayers have been tapped to cover farm losses, the dominant agri-business corporations have consistently racked up record and near-record profits. Many of the worst years for farmers have been the best years for agri-business companies (NFU 2005). This is no coincidence.

Farmers are positioned in the middle of an agri-food chain. On one side, powerful processors and retailers such as Maple Leaf and Loblaws take an ever larger chunk from Canadians' grocery store dollars and pass little back to the farmgate. Moreover, the revenue that does arrive at the farm is quickly snapped up by those on the other side of the agri-food chain — powerful input supply corporations, including fertilizer, seed, chemical, machinery and energy companies.

As detailed above, farmers' profits from the marketplace, in aggregate, since 1985, equal zero. This is a unique occurrence. The only other period of sustained low net farm income in the past century was the Great Depression — a time of drought, unemployment and economic collapse. The post-1985 net income crisis, coming during a relatively buoyant economic period, and coming at a time when the other players in the agri-food chain have been recording record-high profits, demands examination and explanation. I believe the data supports a straightforward explanation: Monsanto, Agrium, Deere and a host of other agri-business corporations have taken advantage of their huge size and the lack of profit-disciplining competition to take for themselves profits that in previous decades would have come to rest in the bank accounts of Canadian farm families. By urging farmers to use ever more of these high-tech, high-cost inputs, Canadian agriculture policies push farmers more deeply into the embrace of profit-extracting giants. Clearly, an imbalance in market power exists between family farmers, on the one hand, and agri-business transnationals, on the other hand, and this has led to a parallel imbalance in the allocation of profits along the food chain, leaving farmers with large losses. In other words, family farmers are making too little because powerful corporations are taking too much.

A Debt Bomb Ticking Beneath Farmhouses and Barns

> Federal agriculture minister Lyle Vanclief said that… increased debt can be a sign farmers are optimistic enough to put more money into their operations. (report for the *Western Producer*, Wilson 1999)

> Farmers are borrowing to make themselves more viable. (Agriculture Canada finances specialist Jack Gellner [quoted in Wilson 2001])

As we see above, farmers' net incomes from the markets are low, or negative. This situation has arisen because, over the past fifty years, farm input prices have increased nearly twice as fast as farm product prices (for example,

Figure 2-6 Canadian Farm Debt: 1970–2010

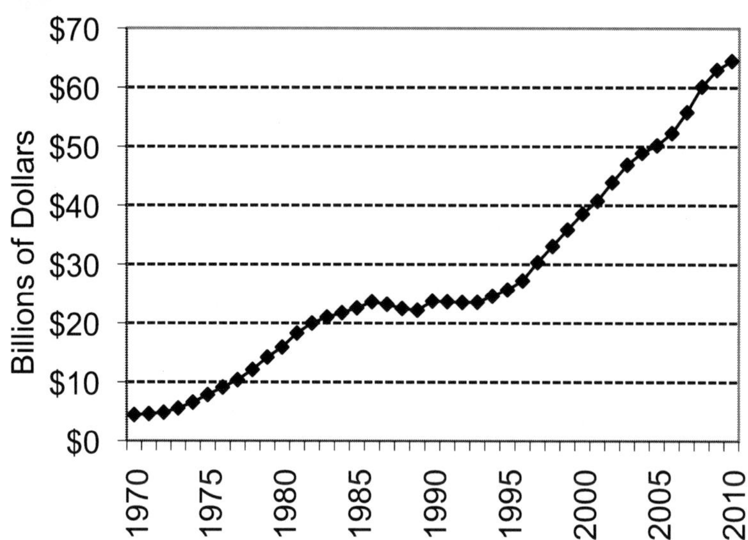

Source: Statistics Canada, 2010b, *Farm Debt Outstanding*, Cat. No. 21-014-X, November, Ottawa: Statistics Canada.

fertilizer and chemical prices have gone up twice as much as corn and feeder calf prices) (AAFC 2009: 115). Prices for grains, livestock, potatoes and other farm products are well below even the most efficient farmer's costs of production. Many farms have been forced to absorb chronic losses. We can see these losses accumulating when we inspect farm debt statistics (see Figure 2-6).

Farm debt levels are now completely out of proportion to net farm income. Furthermore, Canadian farm debt, which now stands at about $64 billion, is rising by about $2.7 billion per year: it has doubled in the past twelve years. Figure 2-7 shows the ratio of debt to Realized Net Farm Income (support payments included); it shows how much farmers owe relative to how much they make. (The graph cuts off possibly anomalous data for 2003 and 2010.[2]) Calculated on a per-dollar-of-net-farm-income basis, debt has skyrocketed. For each dollar farm families earn and keep, they have to shoulder more and more dollars of debt. This is perhaps the clearest proof that government and corporate agricultural policies have plunged our family farms into a net income crisis, and that debt levels are both unprecedented and unmanageable.

In terms of dollars of debt per dollar of income, decade averages are revealing. In the 1970s, for instance, for each dollar farm families earned in net income during that decade, on average they had to shoulder $3.40 in debt. In the 1980s, the ratio rose: for each dollar of net income earned, farmers

Figure 2-7 Canadian Farm Debt per Dollar of Realized Net Income: 1970–2010

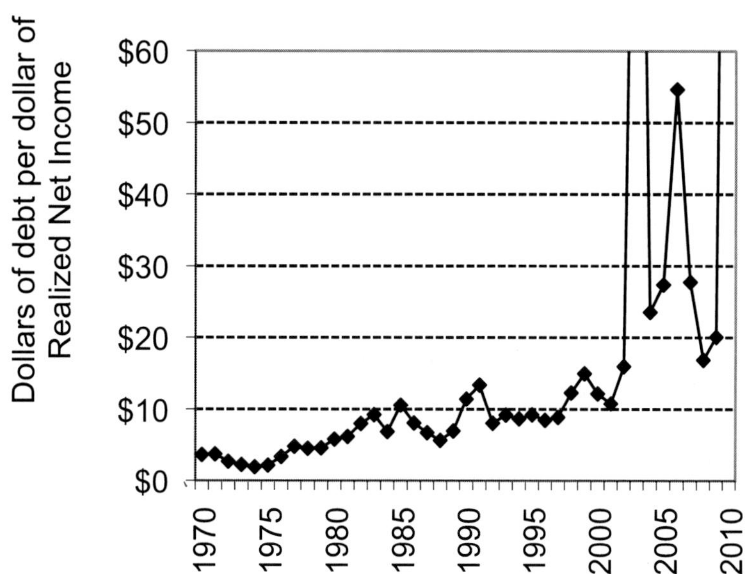

Sources: Statistics Canada, 2010b, *Farm Debt Outstanding*, Cat. No. 21-014-X, November, Ottawa: Statistics Canada; and Statistics Canada, 2010c, *Net Farm Income*, Cat. No. 21-010-X, May, Ottawa: Statistics Canada.

had to carry $7.42 in debt. In the 1990s, for each dollar of net income earned, farmers had to carry $10.47 in debt. In the most recent decade (2000–2009, inclusive, omitting 2003), for each dollar of net income earned, farmers had to carry $23.25 in debt — seven times the level of the 1970s. This last point bears repeating: To earn a net income dollar today, farm families must borrow and risk seven times as much debt as they had to borrow and risk in the 1970s, and three times as much as in the 1980s.

The $64 billion debt farmers now carry makes them excruciatingly vulnerable to interest rate hikes. Each one-percent increase in interest rates will cost farm families $640 million dollars per year. A 3 percent or 4 percent interest rate hike will increase farmers' interest costs by $2 billion to $3 billion per year, thus turning an already bleak farm income situation into a financial cataclysm.

Loss of Farm Families

Low net income, high debt, crop and livestock prices below the cost of production, corporate concentration and profiteering: these and other factors are driving an expulsion of farm families from their land. In many ways, this amounts to a "clearance" policy, led by Monsanto, AAFC and Cargill, not unlike the policies in eighteenth and nineteenth century England, Scotland and elsewhere, designed to remove economically surplus populations from the land.

Official statistics on the number of farmers in Canada dramatically underestimate the rate of expulsion. Government data shows that Canada has lost 22 percent of its farms and farm families over the past approximately twenty years (Statistics Canada 2007, 1987). Those of us who live among farmers know, however, that the actual loss of viable, multi-generational farms in many regions may be much higher than that 22 percent figure.

Most family farms in the 1970s and early 1980s were multi-generational; there were sons and daughters in their teens, twenties, thirties or forties farming alongside their parents, working toward the day when each of them could take over his or her family's farm. In contrast, today, on many of the farms which Statistics Canada counts in its Census of Agriculture, that next generation is missing. Indeed, if we compare the number of viable intergenerational family farms in operation twenty or twenty-five years ago to the number today, we learn that Canada may have lost half its family farms — a truly astounding figure.

Another unsettling trend to ponder is the loss of young farmers— those under the age of thirty-five — in Canada. According to Statistics Canada's Census of Agriculture, in 1991, Canada had 77,910 young farmers. Fifteen years later, in 2006, we had just 29,920 — a drop of 62 percent. In 1991, there was a farmer under the age of thirty-five on one farm in every four; today, just one farm in eight supports a young farmer. Our family farms appear to have gone over the edge of a demographic cliff. Those who doubted the assessment in the preceding paragraph — that Canada may have lost half of its intergenerational family farms — need only look to these young-farmer statistics for proof.

Transferring Land to Local and Distant Elites

Not only has Canada been losing farms and farm families, but those farm families remaining are also in danger of losing their land. A June 2010 report by Canada's National Farmers Union details the rapidly accelerating buy-up of Canadian farmland by investors, corporations and foreign interests. *Losing Our Grip* (NFU 2010a) details how investment companies and others have already bought up or taken control of hundreds of thousands of acres of Canadian farmland. For instance, Assiniboia Capital Corp., Agcapita, Monaxxion, Bonnefield Financial Inc., Hancock Agricultural Investment Group and others are buying up farmland here and packaging it as investments for "high net worth individuals" in Canada and abroad (see Government of Canada 2010). A headline in the April 21, 2008 *Globe and*

Mail stated: "Seeking an agriculture play? Buy Saskatchewan" (Blackwell 2008); a headline subtitle from the June 17, 2006 *Toronto Star* stated: "Asians key investors in 30-farm purchase" (Monsebraaten 2006).

Players in the Canadian farmland buy-up include Brian and Lee Nilsson, owners of Canada's largest meat packing and cattle conglomerate; Jim Rogers, commodities investment guru and co-founder (with George Soros) of the Quantum fund in 1970; and Kenneth Clarke, former U.K. Chancellor of the Exchequer, U.K. cabinet minister and three-time challenger for the leadership of the Conservative Party (NFU 2010a: 4–9).

Canadian governments are supportive of the transfer of farmland from local farmers to foreign and domestic investors. For example, federal crown agency Farm Credit Canada (FCC) is the largest financier of one of our country's largest farmland investment companies, providing multi-million dollar loans to Assiniboia Capital, a company that has already bought up 100,000 acres of farmland on behalf of investors. The federal government's "Invest in Canada" website is promoting "low political risk" and "fertile fields" to international investors. The government website predicts that "Canadian farmers can expect a flurry of international interest in the coming months as investors bet that low commodity prices will rebound," eventually concluding that "Canadian farmland is still affordable by global standards" (Government of Canada 2010). The provincial government of Saskatchewan eased its farmland ownership restrictions in 2003. Speaking at the time, Deputy Premier and Agriculture Minister Clay Serby said the change "sends the message to all Canadians that Saskatchewan is open to outside investment." Since then, often citing that 2003 easing of restrictions, several farmland investment companies have bought up hundreds of thousands of acres of land in the province.

Commenting on the rapid rise in investor ownership of Canadian farmland, National Farmers Union President and Saskatchewan farmer Terry Boehm said:

> There have been two primary models of land ownership and food production over the centuries. In one, land ownership is widely distributed among farmers and other local citizens. In another, a relatively small number of elites owned the land and those who worked it and grew the food were sharecroppers and serfs. Canada has, until recently, embraced the first model. But a corporate and investor farmland buy-up means that we may be in the opening stages of a rapid move to the latter model. Unless we act, our land may soon be owned by modern-day lords and barons, with disastrous consequences for all Canadians. There can be no Food Sovereignty or democratic control of our food system if national and global elites have snatched up the land on which we grow our food. (NFU 2010b)

An Increasingly Unsustainable Food Production System

Canadian farms are growing bigger, using more technology and producing greater output per acre, per animal and per farmer. Many say that our farms today are more efficient than in previous generations. But such assessments are based on a particular, narrow view of what constitutes efficiency. Consider this thought experiment: A century ago, Canadian farms were powered by horses that derived their energy from grass, hay and grain which, in turn, was created largely out of sunlight. In effect, Canadian farms were solar powered. In providing the power to work their fields, these farms required no fossil fuels and emitted few, if any, net greenhouse gas emissions. Today, our farms (and our larger food system) consume massive amounts of fossil fuels and emit large quantities of greenhouse gasses (USDA 2010). Moving all of Canada back to horses, powered by hay — or solar powered farming — is really not feasible and perhaps not desirable; however, this thought experiment does show that there is something odd about how we calculate efficiency: our old solar powered, low emission, fossil-fuel-free farms are seen as inefficient, while our oil-powered, climate-altering modern farms are considered to be efficient. Taking a closer look at how Canada transforms fossil fuels, chemicals, fertilizer, technology, machinery and debt into food further highlights this conundrum.

Canadian farms have been increasing output (at least partly) by increasing their use of pesticides and chemical fertilizers, largely derived from fossil fuels. Canadian farmers use 36 percent more fertilizer today than they did twenty years ago (AAFC 1998: table 2.12; Statistics Canada CANSIM 001-0065 and 001-0068). Nationwide, Canadian farmers now apply 3.5 mega-tonnes of nitrogen, phosphorous, potassium and sulphur per year. Nitrogen is largely a product of natural gas (U.N. 2008: 7). To a significant extent, Canada's increased food and export output can be attributed to increased fossil fuel input. This is, indeed, key to understanding the Green Revolution and much of the post-WWII near-tripling of human population. Canada's food production increases can best be understood if we consider that agriculture is increasingly a way to turn fossil fuel calories into food calories — with each calorie of food requiring multiple calories of fossil fuel to produce.

Figure 2-8 shows that, in constant dollars (i.e., adjusted for inflation), farmers' purchases of chemicals and fertilizers have not only doubled but redoubled. Pesticide purchases increased six-fold between 1971 and 2005, according to AAFC, while fertilizer purchases increased by about 3½-fold. Similar increases are evident using data based on volume (AAFC 1998: table 2.12; Statistics Canada CANSIM table 001-0068).

This data, and data in preceding sections of this chapter, suggest some correlations. First, Canada is utilizing more fossil-energy-derived fertilizer, fuel and chemicals in the production of its food. In the current context, "efficiency" does not mean reducing input and energy use within the system, it means reducing the number of farmers, while the use of every other input is increased. As climate change bears down upon us and as oil supplies become less certain and their extraction more environmentally damaging, we must conclude that replacing farmers with petroleum will clearly reduce the long-term sustainability of the Canadian food supply. Indeed, depending more and more upon something we may soon have less and less of seems the very definition of "unsustainable."

The second correlation suggested by the data is that, as energy, input and technology use has taken off in the past two or three decades, farm income has crashed. This is not surprising. These inputs are sold by some of the planet's most powerful and profitable corporations: fuel is sold by Exxon and Shell; fertilizer by Potash Corporation, Mosaic, Yara and Agrium; chemicals by Bayer, Syngenta, Dow, Monsanto and DuPont; and seeds by Monsanto, DuPont, Syngenta and Bayer. Increased input use and, especially, increased dependence on purchased inputs reduces not only the environmental and social sustainability of family farming, but also its economic sustainability.

A warped view of efficiency (fewer farmers but increased input and energy use) has pushed us away from farm and food-system sustainability. A more genuine approach to efficiency (input reduction and optimization, lower energy use, making space for citizens who want to produce food, reducing transportation distances) will move us toward our sustainability goals (energy savings, lower carbon dioxide emissions, genetic diversity, resilience). The paths toward sustainability and toward true efficiency lead in the same direction — away from Canada's current agricultural policies and toward food sovereignty.

Figure 2-8 Canadian Farm Expenditures on Fertilizers and Pesticides (Adjusted for Inflation): 1971–2005

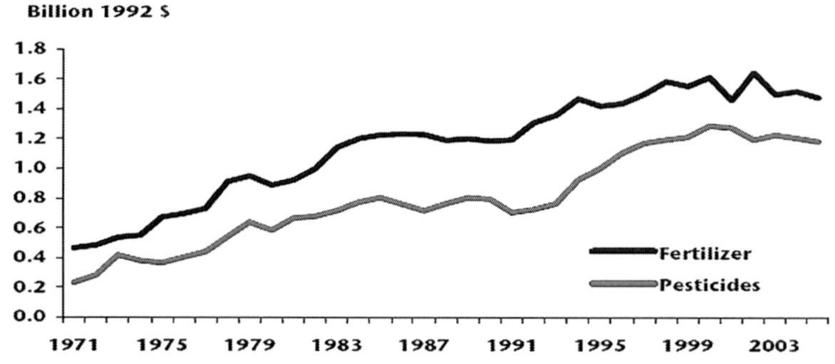

Sources: Agriculture and Agri-Food Canada, *An Overview of the Canadian Agriculture and Agri-Food System: 2007*, p. 124.

The End of Canadian Agriculture?

Is it prudent to raise the prospect of "The End of Canadian Agriculture"? If agriculture is seen as a way that a significant number of family farms make a living by producing and selling food, and if it is seen as a way in which our food, and the people who make it, are woven into the fabric of our nation, its narrative, and our future, then clearly the end may be at hand.

First, it is less and less the case that most family farms "make a living." It is only with the assistance of billions of dollars per year in taxpayer-funded support programs that many farmers can remain on their farms and, indeed, that certain food production sectors (e.g. hog production) can continue to exist in Canada. Second, we are rapidly moving toward a point where it will no longer be true that "a significant number of family farms" exist in Canada. If we continue to pursue policies of farm giantism and policies of replacing farmers with petroleum and patented seeds, then Canada can expect a future wherein perhaps 15,000 farms produce 80 percent of our food output — the largest 7,500 farms today produce 40 percent of Canadian output. If we allow this to happen (indeed, if we continue to pursue federal and provincial agriculture policies that encourage this to happen), then we must admit that we are presiding over the destruction of the family farm in Canada. And if we move to a system without family farms — one in which Canadian foodland is owned by foreigners and investors, one in which the primary financial beneficiaries of food production are transnational agri-business corporations — then we may as well announce the end of Canadian agriculture. There will still be food output tonnage, but there will be no agriculture. In place of agriculture will be something industrial, something corporate, something owned by people most of us will never meet, something apart and alienated from community and culture.

A New Chance for Canadian Agriculture?

Of course, there is another path. The future for Canadian farms is dark; the young people have left and agri-business CEOs have made off with all the profits. Canadian agriculture policy has failed to protect the traditional and diverse forms of agriculture that have supported Canadian families, communities and the environment. This failure is absolute, broad and very visible. But it is exactly this overwhelming and plainly evident failure that now presents hope. By every measure, our agriculture policy model is defective and destructive; to any observer not in the thrall of Monsanto or Dow, it is clear that an alternative is required. The bleakness of the current situation can help give energy to the project of finding and implementing a new model for agriculture. That new model must move us in a direction opposite to the money-losing, production-maximizing, export-focused, technology over-dependent policies that have so ravaged our farms, communities and public purses. That new model is food sovereignty.

The chapters that follow detail the food sovereignty alternative. Suffice it to say here that food sovereignty — applied domestically in Canada and internationally as part of a new trade, cooperation and environment framework — holds the key to a farm and food system renaissance in Canada. Canadian farm families have demonstrated their capacity to produce massive wealth — more than three-quarters of a trillion dollars over the past twenty-five years. And with more appropriate crop and livestock prices, the value of farm production can be even higher. Food sovereignty policies would concentrate on ways to help those farm families hold on to a sufficient portion of the bounteous wealth they create, and stop the bleed-off of wealth to banks, input makers, processors and retailers.

Agricultural policies designed to ensure that Canadian farm families (not foreign-based transnationals) are the primary beneficiaries of the extraordinary wealth created on our food production landscape would have many attendant benefits. If farm families are financially stable, and if additional wealth can be retained in rural areas, then rural communities can thrive and create jobs. Moreover, young and new farmers can enter agriculture and we can restart the intergenerational transfer processes critical to the continuance of our family farm model.

Finally, policies based on food sovereignty (rather than production and export maximization) mean that we can reduce the use of chemical insecticides and herbicides, injected growth hormones and unnecessary antibiotics in livestock. Food sovereignty-based policies seek to maximize stewardship of the land and its long-term sustainable productivity, rather than the short-term extraction of production tonnage.

There is more than enough money in the food system to allow farm families to thrive. There is more than enough will and stewardship ethic among farmers to ensure that our land, water and wildlife are protected. Indeed, there is more than enough land and know-how to ensure that Canadian farmers can produce bountiful and healthy food for our citizens, and, when appropriate, for those in other nations who wish to purchase from us. Our current food and agriculture policies repress and deplete our capacities to produce good food, prosperity and strong communities. Food sovereignty seeks to directly support and nourish such capacities. Our financially devastated farms and towns provide incontrovertible evidence that our current food and agriculture policies are massive failures which have brought us to the brink of a collapse. We must stop administering a corporate-concocted financial poison to our family farms and rural communities and begin administering an antidote. The antidote is food sovereignty. Please read on.

Notes

1. Market net income in this graph takes into account Capital Cost Allowance — the cost of farm machinery and buildings.
2. The graph's ratios are computed thus: farm debt divided by net farm income. Thus, when net farm income (the denominator) falls very low, the ratio rises very high. The ratio for 2003 was 143 dollars of debt per dollar of net farm income. Furthermore, because net farm income denominator is projected to fall so low in 2010, the ratio is projected to rise very high: 220 dollars of debt per dollar of net income. While the 2003 and 2010 values accurately reflect debt-to-income ratios in those years, they probably do not provide a true representation over the medium term: thus, to avoid overstating the case, the 2003 and 2010 are excluded from the graph and from calculations in this chapter. In other words, had the ratio values for 2003 and 2010 been left into the graph and subsequent calculations, it would have been even more apparent that recent debt levels are huge relative to net income levels, and that, in fact, recent debt levels (relative to net income levels) are unprecedented.

References

Agriculture and Agri-Food Canada (AAFC). 2011. "Canada's Farm Income Forecast for 2010 and 2011." February. <http://www4.agr.gc.ca/AAFC-AAC/display-afficher.do?id=1298587468988&lang=eng>

______. 2010a. *Medium Term Outlook for Canadian Agriculture: International and Domestic Markets*. January.

______. 2010b. *Canada's Farm Income Forecast for 2009 and 2010*. February.

______ (Farm Business and Economic Well-being Section, Farm Economic Analysis Section). 2010c. *Structure and Performance of the Agriculture and Agri-Food Sector*. Briefing document, "Agriculture 2020." Ottawa: AAFC.

______ (Agri-Food Trade Service). 2010d. Canadian Trade Highlights. <ats-sea.agr.gc.ca>. Additional data provided by AAFC, via personal communication.

______. 2010e. "Canada Brand International, Market research in key export markets." <marquecanadabrand.agr.gc.ca/research-etudes/research-etudes-eng.htm>

______. 2009. *An Overview of the Canadian Agriculture and Agri-Food System: 2009*. May.

______. 2007. *An Overview of the Canadian Agriculture and Agri-Food System: 2007*. May.

______. 2005. *A Statistical Profile of the Pork Supply Chain*. December.

______. 2002. *Characteristics of Canada's Diverse Farm Sector*. January.

______. 1998. *Fertilizer Pricing in Canada*, June.

Blackwell, R. 2008. "Seeking an agriculture play? Buy Saskatchewan." *Globe and Mail*, April 21.

Canadian Ministers of Agriculture. 2010. *Agriculture 2020: Challenges and Priorities*. Briefing document, "Agriculture 2020." Ottawa: Ministers of Agriculture.

John Deere. 2011. Speech by Samuel R. Allen, John Deere Chairman & Chief Executive Officer, to the 2011 Annual Meeting of Shareholders, Moline, Illinois, February 23. <http://www.deere.com/wps/dcom/en_US/corporate/our_company/news_and_media/speeches/2011feb23_allen.page>.

Government of Canada. 2010. "Hancock Agricultural Investment Group Attracted by Canada's Fertile Fields." Invest in Canada website, Newsfeed: Agri-Food, February. <http://investincanada.gc.ca/eng/industry-sectors/agri-food/news-feed.aspx>

Monsanto. 2008. *Annual Report*. <http://www.monsanto.com/investors/Documents/Pubs/2008/annual_report.pdf>

Monsebraaten, L. 2006. "Banking on a land boom." *Toronto Star*, June 17.

National Farmers Union (NFU). 2010a. "Losing our Grip: How a Corporate Farmland Buy-up, Rising Farm Debt, and Agribusiness Financing of Inputs Threaten Family Farms and Food Sovereignty." NFU brief, June 7.

_____. 2010b. "Corporations and Investors Buying Up Canadian Farmland: NFU Releases Report on Land Grabbing." News release, June 7.

_____. 2003. "The Farm Crisis, Bigger Farms, and the Myths of Competition and Efficiency." November 20.

_____. 2005 "The Farm Crisis & Corporate Profits." NFU brief, November 30.

Statistics Canada. 2010a. *Farm Cash Receipts: Agriculture Economic Statistics*. Cat. No. 21-011-X, May. Ottawa: Statistics Canada.

_____. 2010b. *Farm Debt Outstanding*. Cat. No. 21-014-X, vol. 9 no. 2, November. Ottawa: Statistics Canada.

_____. 2010c. *Net Farm Income–Agriculture Economic Statistics*. Cat. No. 21-010-X, May. Ottawa: Statistics Canada.

_____. 2010d. *The Consumer Price Index*. Cat. No. 62-001-XWE, vol. 89 no. 11, December. Ottawa: Statistics Canada.

_____. 2009. *Statistics on Income of Farm Families*. Cat. No. 21-207-E, June 26. Ottawa: Statistics Canada.

_____. 2007. *The Canadian Productivity Accounts: Data: 1961 to 2006*. Cat. No. 15-003-X, December. Ottawa: Statistics Canada.

_____. 2007. 2006 Census of Agriculture: Farm Data and Farm Operator Data. Cat. No. 95-629-XWE, May 16. <http://www.statcan.gc.ca/pub/95-629-x/2007000/4123856-eng.htm>

_____. 2002. *Agricultural Economic Statistics*. Cat. No. 21-603-E, May. Ottawa: Statistics Canada.

_____. 2001. *Productivity Growth in Canada*. Cat. No. 15-204-X February. Ottawa: Statistics Canada.

_____. 1992. *Agricultural Profile of Canada: Part 1* [1991 Census of Agriculture], Cat. No. 93-350, June. Ottawa: Ministry of Industry and Technology.

_____. 1987. *Census, Canada 1986, Agriculture*. Cat. No. 96-102, December. Ottawa: Ministry of Supply and Services.

_____. CANSIM table 001-0017. Estimated areas, yield, production, average farm price and total farm value of principal field crops, in imperial units, annual. All CANSIM tables available at <http://www5.statcan.gc.ca/cansim/a01?lang=eng>.

_____. CANSIM table 001-0065. Fertilizer shipments to Canadian agriculture markets, by nutrient content and fertilizer year, annual.

_____. CANSIM table 001-0068. Fertilizer shipments to Canadian agriculture and export markets, by product type and fertilizer year, cumulative data, annual.

_____. CANSIM table 003-0026. Cattle and calves, farm and meat production, annual.

_____. CANSIM table 383-0022. Multifactor productivity, gross output, value-added, capital, labour and intermediate inputs at a detailed industry level, by North American Industry Classification System (NAICS), annual.

_____. n.d. "Canadian Farm Financial Database." <cansim2.statcan.gc.ca/cgi-win/cnsmcgi.pgm?Lang=E&ESASaction=Pick1&ESASData=ESAS2008&Res-Ins=CFFD-BDFEAC/ESASPick&JS=1>

Toronto Star 2011. "High fertilizer prices help lift Agrium to record profits." February 9. Canadian Press. <http://www.thestar.com/business/article/935537--high-fertilizer-prices-help-lift-agrium-to-record-profits>

United Nations, Food and Agriculture Organization. 2008. *Current World Fertilizer Trends and Outlook to 2012*. New York: United Nations.

United States Department of Agriculture (USDA). 2010. *Energy Use in the U.S. Food System* (Economic Research Report Number 94), March.

Wilson, B. 2001. "Farm debt a looming concern." *Western Producer*, July 5.

_____. 1999. "Farm debt hits record." *Western Producer*, June 10.

3. GETTING TO FOOD SOVEREIGNTY

Grassroots Perspectives from the National Farmers Union

Interviews with Terry Boehm and Hilary Moore,
conducted by Naomi Beingessner

The National Farmers Union (NFU), the largest voluntary direct-membership national farm organization in Canada, has been a progressive voice for farmers since 1969. The NFU supports family farms and rural communities and actively resists the corporate control of food. It was a founding member of the transnational peasant movement La Vía Campesina (LVC) and is a leader in promoting food sovereignty in Canada.

In this chapter, two NFU leaders in different regions of Canada address the local and national political challenges and strategies involved in the grassroots struggle for food sovereignty. Their reflections also speak to the significance of food sovereignty for achieving economic, social and ecological justice not just for producers, but for all Canadians.

Terry Boehm, President of the National Farmers Union, is a fourth-generation Saskatchewan farmer who has been farming for twenty-eight years near Allan, Saskatchewan. For the first twenty years, he built up his farm while running a manufacturing business building farm and industrial equipment and custom-designed machinery. Now he grows primarily conventional grains, legumes and oilseeds, with a small amount being produced organically, eschewing genetically modified organisms (GMOs). He has been active in politics since his university days, when he studied history and economics; he has a particular interest in issues of power and control, especially the critical issue of intellectual property rights.

Despite not having a family background in farming, Hilary Moore began to farm after completing a degree in environmental studies. She has been a full-time farmer for over a decade: together with her husband, she purchased a farm in Lanark County, Ontario, in 2010. They operate a vegetable Community Supported Agriculture (CSA) program, as well as raising pigs and selling eggs. All of their produce is uncertified organic. A young farmer in her thirties, Hilary's political focus as president of NFU Local 310 is on consciousness-raising and empowerment of new and established farmers.

Naomi: What does food sovereignty mean to your organization?

Terry: Our understanding of food sovereignty for the National Farmers Union is very similar to the conceptualization of La Vía Campesina. It's the ability of the community — whether it's a nation-state, a province, a local community or even a small organization of farmers — to determine what's appropriate in terms of food production and in terms of social and economic justice that flows from growing food. This power includes the autonomy to determine what's appropriate in both those areas and also in terms of the broader economic and ecological context.

From its genesis, the function of the National Farmers Union is really directed toward many of the broader concepts that food sovereignty encapsulates. The NFU's mandate was to advance social and economic justice for small and medium-sized family farms, which the NFU believes are the appropriate units on which to grow food in Canada. This fits rather well with food sovereignty, so in that respect it's quite an important concept. In other respects it's a difficult one to translate because, for some, there is a fundamental conflict between export agriculture and food sovereignty when the latter is associated solely with local food production systems. In many regions of Canada, like here on the prairies, agriculture is export-oriented and indeed was created with an export model in place from the time of settlement. A food sovereignty model means that the trade that does take place shouldn't harm other agricultural producers in other parts of the world.

Food sovereignty changes the discussion around growing food; it is an important contextual piece in terms of how people view food, what position producers are in and the political analysis that flows from that food production. I think a lot of the work that the National Farmers Union has done, at least on the national stage, has been very much about maintaining autonomy and control and translating the benefits of food production back to producers.

Hilary: The NFU is certainly a leader in promoting the idea of food sovereignty, albeit a bit of a quiet leader. Here in Ontario, it seems like the concept of food sovereignty has become a popular slogan that people throw around. So I'm really hoping that the NFU protects the integrity of the concept. I believe so wholeheartedly in food sovereignty and the complexity and radicalness of it that I fret it's going to get manipulated into something less complicated and less radical, and become just like everything else. For example, food security was a big thing for a long time but it actually fits into the dominant program, in contrast to the idea of food sovereignty, which, in the *Declaration of Nyéléni*, says, okay, forget this program — let's get a new model, one that starts from the bottom up.

I'm involved with the International Program Committee of the NFU, and we've talked about the issue of co-optation. There are other organizations that are doing work on food sovereignty, such as The People's Food Policy Project in Canada, and I want the NFU to be right up there, because we've been involved with La Vía Campesina since the very beginning. You can look at everything that the NFU does in its lobbying and rabble-rousing, and you see that it all comes back to promoting the idea of independence and self-reliance on the part of the farmers, and on the part of the nation, for its food sources. Food sovereignty is inherent in the actions of the NFU.

Naomi: Food sovereignty represents a fundamental transformation of food systems. How does food sovereignty challenge the dominant mode of production in Canada and in your region?

Terry: Fundamentally, what's happened with agriculture in Canada and beyond has been dominated by large interests extracting wealth from farmers. Since those interests have been able to influence the political realm and the regulatory realm in such a way as to benefit themselves, it's always been a battle for family farmers to have some economic justice in the system, commensurate with the importance of the work they do. In Canada, the food system has moved away from a national policy to generate economic wealth for the country to a policy that, sometimes by stealth, sometimes by ignorance and sometimes by design, creates a system that facilitates a real transfer of wealth from the land away from farmers. The wealth moves to large, often multinational, interests that both supply farmers with inputs for growing food and buy their products afterwards.

In Western Canada, we've been fighting monopolistic or near-monopoly interests since the beginning of agriculture. The monopoly railways predated agricultural settlement in large parts of western Canada and monopolistic grain companies soon followed. However, at one point, the policy design was ameliorated somewhat when it was believed that the interests of farmers could not be separated from the interests of the economy in general, so we had to stem and control some of these monopolistic influences for the country as a whole to benefit.

But we've lost that now and farmers have lost autonomy — farmers have to organize and fight for their survival and sustainability. In Canada farmers created cooperatives, initiated political parties and pushed for legislative changes to create new institutional frameworks, like the Canadian Grain Commission, supply management organizations and the Canadian Wheat Board. But we're seeing these dismantled because of the acceptance in a neoliberal environment that business is good, big business is good. It's sort of a Darwinistic approach: those in agriculture who will survive will survive, and those who can't — we didn't need them anyway.

Hilary: In Canada and in my region, food sovereignty challenges the dominant mode of production in every way. The dominant mode of production is export-based and it's looking at food as a commodity, not a means for survival. It comes down to culture, really. The culture of Canada and the United States is a money culture, it's a consumer culture. We're constantly peeling away at all the social components of our culture in favour of higher financial efficiency and making more money. Every single part of the global economic system is based on these values.

These values have permeated the food system all over the world and our own people, the citizens, don't take pride in "Made in Canada." The government certainly doesn't encourage people to take pride because the government itself does not make any movement towards Canada being a self-reliant nation of any capacity. The concept of food sovereignty is on another planet if you compare it to our culture and our way of governing.

Naomi: What are the most significant challenges to implementing food sovereignty in Canada, and in your region/province?

Terry: In general, Canada has not been immune to the prevailing economic influences in the world — the neoliberal free market that is able to decide all. The bureaucrats have all adopted the neoliberal economic jargon. So there's always a very simple solution, and it's always the market, for whatever problem prevails. I have huge difficulties with that concept because in other political contexts no one would have imagined making decisions wholly based on market economics, particularly when its underlying concepts, such as competition, for the most part don't exist. The power imbalances are so out of proportion from a farmer to a grain company, a seed or herbicide company, a fertilizer company, or an oil company — it's unbelievable the scale and the differentials in power and influence. Related to that, Canadian farmers are shouldering huge debt loads; currently, the 220,000 farmers in Canada are carrying sixty-one billion dollars of debt. That really restricts a farmer's ability to engage in activities that might advance his or her own autonomy or food sovereignty. A solution first requires the farm community to recognize the pressures and the co-optation that they're under. Then, how does one act? What political measures, activities, production methods will farmers engage in? Or which are they able to do, when they're dependent on these huge companies to finance their farm operations?

The political acceptance of neoliberal market ideas also replaces governing in the public interest or on its behalf. It was recognized in the past that well-paid civil servants with job security could advise and act in the public interest, relatively free of outside influences. This also has been eroded in Canada, and there's increasing emphasis on contracting out. Civil servants don't see their entire career being spent in the civil service, so they start to focus on climbing within the service itself and acquiring enough of a base to go out as private consultants. Consequently, civil servants tend to advise and influence very negative policies for farmers and, actually, for Canadians, and very positive policies for those same corporate interests that they may be working for in the future. A related issue is that private consultants are hired to conduct consultations, write ensuing analysis, and highly direct how meetings are conducted, for predictable results. That divorces citizens from their own government; it inserts another layer between what they want to do and what government is trying to manage or manipulate or facilitate. People now understand that this "democratic model" is really not designed to consult as much as to manipulate. People are naturally frustrated and demoralized by these processes.

I've also been focused for a long time on issues around seeds and intellectual property. In Canada, there's real recognition on the part of those who seek to control seeds, like the Monsantos, Syngentas and Bayers of the world but others too, of just how much wealth can be extracted and how much control can be exerted through those intellectual property controls, contract law and other controls around seeds. We see a real erosion in farmers' ability to use, reuse and exchange and sell seeds as they see fit.

As well, we've seen real erosion in the purpose and financing of agricultural research, which formerly was for the benefit of farmers and beyond. There's been a demoralization of that public interest research community. It's now being seen as a vehicle to generate revenues for the universities and other research institutions, including Agriculture and Agri-Food Canada. At the same time agricultural research is also seen as an unnecessary expense so that corporations need to be given unbelievable rights of control in order to facilitate privately-run research. A system of matching investment initiatives has been created where public researchers need to source 50 percent of their funding from a private source and then it's topped up with public monies. That directs research down a particular path and influences researchers to be supportive of these intellectual property controls and other control mechanisms.

International trade agreements — the Trade-Related Aspects of Intellectual Property Rights (TRIPS) agreement, the World Trade Organization (WTO) and now bilateral agreements like the Comprehensive Economic and Trade Agreement with Europe (CETA) — are all imposing these conditions and many more: they're attacking our supply management system used in the production of dairy, poultry and eggs in Canada. These are all real threats to food sovereignty and autonomy and really, the whole social justice, economic justice model that we should be thinking about with our food and those people that grow it.

Farmers are being forced off the land, the debt crisis continues, agricultural commodity prices are almost universally depressed, farmers have to work off-farm to make a living, they're tired, they're overworked, they're stressed and their space to act politically, in a lot of ways has been exhausted or enclosed also. So the challenge is, how do you organize a community that's under such stress and pressure and is mainly focused on surviving the next year or growing cycle? It's difficult for farmers to think beyond that, and that's completely understandable. Nevertheless, food sovereignty challenges conventional thinking in very important ways. It's just difficult in the conditions under which farmers are living.

Hilary: A big issue in Ontario is land use, development and ensuing land prices. Here the competition for land use comes from the cities, with their sprawl and the giant homes with five acres of lawn. Farmers want to be as close as possible to a centre because that's our market, but it's becoming prohibitive. Forget buying land in the really good farming country down around Toronto and just west from there. You couldn't afford it, because the value is based on its development potential. In this province there is a terrible disregard for open space. It's considered useless unless it's being built on. Around Toronto is the best soil that this country has, and it's under concrete.

The provincial government is creating greenbelts around cities — a certain amount of land in a ring around the city that you're not allowed to develop on — but you can just leap over that ring and keep going. And meanwhile, in that ring, the real estate value has gone through the roof because it's this little bit of green in a sea of grey. And so that's certainly not what food sovereignty is all about. The greenbelt doesn't excuse the development that the government engages in — it's almost there to pacify environmentalists.

And you don't have the resources in these belts. You don't have the tractor repairs, the auto parts stores to get your filters, the abattoirs, the co-ops. It's horse farms or pastoral cottaging. The loss of processing resources is also a big issue. Our village here in Lanark used to be a cannery village and used to be quite a thriving place, actually. But canneries, granaries, local mills, commercial kitchens — those don't really exist in any capacity. And, of course, government regulations are an obstacle for farmers wanting to sell to a local market. There used to be many small abattoirs around here until the new provincial guidelines started being applied to small facilities in the last few years. The fact of the matter is these abattoirs can't invest another hundred thousand dollars into the business to comply with the guidelines. And there's not a lot of government support or enticement for those things.

You even have tractor dealerships disappearing. There's been a relocation of tractor dealerships from out in the countryside to a tract housing suburb for Ottawa. They're moving in there because of course they're selling more lawn tractors than they are other tractors. So now I have to truck almost an hour to go and get a part that used to just be here fifteen minutes away. Transportation in general is really expensive. As my friend Bruce would say, everything just keeps getting more expensive and we're getting less and less for what we're making.

Naomi: What are the most significant activities and strategies that the National Farmers Union is engaging in to build food sovereignty? Which have been most successful and why? Can you talk about some that have failed and why?

Hilary: In Ontario I see a lot of really positive activity at the local level. At the last NFU convention, for the first time in four years I was the oldest person in my social group. I know that there are a lot of young people becoming interested in farming, but I was really happy to see that they're also becoming interested in the politics of it. There's a real positive momentum growing.

I know the NFU locals around here in Eastern Ontario are doing quite a bit in our own counties. Renfrew membership has been going up steadily, because they're out there writing and publishing letters in the newspapers all the time, addressing injustices on a real public scale. Kingston is really involved with their local food movement. The NFU locals are also having an eastern Ontario supper on Wednesday nights to get together and talk about what everyone's doing, how we can support each other and how we can recruit more members. It's from the bottom-up, it's shaking up community.

Here in Lanark, we get people together for information sessions, open to the public. We just had one about the microFIT (micro Feed-in Tariff) program that our provincial hydro company is offering, trying to outsource solar generation to private homeowners for them to make money. Last week we showed the movie *The World According to Monsanto*, which was packed and evoked a whole lot of interesting conversation, but in a gentle way. I think it's important to have these open forums on subject matter that's intriguing to all sorts of people but not coming from a particular point of view. To some people the National Farmers Union is too left-wing and so you want to appear sort of neutral: like, we're showing this movie, you can take from it what you want. It seems to work and people come to our events. The most recent session we had was on the effect of urbanization on agriculture. That had a small attendance, but the Ontario Landowners Association was there. They're a pretty radical group of anti-government landowners — anti-regulation — but, despite some friction, the NFU and the landowners have a lot of commonalities. At this meeting we had a really good discussion, and, out of that, some letters are going to be written. What the letters do, who knows? At least you write them, at least you feel like you're doing something; it is empowering to do something at some point.

Terry: The development of supply management models in dairy, poultry and eggs — while there are some problems with overcapitalization of quota, the high and increasing cost of the quota which effectively blocks entry into the supply and management system for many — is nevertheless looked at around the world as a real example of food sovereignty in action in that it actually allows farmers in those sectors to earn a decent living from their activities. The fight for the Canadian Wheat Board as a marketing agency that maximizes returns for farmers in wheat and barley is also a positive activity. We are fighting constantly to maintain those two mechanisms as they're under severe attack from all quarters: from our competitors, the World Trade Organization (WTO), our provincial and federal governments. There have been relentless attempts to wipe out the Canadian Grain Commission (CGC) or to change its fundamental mandate so that it would essentially function as a service provider for the grain companies instead of in the interest of grain producers. And we've been able to preserve it.

Unfortunately, since a lot of these institutional legislative frameworks are older than two generations, some farmers don't actually understand a time where these protections were not in place. If and when they disappear, then they will very quickly understand how important these are. So, for us, it's vital to recognize their significance and be able to maintain them. Defending these institutional legislative frameworks has been extremely hard work; in many respects the NFU has been involved in a rearguard action and fight. In the political context we are in, however, these are huge victories even though they may not appear to do more than maintain the status quo. These victories are also important to help people understand their interests and to allow these mechanisms to translate into some economic justice. When you have economic justice you start to have space for social justice too. When people are not totally focused on surviving they can start to develop ideas and improvements and think about aspects of food sovereignty, whether they call it that or not.

The NFU, more than any other farm organization, has been able to work with other organizations to advance the general well-being of society. That's incredibly important, as farmers are just one percent of the Canadian population, and not all farmers in Canada are members of the National Farmers Union. From an organizational, tactical and political perspective you absolutely need these alliances and cooperation with other organizations and political parties.

For example, we worked with a large coalition that opposed GM wheat, and its work was successful. For that struggle, having an old institution like the Canadian Wheat Board (CWB) was an important tool. They had the international marketing information expertise to be able to go out and survey our international customers, who, in the high 80-percentile range, came back and said that if Canadians grew GM wheat they'd either buy from other countries or severely discount our wheat. Unfortunately, our regulatory system refuses to recognize market harm issues — if it hadn't been for political pressure and organization of consumer groups, environmental groups, the CWB, the National Farmers Union and others, we would have GM wheat. The fight against GM flax wasn't successful but it's a good example of the difficulties, the market losses and the harm that can result from GM. And now we're under pressure again: UPOV (International Union for the Protection of New Varieties of Plants) is rearing its head in the Canada-European Trade Agreement (Canada-E.U. Comprehensive Economic and Trade Agreement or CETA) under negotiation right now. UPOV '91 was the plant breeders' rights legislation that would have, for all intents and purposes, eliminated farmers' ability to save and re-use, exchange and sell seeds. This is now a central part of CETA's program as are many other draconian measures for imposing intellectual property rights and control, and eliminating the possibility for food sovereignty by controlling seeds. So we're fighting back on that with coalitions — that one's just getting started. It's incredibly important.

A successful campaign is one where you can communicate why the issue is important to everyone, not just farmers. In the UPOV campaign we had difficulty translating these issues in the mainstream media, but through our coalition work — with church organizations, environmental and consumer and social justice organizations that spread the word through their networks about what was happening and what it meant — we did public meetings, we developed fact sheets and analysis briefs that were widely distributed and actually are used internationally. However, many of these issues are difficult to discuss even within the agricultural community that is directly affected. Then to translate the nuances for an increasingly urbanized public is always a challenge. Some campaigns lend themselves to that automatically and others are much more difficult.

The other strategy in terms of mobilizing people and getting them to engage in the political system is to encourage them to write Members of Parliament, to phone, send faxes or emails, sign petitions — this is all basic stuff, but it takes surprisingly few to generate the sort of public backlash that politicians will start to listen to. All of these things are important for a successful campaign. Although governments largely have been ignoring protests and proceeding with their business as usual, which seems to be corporate business, every now and then they realize that they have to respect the public opinion that's out there.

From a tactical perspective, working with the agriculture critics and others in political parties has been important in delaying or amending legislation. Then it falls off the order table when an election is called and either has to be reintroduced or is forgotten altogether. But it's unfortunate that we haven't been able to initiate very much positive legislation to advance food sovereignty and autonomy and the interests of farmers and ordinary citizens. We've largely been working from issue to issue, so that comprehensive idea of food sovereignty hasn't been developed enough, although aspects of it are part of many of these struggles and fights.

Naomi: In addition to the NFU, who else is working towards food sovereignty in Canada and/or your province? Are some organizations more successful than others? Why?

Terry: There's been a wide scope of organizations working with the NFU or working on similar issues: the Saskatchewan Organic Directorate (SOD) and broader organizations, the Canadian Biotechnology Action Network (CBAN), Ecological Farmers Association in Ontario (EFAO), environmental organizations, churches and the Council of Canadians. The labour movement has been important many times in moving the debate to a broader public. And of course, we work with other farm organizations where our interests are the same.

Some of these organizations are more successful than others because they have a good understanding of political process; they understand how to engage and influence it, how decisions are made and how to participate. Other organizations could have that same understanding but the problem is always one of people capacity and financial capacity. We're often outclassed — not in people, we always have more people, and we have bright, intelligent people — but certainly in the financial capacity. To sustain long-term, successful campaigns is always a struggle. The dependency of some organizations on government financing and grants hobbles them too in terms of just how far they're willing to go on a given campaign. So that's an issue.

One strategy at one moment will work in terms of influencing government and at another time operating totally outside of government is a better strategy. But for me anyway, although food sovereignty is a comprehensive strategy, at this point in time it's largely a political strategy. The rethinking of production methods, ecological production, issues around land ownership and all of those things, while important, will come — but we need to generate political space, maintain it and make the governmental processes work to allow those other things to come.

For local food movements and consumer-based food movements, small regulatory changes and legislative pieces make huge differences, so that political piece is terribly important. We've often been told that governments have to act a certain way because of this international obligation or that trade agreement. But really it's a national political decision for governments to participate in those agreements and then to behave how they want to behave using those agreements as a justification. So I can't emphasize enough, whether it is on seed sovereignty, genetic sovereignty, control issues, autonomy, the ability to organize cooperatives, to engage in class action lawsuits, whatever it might be, it's all about political engagement in that respect.

Hilary: There is the People's Food Policy Project, whose main focus is food sovereignty. There's the Union Paysanne in Québec, and the Canadian Biotechnology Action Network, Heifer International and Inter Pares through their work with La Vía Campesina.

More broadly, there's a myriad of organizations that are promoting local food production and consumption. FarmLink Ontario is an organization trying to link young farmers up with people with land to secure land access. FoodShare, in Toronto, focuses on food access that in its own way promotes food sovereignty. There's a lot of collaboration among groups as hosts for key events. In Ottawa, three groups host Reel Food, which shows documentaries relating to food. Another example of collaboration is the different craft nodes: three collaborative regions in Ontario will align for farmer training, which is geared towards apprentices. Each group hosts activities such as farm tours and educational get-togethers.

What I would like to see groups do, instead of trying to work within the system, is to radically challenge the status quo. In the non-profit world, the money's never there for something that's really earth-shattering or long-term — infrastructure of any sort, job security of any type. So the projects that come out of that short-term thinking have a lot of discontinuity because staff people are coming and going, but you also have a lot of projects that come out that are flogging a dead horse. How many groups need to be doing the same thing? What is the effectiveness? The Toronto Food Policy Council (TFPC) really pushes the city of Toronto to change their ways, and I would love to see more radical challenges. I think that would be the beginning of some serious change, where we're not just working within the paradigm of capitalism.

Naomi: Food sovereignty poses a fundamental challenge to the status quo. It requires radical change not just to food systems but also to the whole of society. What are the conditions that need to exist to successfully implement food sovereignty in Canada?

Hilary: There needs to be a cultural shift. You almost wish for a sense of wanting to be self-reliant and the national pride that goes with that. You need that specifically in the rural parts of the province or the country, because food sovereignty is a movement coming from the rural people and the people need to feel like it matters. The sense of empowerment is missing in rural communities. Around here, anywhere, farmers' ages are getting up there and when you're approaching retirement, you probably don't have that zeal to change, to fight for your right to have what it takes to be food sovereign. This new generation of farmers is sort of an alternative generation because it's mostly people like myself that are coming from university and, for whatever motivation, deciding farming is what they want to do. I think that provides an interesting possibility in forming and building that rural voice.

There's also knowledge that we need to cling to, rural knowledge. I think it's really essential for the new generation of farmers to integrate into the rural communities. People in the county think that I've lived here forever when I've only lived here for seven years or so, because I get the culture, I fit into the culture. That's the only way to understand history — geographical history, cultural history, weather history, that sort of thing. And that's how you're going to keep a lot of these resources alive too, like all the different co-ops. You need to talk to old farmers and learn the ways that they do things, ways to save money — there's just so much to that. The young farmers today might buy something brand new off the Internet, for example, as opposed to going to auction sales, or figuring out how to do with a little less, and using more local resources — like going to your neighbour's place as opposed to some big box store. Part of the rural culture is all these little pockets of wealth and knowledge. But you have to seek them out; that's also part of the culture, not everything is out there on the main street with big signs. I think it's really important for young people to not just want to farm, but to want that lifestyle. I think that that's part of the puzzle too, that we all have to be on board. You have to have faith that the collective will benefit everyone.

The age-old dichotomy between rural people and urban people is almost like colonialism on a small scale — urban people feeling they know better than those in the countryside; there's a sense of better and worse. I think that there needs to be a bit of respect from urban centres and urban organizations for the way that rural communities work. Remembering that food sovereignty is starting in the rural communities, we need to blow the dust off, wash the curtains and let the light come in on our rural communities. So I think that's the biggest challenge: how do you start from the bottom up as opposed to the top down? What doesn't need to occur is pooh-poohing the rural communities and thinking that the way to go is through the city centres because they have a greater population. The city centres are not going to spring forth food sovereignty at all.

Terry: In many historical instances where social and economic justice for farmers has been advanced, government and broader society and farmers' interests have not necessarily been the same but have coincided. It mattered to the broader interests of the economy that farmers needed assistance or that they couldn't be killed off by monopoly railway influences or grain company influences. So you ended up with progressive legislation.

For food sovereignty, one has to take a long-term view. When you're constantly reacting and struggling on a daily basis with the issues that come up that erode the possibility of food sovereignty, it requires a lot of debate, discussion, education and doggedness to make the concept interesting to broader society and government. But I think there's a lot of pressure in terms of the productivist agriculture that we're engaged in right now, even from an ecological standpoint, where those moments will come. There is resistance to dominance and extraction such as intellectual property controls on seeds and forces such as climate change, where pressures on the planet and on governments will become large enough that different interests will converge.

Naomi: In some countries, local and even national governments are engaging with food sovereignty. For example, it was included in Bolivia's constitution in 2009. How are local and national governments in Canada responding to the call for food sovereignty?

Terry: I would be surprised if they even recognized the concept. On the national stage, there's no particular understanding or actual internal debate taking place about food sovereignty at this moment in the Canadian government. It's something that hasn't been systematically inserted into the political debate. In fact, they're doing almost everything in their power to prevent food sovereignty from happening. But that isn't because of an attitude per se to food sovereignty, it's just a belief in market economics which excludes any other possibility: there are no other options, no other solutions. It's an ideological approach that's fundamentally opposed to a food sovereignty approach.

Hilary: There's some really nice people that work in the Ontario Ministry of Agriculture, Food, and Rural Affairs (OMAFRA) who would really like to see some different things happen within the province and OMAFRA, but those things aren't happening. The day that I'm allowed to sell ungraded eggs at the farmer's market I'll have an example for you of a positive step governments are taking.

The provincial government here wants to support this new local food movement. I am sort of cynical about that, because they want to support non-profit organizations shuffling paper and having six- or twelve-month annual projects that are not going to make any substantial changes. That's what the money is going towards. The government is not reflecting on changing their policy. They're certainly not reconsidering their position on exports. There's not a sense in Ontario that the government's on side. That's a huge issue, because as much as you can be anti-government, in order for food sovereignty to take off you really need their support.

Naomi: Food sovereignty calls for ecologically sound and sustainable production that embraces biodiversity. What would food sovereignty's implementation mean for the environment?

Hilary: All good things. Not just because of food sovereignty in its own right, but also because of all the ripple effects it would have in community structures and the values we place on different things. I think you would be recycling a whole lot more, and by that I mean re-using resources and frugality. Oh, to think of all the gas that wouldn't be burned, just the impact of all the heavy machines, all that effort! It's just baffling to me how industrial agriculture could be cheaper than growing it here and selling it here.

The few things that we need for survival are being compromised. The strength of the sun, the water, our health is deteriorating globally. Contrary to popular belief, you don't just buy soil. That soil took billions of years to make and it's been robbed. Water quality or even water usage — there's just such an inane overuse of irrigation water that we're running out. And the wonky weather systems that we've been having — I used to be able to tell you the trends of the seasons, the months. There's no telling that anymore.

When I think about food sovereignty I'm also thinking of a whole lot more people growing their own food, not just huge farms growing food. People would have a lot more connection to their food production, whether they have a small garden, or a couple of hens outside, or they go to the market — kind of like it used to be. That way, you're more aware about everything around you. I know that as a farmer. For example, when you depend on the weather, you pay a whole lot more attention to it. I can't stand listening to the radio, because all I hear when I haven't seen a drop of rain in a month is, "And another fantastic weekend!" You get everyone else thinking rain equals bad, sun equals good. And so I think food sovereignty would be a real wake-up call. I yearn for it, because I think after being connected to the world around them a little more, people would be a little more connected to themselves.

Terry: Productivist agriculture looks at the environment as pieces to be used to generate as much yield and as much economic activity as possible. It's largely an extractive model. The productivist model also looks at what's as profitable as possible and then creates uses for land and the ecology that may not be appropriate in the long term for that particular region. The economic pressures and supposed opportunities create activities that go in a certain, usually unsustainable, direction. As well, because farmers are threatened with being driven off the land both in Canada and elsewhere, they adopt methods that may not be appropriate environmentally, such as GMOs. It's not the increases in production of GMOs that have led to adoption in certain areas, it's because there are vast areas to cover in a short window of time: GMOs have simplified production and given farmers a broader window for herbicide application in those models that use it.

Food sovereignty, by looking at food-growing in a wide context, challenges what we're doing to the environment and allows people, on a human and an ecological scale, space to act in a manner that is socially and ecologically appropriate for their locality, for the land. The consequences of this perspective are ecologically important for the planet as a whole. I think ecology is an incredibly important aspect of food sovereignty; that's what local food movements, consumers' interests in food quality, environmental organizations and of course farmers are interested in. Their restrictions and pressures from such problems as debt loads might force them down another path, but I think most farmers really do want, as much as possible, to maintain the fertility of the land, so they pass something on that's still productive and healthy.

Naomi: A wide diversity of organizations in the North and South has embraced food sovereignty. What are the challenges of working with such a diverse set of organizations and cultures that practise very different kinds of agriculture?

Terry: I think time pressures present an important challenge in food sovereignty, as well as agriculture and ecology. Whether it be the time to cover the ground that you have to cover, the pressures of debt servicing in "X" amount of time, the challenges of working organizationally, the amount of time one can dedicate and the amount of time one feels is available — all of these factors can affect people's involvement in bringing abut change. In terms of meeting with practising farmers, the seasonal constraints, just from a timetable perspective, often get in the way. The other difficulty is that we have a very small pool of people to draw from to participate in assorted events and meetings, which also adds to time constraints.

It's also a challenge to set aside, in some ways, our sense of time. We have a very short view of time: we want things to happen very quickly and in a linear manner. People from other organizations have a longer view. It's a challenge, given the pressures that we see, to adopt that longer view even in terms of the time it takes for processes to unfold. My personal experience has been that actions do come out of organizations like La Vía Campesina, but it has been a challenge, from a North American perspective, to loosen up on the concept of time or speed and take a long-term perspective.

Hilary: Because we all come from different cultures, understanding and respect is important. I went to the Terra Madre, which is a big world summit, if you will, for food-connected people, in Italy. I sat in a few workshops where I found that what people were really good at was pointing fingers at countries. I think that we need to understand, especially when we're thinking about members of La Vía Campesina, that we are all small-scale, peasant-farming type people who are all under the same stresses and challenges in our different countries, and that we're often politically isolated. Maybe there is some solidarity between other nations' farmers and the Canadian farmer, who is faced with heavy debt load and is confused and maybe morally conflicted. I think it's critical, and a huge challenge, to not just pinpoint and generalize, but also to respect the different ways that people do things, and not value things as primitive versus modern. Judgment is never a good place to go.

Naomi: What is the primary aspect of food sovereignty that you would like to emphasize for our readers?

Hilary: In my opinion the idea of food sovereignty is groundbreaking because it's talking about empowering all the people, prioritizing all those little elements that have been shoved to the back — the people, the rural people, the food. That idea that people have where food is a last priority — that I'll spend oodles on a new sofa and I'm going to find the cheapest can of corn I can and not care where it comes from — has to go. Food sovereignty is just groundbreaking: I hope that it maintains its integrity as it becomes more popular and more well-known, more discussed.

Terry: The fate of cooperatives in Canada has lessons for food sovereignty. Cooperatives had a very real social justice aspect to their existence — they had a democratic element, an educational element and an economic element. One of the unfortunate things that has contributed to the demise of cooperatives in Canada has been that we've forgotten their reason for existence and we've lost sight of those three component parts that food sovereignty is actually attempting to encapsulate.

So in the food sovereignty debate, one always has to be vigilant. When we engage with government, we have to hold politicians' feet to the fire and say, "What is the end goal here, what is the likely result and what is it going to mean to farmers or citizens, or ultimately for the ecology of the country or the planet?" So often, within government and organizations, things are compartmentalized, taken out of context. And they need to be contextualized in the broadest possible manner. That's what the NFU and food sovereignty seek to do.

Compartmentalization in the regulatory system, for example, has led to all sorts of huge problems that have eroded people's interests in general and farmers' interests in particular. So you have a situation where the Canadian Food Inspection Agency (CFIA), in reaction to consumers' concerns about meat contamination issues, imposes conditions that destroy local abattoirs because these can no longer afford to exist in the new regulatory environment. Effectively, concentration is facilitated. And we have to ask the question, "Do the conditions imposed in the name of consumer assurance and safety achieve their objective or do they just create a situation where everything is centralized with one company?"

You have to constantly question, what is the goal and what are the consequences? So many times other organizations focus on the very specific, and often one needs to, but you'll always need to have underlying fundamental principles in order to frame the context. And I think in many ways that's what food sovereignty seeks to do.

4. TRANSFORMING AGRICULTURE

Women Farmers Define a Food Sovereignty Policy for Canada

Annette Aurélie Desmarais, Carla Roppel and Diane Martz

Food sovereignty demands fundamental changes in power relations. It demands equality and the end of all forms of violence against women, and as such it seeks to transform existing unequal gender relations. Food sovereignty recognizes the distinct and key roles women play in agriculture, food distribution and consumption; it also struggles for the equitable distribution of resources, including men and women's equal participation in decision making in the development of policy and programs related to food and agriculture.

Many agrarian movements are tackling the gender dimensions of food sovereignty head on. For instance, during its Fifth International Conference held in Maputo, Mozambique, La Vía Campesina (2008) launched an international campaign with the slogan, "Food sovereignty means stopping violence against women." As the Declaration of Maputo states: "If we do not eradicate violence toward women within our movement, we will not advance in our struggles, and if we do not create new gender relations, we will not be able to build a new society."

As part of the process of creating new gender relations of equal participation and representation in farmers' organizations and decision making, the Status of Women Canada report, entitled *Farm Women and Canadian Agricultural Policy* (Roppel, Desmarais and Martz 2006), was one of the first in-depth studies to propose food sovereignty to Canadian policy makers. The report is especially important because it reflects the needs and interests of Canadian farm women — a sector of the rural population that historically has been largely absent in agriculture and food policy development. Farm women are significantly involved in decision making on matters concerning the ongoing operation and management of the farm. In addition to community and family work, farm women are also increasingly involved in a broad range of farm field work and taking care of livestock. As these roles increase, many farm women are identifying themselves as joint operators of farms or are specializing in their own on-farm enterprises (Martz 2006).[1]

Women farmers have a distinct analysis of agricultural policy and specific ideas about what an inclusive agricultural policy would look like. Yet, farm women were conspicuously absent in the Department of Agriculture and Agri-Food Canada's (AAFC) consultation process leading up to the Agriculture Policy Framework (APF), and it appears that no specific efforts have been made to include them in subsequent national agricultural policy development.[2]

We have to ask what kinds of issues would women have raised if they had participated in the consultations. This is precisely addressed by the *Farm Women and Canadian Agricultural Policy* (subsequently referred to as *Farm Women*) study. Conducted in 2004, one year after the APF was put into place, the participatory study involved 105 farm women from Saskatchewan, Ontario, Prince Edward Island, New Brunswick, Manitoba and Alberta. Containing excerpts from, and building on, the results of this study, this chapter explores the limitations of "participation" in AAFC's policy development and summarizes what kind of agriculture and food policy women farmers in Canada might propose in its place.

"Participation" in Government Agricultural Consultations

At the heart of food sovereignty is the idea of farmers' and local communities' meaningful and extensive participation in decision making on agriculture and food policies (La Vía Campesina 2000, Pimbert 2006, Nyéléni 2007). On occasion, agricultural policy development in Canada has involved "participation," of sorts. Indeed, the government of Canada has established an international reputation for promoting and engaging civil society in democratic debate through the practice of multi-stakeholder consultations.

At the turn of the twenty-first century, when the Canadian government sought to better integrate agriculture into the global marketplace by developing a policy geared to ensure the industry's growth and profitability, AAFC held a series of fairly extensive multi-stakeholder consultations across the country. Leading up to the APF, the federal government conducted two "phases" and "waves" of consultations in 2002. Phase One (Wave One and Wave Two) involved fifty-six sessions across the country with 1417 participants and 320 observers. Producers represented 60.6 percent of the participants, government representatives accounted for the overwhelming majority of the observers and the remainder of participants were processors, distributors, retailers, academics and representatives of consumer organizations and environmental non-governmental organizations (Roppel et al. 2006: 64–65).

Yet, the extensive consultation process used by the AAFC to establish a national agricultural policy was deeply flawed. First, there was a significant lack of women's participation. Second, the consultation process reflected a very limited understanding and practice of "participation."

Farm Women's Involvement in Agriculture Policy Consultations

Women play a critical role in the day-day operation of Canadian farms and often have different roles and responsibilities than their male counterparts (Martz 2006), yet the various waves and phases of government consultations on the APF ignored women farmers. For example, a survey of 105 rural women from six provinces, all active in farming, farm issues, farm organizations and/or rural community affairs, reveals that only 10.5 percent of them had been informed of the consultations, 8.6 percent were invited and only 6.7 percent actually participated in the government consultations that led to the APF (Roppel et al. 2006: 69).

The lack of farm women's participation is striking given that, in 1995, the Government of Canada committed itself to gender equality at "all levels of decision making," as outlined in *Setting the Stage for the Next Century: The Federal Plan for Gender Quality* (SWC 1995). According to the plan, the federal government aims to "incorporate women's perspectives in governance"; they state that, in order to

> achieve gender equality, the social arrangements that govern the relationship between men and women will have to change to give equal value to the different roles they play, as parents, as workers, as elected officials and others; to foster equal partnership in the decision making process; and to build a just and equitable society. (SWC 1995: 14)

The government plan goes on to note that

> introducing gender analysis in the developmental stage of a policy is more efficient and potentially less costly in human and social terms for women. Since it helps identify any negative impact the policy might have on women, it leads to more effective public policy while providing greater opportunities for economic and social development of Canadians. (SWC 1995: 19)

Furthermore, the plan's "Priorities for Action," among other things, seeks to "accord women an equitable share of power and leadership in decision making processes affecting Canada's social and economic development" (SWC 1995: 54).

One fairly easy and basic measure of accountability toward realizing Canada's commitment to gender equality in policy making is the development of specific mechanisms to ensure women's participation and the collection of gender-segregated statistics in every arena where policy development and decision making occur. This, however, did not happen during the APF consultation process.

In our analysis of the APF process we found no gender-segregated statistics of participants in the on-line meeting reports. An email query to AAFC about the availability of such data reveals that the Department "didn't track gender, nor do we have suffixes (e.g., Mr./Mrs.)" by which gender might be inferred (Chartier 2003). Understandably, individual participants may have chosen not to use a title (Ms., Mr., Mrs.), but it would have required little effort for organizers to count and record the number and affiliation of the women and men who attended the consultations.

Essentially, the APF consultation process failed to take account of the Government of Canada's own commitment to achieving gender equality. For example, a keyword search of APF-related documents available on the Internet revealed there were no hits for the keywords beginning with "wom," nor were there any references to gender, youth or young (Roppel et al. 2006: 68). Similar results emerged in a search for the same keywords in articles about the APF consultation process in *The Western Producer*, a major weekly prairie farm newspaper. The absence of women's participation meant that the resulting APF was not likely to reflect women's specific needs and interests.

Nominal Participation in APF Process

The government consultation process was also problematic in that, despite a significant producer presence in the consultations, it produced a policy that did not adequately reflect the interests of Canadian farmers. For instance, the two major national farm organizations — the Canadian Federation of Agriculture (CFA) and the National Farmers Union (NFU) — voiced strong opposition to the policy: the NFU ultimately rejected the APF as a whole (NFU 2002) while the CFA wanted fundamental changes to important elements of the policy (CFA 2003a and 2003b). In addition, at the Wave Two consultation meeting held in Montréal, fifty-one representatives of Québec's main farm organization, the Union des Producteurs Agricoles (UPA), left the meeting in protest while expressing deep dissatisfaction with the fact that the concerns they had expressed earlier on in the APF process (Wave One) were not being addressed (GPC Event Report 2002). Since the UPA delegation represented over half of the participants at the meeting, its action should have registered some concern. Yet, the most accessible AAFC website report of the consultations does not mention the position of the UPA delegation. It states:

> In Wave Two there were few criticisms of the process. Participants indicated that they felt their views from the first wave had been accurately reported and that some of the views had been reflected in the APF documentation. This, in part, explains why participants were less skeptical of the process in Wave Two. (AAFC 2002)

The AAFC's consultation process and documentation reflect a particular type of participation. Sarah White (2000), an academic based in the United Kingdom who has analyzed the purpose, characteristics and interests reflected in participatory processes in several countries, identified four types of participation: nominal, instrumental, representative and transformative. The very limited understanding and implementation of participation in the consultative processes used by the federal government would meet White's definition of "nominal" participation where the purpose of participation is restricted to demonstrating that those in power are "doing something" with particular groups (White 2000: 144–45). We argue that this is exactly what the APF process entailed: the main parameters of the policy goals and content were already largely defined by government bureaucrats who had prepared the policy documents. Farmers were invited to participate in consultations across the country but they were restricted to debating only the issues raised in the draft policy documents. This approach yielded quite predictable results, while, in the process, it ignored farmers' concerns. For instance, farm on numerous occasions, organizations had stressed that the new APF must focus on resolving the roots of the farm financial crisis. Yet this is precisely what the consultations failed to do.

Participation that Transforms

Unlike the nominal participation approach used by AAFC, *Farm Women* used what White (2000: 146) calls "transformative" participation. This is a type of participation in which those who design the process and the participants share the common interest of empowerment, and participation functions both as a means as well as an end. As White explains:

> The idea of participation as empowerment is that the practical experience of being involved in considering options, making decisions, and taking collective action… is itself transformative…. It leads to greater consciousness… and greater confidence in their ability to make a difference…. Participation is therefore at one and the same time a means to empowerment and an end in itself. (2000: 146)

Farm Women stemmed from the NFU women's initial critique of the consultation process and the content of the APF, and it sought to empower. There are three aspects to this empowerment. First, the participatory research project was developed as a leadership capacity-building tool among the NFU members in their regions. Given women farmers' already over-stressed and busy lives, the research workshops sought to provide a rare opportunity to build community. Second, the research aimed to strengthen NFU women by creating the space for direct engagement in policy analysis and policy development in ways that validated their own personal lives and experiences and then collectivized/socialized these. Third, the research project went beyond the NFU membership to include the participation of women from other farm organizations and rural community groups.

The research team — involving the authors and twelve NFU women leaders — worked as a collective to establish the research questions and a research design that included five participatory workshops in which 105 farm women analyzed their policy needs and developed a vision for an inclusive Canadian agricultural policy. The workshops were designed to move the analysis of individuals' realities to collective reality and from the personal to the political.

Because *Farm Women* is the largest existing recent research of its kind to consider farm women's views of agricultural policy, it is worth providing a snapshot of those involved. Workshop participants reflected a wide diversity in age, type and size of farm operation and farm organization affiliation. Of the 105 women, five were under the age of twenty-five years, twenty participants were between twenty-five and thirty-five years of age, while twenty-nine were older than fifty-five; and almost half of the group was between the ages of thirty-five to fifty-five. The type of farms included dairy, poultry, grain/oilseed, livestock, market garden, potato, dry edible bean, soybean and honey producers. The size of landholding also differed: only five farms were larger than 2,401 acres (two of these were in Saskatchewan while three were in Manitoba); forty-two operations ranged between 640 to 2,400 acres; twenty-eight were between 161 to 640 acres; and twenty-three were smaller than 160 acres. Fifty-one percent of the participants were members of the NFU while the remaining 49 percent were members of other farm women's rural and/or community-based organizations.

Farm Women may not be representative of the views of all women farmers across the country. To our knowledge, no such comprehensive study exists. Rather, the remainder of this chapter explores the views about food and agricultural policy expressed by 105 women farmers from six provinces who participated in the research workshops. These views emerged in their answers to several key questions: What is happening on farms today and what forces have led to the current situation? Is the APF a solution or does it make things worse? What critical issues must be included in agricultural policy? and What kinds of recommendations could we make to ensure an increased participation of farm women in policy development and to ensure that their interests are reflected in agricultural policy?

Down on the Farm

> Farming is a huge passion for us and I think it's a spiritual experience too. There is a spirituality about farming that is hard for us to articulate. (Manitoba woman farmer)

Figure 4-1 Key Themes Affecting Life on the Farm

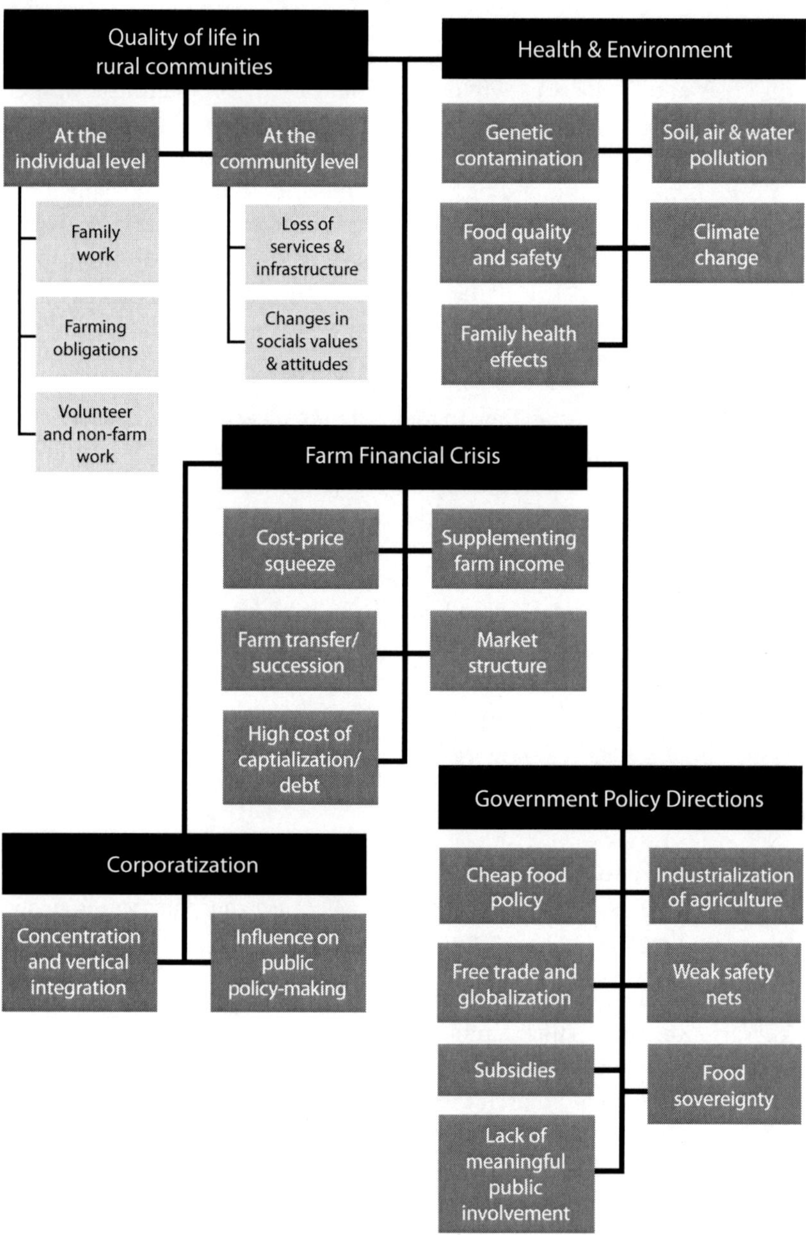

Source: Roppel, Desmarais and Martz 2006: 36.

How one defines a problem has crucial implications for the kinds of policies and practices that are developed to solve it. In spite of the overwhelming pressures of poor finances, animal health concerns, trade actions, a recurring farm crisis and an increasingly hostile political environment, the women farmers involved in this study retain deep attachments and commitments to their farms and communities.[3] They spoke of feeling a sense of rootedness — a deep connection to and passion for the land — that they value, both for themselves and their children. Farming is deep in their spirit, heart and blood, and, for many, farming is all they have ever wanted to do. They value living and working closely with their spouses, their children and relatives; they spoke of peace and quiet, the beauty of landscape, starlight and moonlight, and of being outdoors and experiencing the seasons.

> You know you can look in four different directions and get four different landscapes. The lighting is beautiful; it is a place I would like to live until I die. (Alberta farm woman)

The women feel a deep sense of responsibility to build strong communities, maintain a healthy environment and produce healthy food safely. They see farming as a valued and valuable occupation — one of the most important jobs on earth.

While the women's connections to family and community, appreciation for beauty and nature, place in family and community history, responsibility for environmental stewardship and the desire for independence kept them tied to their farms, they are also deeply affected by an acute financial crisis.

> Farming to me, it can steal, it's a thief. It robs you of your spirit, it can even rob you of your marriage because your husband is always on that tractor. (Maritime woman farmer)

These women see this recurring crisis as the major stress in the lives of many farm women and their families. and they consider it to have been created primarily by current government policy directions and the corporatization of agriculture. They noted that, if these root causes of the financial crisis were solved, the quality of life in rural communities, as well as their health and environment, would improve significantly (Figure 4-1).

Farm Financial Crisis

> Everything is about money. And everything is about debt. That's what drives my life. (Ontario woman farmer)

> We are working harder to stay at the same spot financially. Ten years

> ago we had the same income. Now, we just have less time because we are working harder. (Manitoba farm woman)

> Right from the beginning we diversified and diversified and got larger and did all these things, but we just actually always held our net income to the same level. (Saskatchewan woman farmer)

The women view the crisis as largely driven by inequitable and corporate-dominated markets combined with government policies that are limited to encouraging entry into those very markets. The impact of the crisis is multi-dimensional. Farm families are forced to seek other sources of income to supplement their livelihoods, thus adding to their workload and stress. Moreover, succession plans for family farms are uncertain, as retiring farmers need to "cash in" the retirement equity they have invested in their farms, while at the same time not burying their sons and daughters in debt. Given low prices and high input costs, many of the women questioned the wisdom of advising their children to take over the family farm. Consequently, rural communities are doubly disadvantaged. They lose people, businesses and services through depopulation; then, as a result of this, there are fewer people available to do the critical activities that keep communities vibrant.

Quality of Life, Health and Environment

> We aren't respected by anyone. No one wants to be a farmer. I don't call myself a farmer, because when I do, I get no respect. (Ontario farm woman)

> So we spray before we seed, we seed, we spray again. … We watch our crop grow but there is a disease there, so we spray again. And, of course, we spray before we harvest, we harvest our grain and then we spray after harvest. (Alberta woman farmer)

> GMOs are a tremendous threat. If our crops are contaminated or polluted by it, we cannot sell our products as organic. We will lose everything. (Ontario woman farmer)

The population decline in rural communities greatly affects the quality of life in these communities at the individual and community levels. The women reported that they are much busier with farm work, non-farm work and community volunteer work. They and their families now travel further to access everything — banking, shopping, health, education and recreational services — as rural services and businesses have closed. Changing social and cultural attitudes are leading to more competition and less cooperation among farmers, while food production and farmers are accorded less respect by the general public, politicians and bureaucrats. The women identified a number of driving factors contributing to changes in social and cultural attitudes: the loss of traditional knowledge, resulting in changes in rural culture and farming practices; a shift from knowledge to information overload; privatization of research and subsequent shift in research priorities; and mass media's oversimplification and often misrepresentation of rural issues.

The women expressed deep concerns about the threats to food quality and safety resulting from the high-volume, high-input farming systems now used to grow most food. Many believe that organic foods are more nutritious and less likely to be contaminated by genetically modified seeds, pesticides and food pathogens. They also highlighted the lack of research on long-term effects of low-level exposure to multiple chemicals, chemical combinations and genetic contamination of seeds on human and environmental health. Many talked about how current farming practices endanger soil, water and air due to contamination and pollution by fertilizers, pesticides and animal waste. Global warming and its effects on farming, as well as the impact of farming on the environment are sources of unease.

Government Policy Directions and Corporatization

> One of the big issues is corporate control, 90 percent of them are U.S.-based. So they've really got the farmers on a string. They've also got the federal government on a string. (Saskatchewan farm woman)
>
> But now President's Choice products are really undercutting everything and everyone, and keeping everybody out of the distribution system. It's hard to get into the stores. (Ontario woman farmer)
>
> I'm talking about production dollars and value-added dollars. The government told us, "if you can't get enough dollars in this, then add something else," thinking that with extra income you don't get extra expenses. And then, "if that isn't making it for you, go do marketing too!"… I used to say we had one job that didn't pay. Now we have three that don't pay. (Maritime farm woman)

The women saw government policies as overwhelmingly influenced by corporate rather than citizen interests. Consequently, they saw government policies contributing directly to industrialization of agricultural production — a focus that economically excludes small farmers. In "bigger-is-better" factory farming, concentration offers economies of scale that reduce production costs, thus supporting a cheap food policy and high corporate profits. The result is a policy environment that is detrimental to family farmers. To be sure, the terminology of "cheap food" voiced by the farm women who participated in the study might have also been in reference to low farm-gate prices. Historically, the implementation of a cheap food policy was a mechanism to enable low industrial wages. At that time, farmers received a greater share of the consumer food dollar. However, in the current environment where low-priced food is imported and discipline in wages is accomplished through the possibility of exporting jobs, the price of food is no longer determined by government policy. Instead, food prices are determined by an international marketplace that is increasingly controlled by transnational agri-business corporations. Consequently, farmers' share of the consumer dollar has decreased considerably over the past thirty years, as corporate entities have inserted themselves in the food chain (see Martz [2004] for an analysis of the farmers' share of the consumer food dollar in Canada).

When analyzing the current realities on their farms, the women noted that agri-food corporations are consolidating their control and influence on all aspects of food production, processing and distribution through mergers and vertical integration. Fewer corporations supply farm inputs, and, through vertical integration, they are the same companies that buy agricultural commodities from farmers. Individual family farmers with no large collective market presence have little negotiating power in the context of increasingly powerful and profitable large corporations.

Women Farmers Analyze the APF

In analyzing the impact of current agricultural policy on their daily lives, the women argued that the APF has not and will not lead to economic stability primarily because it does not address the root cause of the farm income crisis — the cost-price squeeze. A cost-price squeeze occurs when production costs are higher, and/or increase faster, than the commodity prices received. Farmers do not receive prices for their commodities that cover their production costs and thus do not provide a return on investment.

Women also felt that the policy will not contribute to environmental and social sustainability, since it separates agriculture from everything else in a piecemeal fashion, thus reflecting a narrow approach to environmental and food safety/quality issues rather a holistic view of rural communities, food production and consumption. They felt, in addition, that the APF fails to establish new and/or expand existing farmer-friendly supply-managed production (such as in dairy and poultry) and orderly marketing structures (like the Canadian Wheat Board) that would benefit small and medium-scale farmers. The women noted that the APF does not include a domestic food policy that encourages and supports local production for local consumption, not does it provide adequate farm safety nets. Indeed, the women argued that, in the long term, the APF would harm farm families and rural communities in significant ways (Box 4-1).

Box 4-1: APF Impact on Farm Families and Rural Communities

- Larger, more industrialized farms; fewer neighbours; loss of community; loss of rural tax-base and therefore, of services and infrastructure; more driving time; and more stress and family break-ups;
- Reduced farmers' market power because of continued corporatization and consolidation in the food chain;
- Greater dependency on expensive technological solutions;
- Tighter cost-price squeeze, more financial insecurity and more debt due to lack of market mechanisms that would improve commodity pricing or increase the farmer's share of consumer dollars;
- Government programs that continue to favour the largest operators;
- Increased need for off-farm income;
- Greater on-farm responsibility for, and cost of, implementing food safety/quality and environmental programs, for which farmers will not be compensated;
- More on-farm work, especially paperwork; and
- Increasing threat to the environment and to human and animal health from chemicals and animal wastes.

Source: Roppel et al. 2006: 69–75.

Women Farmers' Vision for an Inclusive Agricultural Policy

> I'm not ready to hang up yet because I still believe the family farm has to stay. It has to be the vehicle to provide food for Canadians. (Maritime farm woman)

Since the women considered the APF so deeply flawed, they argued for a fundamental rethinking of agricultural policy and how that policy is defined. An effective agricultural policy, for these farmers, entails creating the necessary structures, processes and mechanisms to ensure that the needs, concerns and interests of farmers, farm women and youth are heard and responded to, and are given equal weight in policy development. What is needed is a holistic policy, one that addresses the social, cultural and environmental aspects of life and community, as well as economic well-being. This would be a policy that

- Strengthens the voices of farm families;
- Involves a practical policy process that starts with farmers' needs;
- Respects farmers by acknowledging farming as a full-time profession/occupation;
- Is accountable and responsive to farmers;
- Benefits farmers and centres on fair trade, not free trade;
- Solves the financial crisis and provides long-term economic, environmental and social stability;

- Provides mechanisms to support and enhance the quality of life in rural communities;
- Ensures that both food and the environment are safe and healthy;
- Educates consumers about the contributions that farms and farmers make to society; and
- Bridges the rural/urban divide.

These specifications constitute the essential foundation of an inclusive agricultural policy that is grounded in food sovereignty. The women's vision for agricultural policy rests on four pillars: financial stability; domestic food policy; safe, healthy food and environment; and strengthening the social and community infrastructure (Figure 4-2). The women also defined specific strategies for each of these policy pillars. Needless to say, these pillars and policy strategies differ considerably from those of the APF.

Farm Financial Stability

> In my life I never wanted to do anything but farm, and I still don't. But I have an awful lot of concerns about the future of our industry. (Manitoba farm woman)

Because the farm financial crisis is at the core of women's concerns about agriculture, farm financial stability must be at the heart of agricultural policy. Such stability requires fair pricing, family-farm-friendly production and marketing structures and limitations on corporatization. Overwhelmingly, the women preferred that their families' fair income be generated by production rather than from government support programs. Figure 4-3 highlights policy directions and programs that the women believe would make farming more economically sustainable by ensuring a secure, stable income for producing quality food and increasing farmers' market power in the food chain.

Domestic Food Policy

The women also stated the need for a strong domestic agricultural policy. Such a policy would enable Canadian governments, consumers and rural communities to construct a food system of the highest possible quality — one that, because it operates at a smaller and more local scale, can provide food that is safer and healthier, produced in ways that have less environmental impact. They argued that, based on their experience, smaller, more local and domestic agri-food businesses would enable fairer distribution of benefits arising from agricultural trade.

> Consumers are more concerned, are becoming more aware of where their food is coming from. They see what is going on and they're demanding more, and I see that in the future it is going to be more

> community again, smaller farms, more mixed farms, and we're going to think about our environment. (Maritime farm woman)

The women identified four major policy strategies to be included in a domestic food policy: shift government focus from free trade to fair trade; shift government focus from cheap food to quality food; emphasize production for local and domestic consumption; and reduce importation of foods that can be grown domestically.

Social and Community Infrastructure

For the women, the economics of farming are inextricably linked to the communities in which farming occurs. Having identified the depopulation and decline of rural communities as a consequence of narrowly focused government policies, farm women defined an agricultural policy that is holistic — one that gives equal weight to the economic, social and cultural aspects of rural communities:

> It is the farm that is the core of our system, and around that is the family... and around that is our community, our school, church organizations and the volunteering that we do. Around this core are the external pressures over which we seem to have no control. (Manitoba woman farmer)

Like an agricultural policy that addresses only economic issues, an agricultural policy that excludes farm women's voices and their concerns is only half-complete. Structures and mechanisms need to be established to ensure women's equal participation in decision making and policy development. Moreover, as urbanization widens the gap between food production and consumption, there is a loss of understanding about the critical role that farmers play in the food chain. Consequently, government policy needs to foster consumer education to rebuild and strengthen food–farm relationships. Figure 4-4 compiles the strategies and actions that farm women identified as enhancing the quality of life in rural communities.

Safe, Healthy Foods and Communities

> For our future we have to have healthy farms, we have to be able to work with the people in the cities to educate them about what actually goes on on our farms.... I think it's health not only for us as farmers and health for our farms, but also health for people all the way around. (Alberta woman farmer)

A holistic Canadian agricultural policy would equally address economic, social, cultural and environmental needs. The women talked about the need

Figure 4-2 Farm Women's Vision for an Inclusive Canadian Agricultural Policy

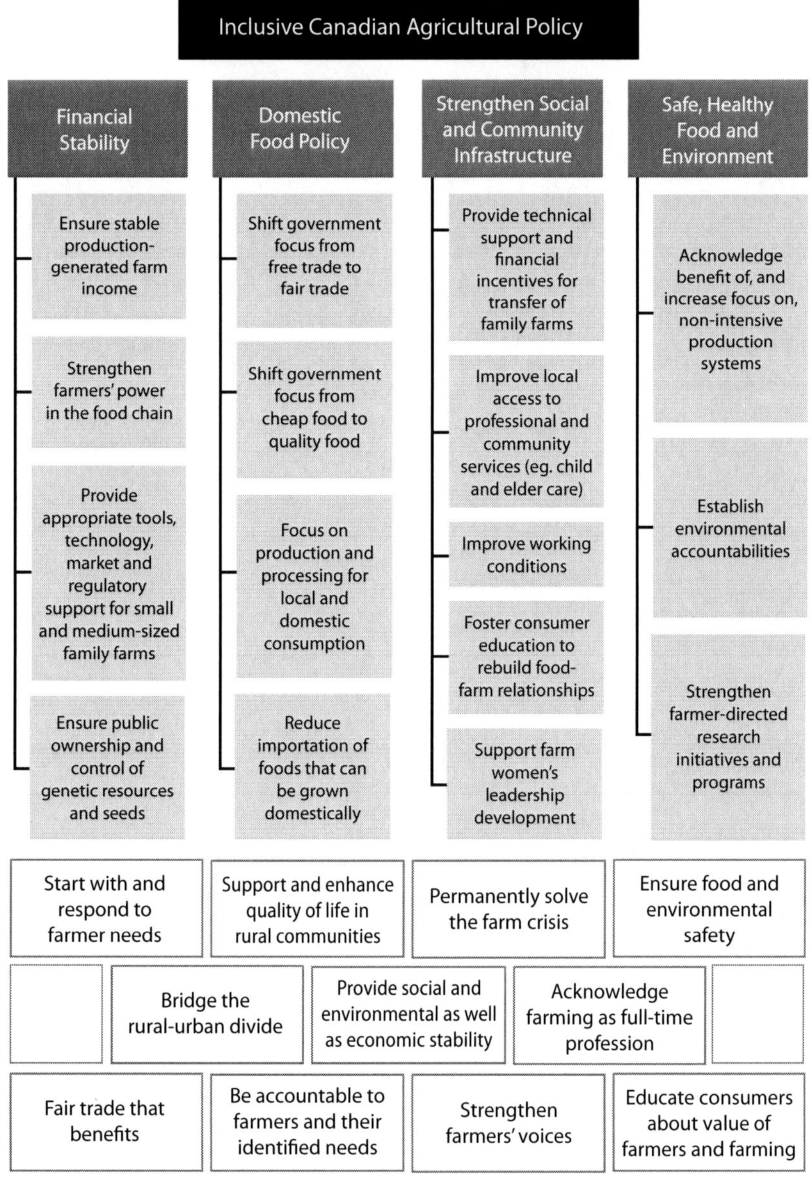

Source: Roppel et al. 2006: 77.

Figure 4-3 Policy goals and strategies for financial stability

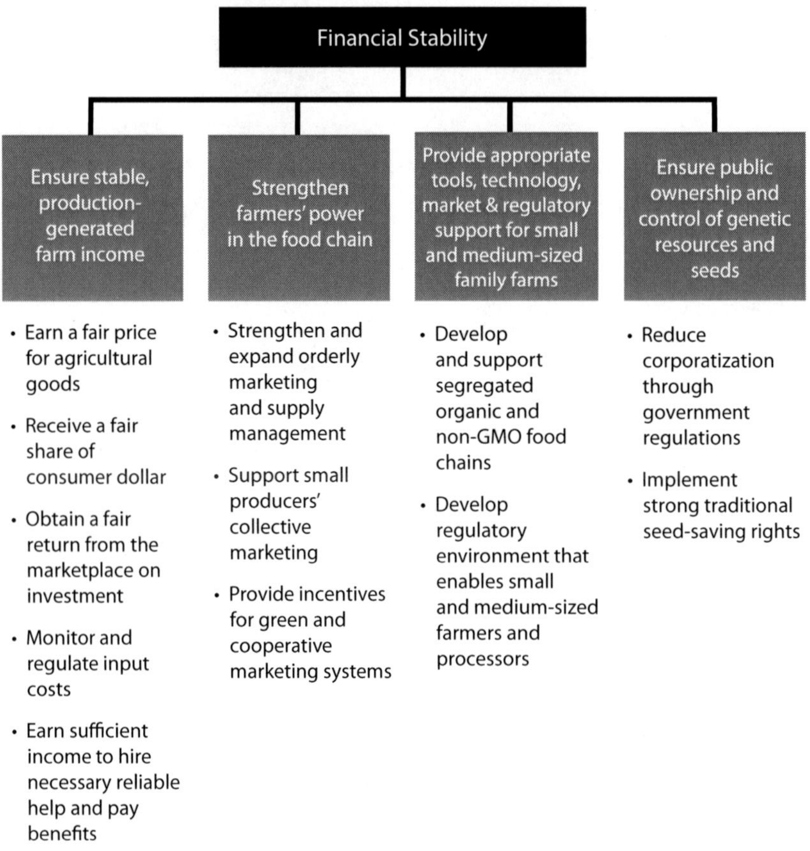

Source: Roppel et al. 2006: 78.

to develop agricultural practices that are more respectful of nature. They highlighted their assessment that safer food is a product of smaller, diverse and less-intensive farming operations, requiring size-appropriate regulation and using alternative energy sources and on-farm nutrient cycling. Agricultural policy must respect, protect and fulfill the human right to a healthy and safe environment, and thus hold citizens, governments and corporations accountable for their actions (Figure 4-5).[4]

In the Canadian agricultural context, a food sovereignty policy process begins with the lived realities of farming families to better understand what is actually happening in rural Canada and then moves to articulating policy solutions. When 105 women farmers from six different provinces were finally brought to the policy table, they highlighted a radically different vision of agricultural policy than that reflected in the APF and its predecessor, *Growing*

Figure 4-4 Policy Goals and Strategies to Strengthen Social and Rural Community Infrastructure

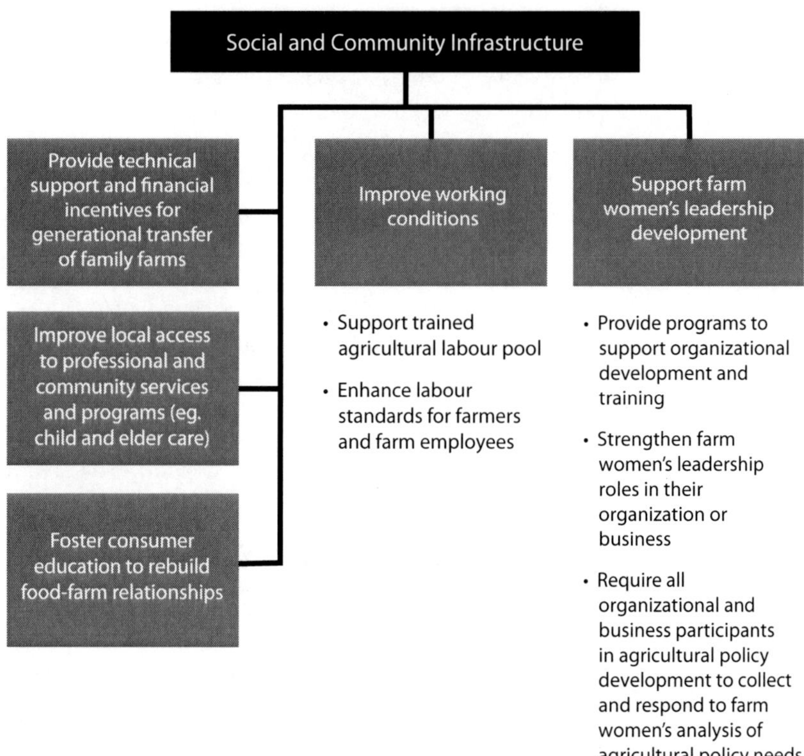
Social and Community Infrastructure
Provide technical support and financial incentives for generational transfer of family farms
Improve local access to professional and community services and programs (eg. child and elder care)
Foster consumer education to rebuild food-farm relationships
Improve working conditions
• Support trained agricultural labour pool
• Enhance labour standards for farmers and farm employees
Support farm women's leadership development
• Provide programs to support organizational development and training
• Strengthen farm women's leadership roles in their organization or business
• Require all organizational and business participants in agricultural policy development to collect and respond to farm women's analysis of agricultural policy needs

Source: Roppel et al. 2006: 80.

Forward. The final set of policy recommendations articulated by women farmers (see Appendix) reflects an alternative, comprehensive and inclusive policy framework — one that is firmly grounded in food sovereignty.

"It's the Same Old Song," or Implementing a Radical Alternative?

The AAFC's version of "participation" in policy development is very limited. In the context of the APF, farmers' key interests were effectively excluded, and the consultations ignored a significant part of the farm population — women. Judging from the media reports of the round of government consultations conducted in the winter of 2007 to finalize the *Next Generation of Agriculture and Agri-Food Policy* — now called *Growing Forward* (AAFC 2008) — it appears that the same blinkered view of participation was repeated.

There is no evidence, for example, that the government introduced mechanisms to ensure women's participation and representation in these discussions. And, even though the Parliament Secretary's report *Empowering Canadian Farmers in the Marketplace* (Easter 2005) emphasized the need to focus on resolving farm-income issues, the consultations failed to do so. Commenting on the Next Generation Agri-Food Policy consultation documents, Bill Anderson, a farmer in Manitoba said, "Every word in there could have been, or probably was, written twenty to twenty-five years ago in an earlier vision statement" (quoted in Winters 2007: 96). Another farmer interviewed by Daniel Winters from the *Western Producer* said, "It's the same old song; the tune is the same, only the words keep changing." Also, Larry Powell, a Manitoba vegetable farmer commenting on the Next Generation APF consultations, noted that terms like "sustainable" and "sustainability" barely appeared in the policy documents. This prompted him to insist, "We have to start doing things differently. We have to start promoting local markets. The present way we are doing things just doesn't stack up with our commitment

Figure 4-5 Policy Goals and Strategies to Achieve Safe, Healthy Foods and Environments

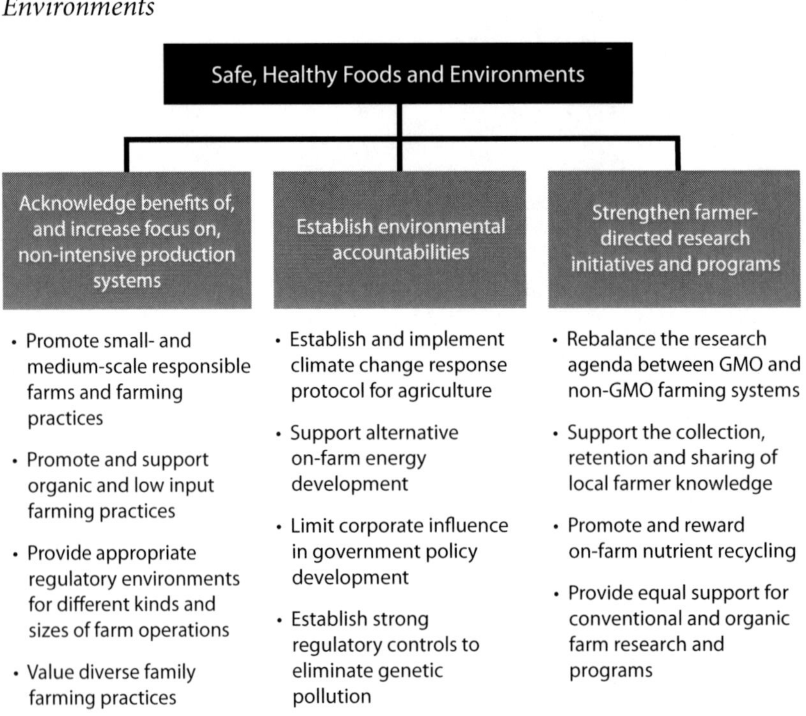

Source: Roppel et al. 2006: 86.

to the environment and being producers of good-quality, safe food" (quoted in Winters 2007).

A food sovereignty framework differs considerably from the multi-stakeholder consultative approach used by the AFFC, and consequently it yields different results. The agricultural policy that the women farmers envision is grounded in their daily experiences: it responds to the needs of their families and their communities, and it addresses social, cultural and environmental aspects of life and community, as well as economic well-being. The women were not constrained by an exclusive focus on increasing production for export and policy directions that favour agri-business corporations. Instead, they argued for inclusive policies that aim to increase farmers' power in the food chain, to enhance production and processing for local and domestic produce and to strengthen rural communities. Importantly, the farm women also developed a series of recommendations geared specifically to increase women's presence and participation in future policy making processes.

The women farmers' vision for agriculture and food holds some important insights that can contribute to a more sustainable agricultural policy that actually keeps farmers on the land, helps to create vibrant rural communities, supports socially and environmentally sustainable agricultural practices and produces good-quality and safe food. This, after all, is what food sovereignty is all about.

Notes

1. This chapter uses the terms "farm women" and "women farmers" interchangeably to reflect the fact that rural women often self-identify as belonging to one of these two categories.
2. The Agriculture Policy Framework (APF) was a five-year national agreement that was launched in 2003, and ended in March 2008. It was followed by the five-year Next Generation Agri-Food Policy which was subsequently called the Growing Forward Policy Framework, endorsed by Canada's federal, provincial and territorial governments in July 2008.
3. All of the quotes, unless otherwise indicated, are from women who participated in the study. The rather than using descriptors such as "the women farmers involved in this study" or "the study participants," in the remainder of this chapter we refer to the study participants as "the women."
4. According to the United Nations' international human rights framework, signatories to human rights agreements have three types of obligations: to respect, protect and fulfill the human rights outlined in the agreements. The obligation to respect means that the state parties must refrain from interfering directly or indirectly with the enjoyment of the rights in question. The obligation to project requires the state to prevent third parties from interfering in any way with the realization of those rights. Finally, the obligation to fulfill means that

states must adopt the necessary measures directed towards the full realization of the rights.

References

AAFC (Agriculture and Agri-Food Canada). 2008. *Growing Forward.* <www4.agr.gc.ca/AAFC-AAC/display-afficher.do?id=1238606407452&lang=eng>.

___. 2002. "Agricultural Policy Framework Consultations: Phase 1 Final Report. Agricultural Policy Framework Consultations March 27–June 19." <www4.agr.gc.ca/AAFC-AAC/display-afficher.do?id=1184868161653&lang=eng>.

CFA (Canadian Federation of Agriculture). 2003a. "The Message Has Not Changed." News release, March 17.

___. 2003b. "Farm Leaders Discuss BSE, Business Risk Management and Other Issues." News release, July 25.

Chartier, Guy. 2003. Senior Communications Advisor. Saskatchewan Region, Communications and Consultations Team, Agriculture and Agri-Food Canada. Personal Communication. August 9.

Easter, Wayne. 2005. *Empowering Canadian Farmers in the Marketplace.* A report by the Parliamentary Secretary to the Minister of Agriculture and Agri-Food. Ottawa: Minister of Agriculture.

GPC International. 2002. "Event Report: APF — Wave Two Consultations." <www4.agr.gc.ca/resources/prod/doc/cb/apf/pdf/wave2-QC_e.pdf>.

La Vía Campesina. 2008. "Declaration of Maputo: V International Conference of La Vía Campesina, Maputo, Mozambique." October 19–22.

___. 2000a. Vía Campesina press release at the Global Forum for Agricultural Research (GFAR,) May 23, Dresden, Germany.

Martz, Diane J.F. 2006. "Canadian Farm Women and their Families: Restructuring, Work and Decision Making." Doctoral dissertation, Department of Geography, University of Saskatchewan.

___. 2004. *The Farmers' Share: Compare the Share 2004.* Muenster, SK: Centre for Rural Studies and Enrichment.

NFU (National Farmers Union). 2002. "Vanclief Hires World's Largest PR firm to Manufacture Farmer Consent." News release, March 28.

Nyéléni 2007. "Forum for Food Sovereignty: A Synthesis Report." <foodsovereignty.org/public/terrapreta/31Mar2007NyeleniSynthesisReport.pdf>.

Pimbert, Michel. 2006. *Transforming Knowledge and Ways of Knowing for Food Sovereignty.* Reclaiming Diversity and Citizenships Series. London, UK: Institute for Environment and Development.

Roppel, Carla, Annette Aurélie Desmarais and Diane Martz. 2006. *Farm Women and Canadian Agricultural Policy*. Ottawa: Status of Women Canada. <foodstudies.ca/Documents/Farm_Women_and_the_apf.pdf>.

Standing Committee on Agriculture and Agri-Food. 2007. 39th Parliament, 1st Session, Draft transcript of evidence, February 22.

SWC (Status of Women Canada). 1995. "Setting the Stage for the Next Century: The Federal Plan for Gender Equality." <swc-cfc.gc.ca/pubs/066261951X/199508_066261951X_e.pdf>.

White, Sarah C. 2000. "Depoliticising Development: The Uses and Abuses of

Participation." In Development NGOs and Civil Society: A Development in Practice Reader. (Originally published in *Development in Practice* 1996: 6, 1. <developmentinpractice.org/.../development-ngos-and-civil-society>.

Winters, Daniel. 2007. "Producers Skeptical of Ottawa's APF Vision." *Western Producer* February 22.

5. FOOD SECURE CANADA
Where Agriculture, Environment, Health, Food and Justice Intersect

Cathleen Kneen

The vision behind Food Secure Canada (FSC) was ambitious: to create a coherent food movement in Canada that could strengthen local projects and support a national food policy for a just and sustainable food system. The idea was to bring together all the very different perspectives of groups working on food issues, insisting that ending hunger, supporting population health through healthy and safe food and ensuring the environmental (and economic) sustainability of the food system are necessarily interlinked. Of course for many groups and individuals engaged in food projects and programs, such a link is neither inevitable nor, indeed, intelligible. For example, there are farmers who see "environmentalists" as threatening their livelihoods, and food bank operators who dismiss farmers as only looking for the highest price for their produce (thus placing it out of reach of the poor). Nevertheless, as the consolidation of Food Secure Canada in 2006 attests, there are many social actors within the food system who recognize the links and are prepared to devote considerable energy to strengthening them. As one such actor, I was part of the group that created Food Secure Canada, a high point in my personal history of nearly thirty years of active participation in food system and justice issues.

The Social and Historical Context

During the Depression of the 1930s, people across Canada established soup kitchens to feed the unemployed. Many of these soup kitchens were charitable, run by church groups who saw this service as a religious duty (and in many cases as an opportunity to save souls as well); but some, like the one in the mining town of Sudbury, were centered in political organizing to gain worker power. Still, it was not until panic about rising oil prices led to a food-price crisis in the 1970s, that there was an opening for public discussion in Canada on the food system as a system. In response to the government stance that the high food prices of the time penalized consumers and benefited farmers, a group of young activists from church, trade union and non-profit groups came together to uncover and articulate a different perspective. The result was the People's Food Commission (PFC), which ran from 1978 to1980. It consisted of volunteer commissioners who held about seventy hearings organized by local groups from coast to coast, and heard testimonies from people representing virtually every walk of life. The PFC concluded that, behind the rise and fall of food prices, there were a handful of corporations who controlled and profited from the food system. This insight was reflected in the title of its final report, "The Land of Milk and Money" (People's Food Commission 1980). The analysis was further laid out in Brewster Kneen's (1989) book, *From Land to Mouth: Understanding the Food System*, which described the logic and effects of this industrial food system.

Despite this thorough analysis, problems of hunger continued to be framed simplistically by policy makers, and issues such as the corporatization of the food system were generally left out of the mainstream policy debates. As a result, the main response to the food-price crisis in communities across the country was the establishment of food banks. The first Canadian food bank was started in Edmonton in 1981, and the first national food-bank conference was held in Toronto in 1986. Although community-based programs for self-reliance, which had a broader frame of reference, were also established, particularly in the cities, emergency food provision through food banks and other charitable programs remains the standard response to hunger in Canada even today.

Since the 1970s, many different initiatives have begun to address issues related to food and the food system in Canada. Although a national standard for organic agriculture was not adopted in Canada until 2009, farmers across the country had started developing and certifying organic production in the late 1970s through farmer-to-farmer mechanisms. Québec saw the rise of community kitchens in the mid-1980s, set up predominantly with poor women cooking collectively to save money; a formal organization of community kitchens was formed in Québec in 1990, and the practice has since spread across the country with literally hundreds of projects in each province —more than five hundred were reported in B.C. alone in 2004. Also in the last two decades, as rates of obesity and related chronic disease have soared, health practitioners have made the link between food and public health (see Chapter 8 for more discussion of the links between collective kitchens and public health and nutrition). The Toronto Food Policy Council was formed in 1991 under the city's Board of Health with a professor of nutrition as chair. Across the country local health units have also been developed; these support a range of community-based initiatives, including community gardens and farmers' markets, which work to get healthy food to people.

When a young couple in Vancouver popularized the term, "the 100-mile diet" (Smith and MacKinnon 2007), the notion of eating local food to reduce our "ecological footprint" found a ready audience and sparked Eat Local campaigns in cities, towns and villages throughout Canada. Growing rates of cancer, asthma and allergies in the general population have also increased support for organic and local foods, which are seen as more conducive to good health than the chemical-dependent produce and manufactured foods of the dominant food system. These concerns have given impetus to increased urban agriculture, for both family sustenance and for sale, as well as the immensely popular direct farmer-to-consumer programs called Community Supported Agriculture (CSA). They also have encouraged restaurants to feature local and seasonal ingredients on their menus, largely because of customer demand. Since 2000, when the Slow Food Movement, based originally in Italy, was established in the U.S., local *convivia* supporting small-scale, "artisanal" food production have been springing up across Canada, supported by food producers, chefs and citizens.

The development of direct relationships between farmers and their customers has also challenged the marketing boards. These were originally put in place to protect farmers in a market of undifferentiated commodities and to ensure a fair return to farmers (based on their real costs of production) by limiting supply to actual market demand. While these supply-management marketing boards have succeeded in ensuring that farmers in dairy, poultry and eggs are able to make a living, they are having difficulties adapting to markets based on a plethora of products identified by production method and location. The direct-to-consumer markets, with their focus on local or certified organic foods, are built on personal relationships, which typically develop outside of the conventional marketing systems in which the boards operate. For example, there was a prolonged struggle between the British Columbia Egg Marketing Board, which insisted that "an egg is an egg" and that direct sales of organic eggs are a violation of the marketing board legislation, and farmers and consumers, who insisted that, because the people who want to buy organic eggs will not purchase conventional eggs, organic eggs should stay outside of the system (Shore 2010).

Not all marketing boards have supply management powers, of course. The Canadian Wheat Board (CWB) — which the current federal government is determined to destroy — is based on the advantage of single-desk selling of wheat and barley. It ensures that all producers have more equal access to the market: because of the volume that it handles and the premiums it obtains for consistent quality and reliable service, it also achieves the best available prices. It spreads the marketing risks among farmers in a fair way and protects them to some extent from the monopolistic power of the large grain traders (see Chapter 7 for an in-depth analysis of the CWB.)

Meanwhile, back in Ottawa, the policies of the federal government affecting the food system have remained essentially unchanged since 1969. They are based on an industrial, monoculture vision of food production and distribution and an abiding faith in technology to address food safety, and environmental and health issues. For example, Health Canada's assessment of the products of genetic engineering uses the concept of "substantial equivalence" to ensure the rapid approval of novel organisms in food production and processing. Based on the completely unscientific notion of "familiarity," substantial equivalence[1] has been explained as a process of deciding, in effect, that "if it looks like a duck and quacks like a duck, it's a duck and we don't need to do any further study before approving it for human consumption." The influence of the food-chemical-pharmaceutical-biotechnology industry is enormous: even though the vast majority of Canadians have shown in repeated studies and polls that they want mandatory labelling of foods produced with genetic engineering, the federal government has steadfastly refused to implement such labelling in deference to its industry partners.[2]

The Formation of Food Secure Canada

By June 1999, when the first formal discussion of a Canadian food security network took place, a large number of people across Canada were actively working on issues to change the food system. They joined together through a wide variety of community-based projects, food banks and public health promotion groups, as well as farming, fishing and environmental organizations; while the goals were diverse, they included increasing food self-reliance among poor and marginalized populations and supporting sustainable livelihoods, as well as opposing genetically modified organisms (GMOs). Consumer consciousness, in addition to increasing interest among academics in the relationship between food and health, had begun to emerge. People began to recognize the importance of direct relationships between food producers and consumers, which could be achieved through farmers' markets and food box delivery programs. The idea was to bring all of these groups and interests together to create a national network for information sharing and policy advocacy.

Such networks had already existed locally and regionally. For example, the Nova Scotia Nutrition Council (NSNC) was formed in 1985. In 1992, *An Action Plan for Food Security for Manitobans* was published, marking the establishment of the Nutrition and Food Security Network of Manitoba. In British Columbia, a Vancouver-based organization called FarmFolk/CityFolk started in 1993; by 1999 the British Columbia Food Systems Network (BCFSN) had brought together participants in community-based food security projects and programs, in particular those involving marginalized communities, pregnant women and young mothers and Indigenous Peoples, to discuss strategy with provincial policy analysts.

Meanwhile, Canadian civil society had played an active role in trying to shape the Government of Canada's position at the World Food Summit (WFS) held in Rome in 1996. Citizens had debated food policy through meetings and teleconferences, and a joint government-civil society committee was formed to seek consensus on Canada's contribution. This was perhaps the first time that the Canadian federal government sought civil society participation in international food policy so enthusiastically. Representatives of Canadian grassroots organizations and non-governmental organizations then participated in the NGO Forum (held parallel to the World Food Summit). This forum developed the NGO Statement to the World Food Summit, "Profit for Few or Food for All? Food Sovereignty and Security to Stop the Globalization of Hunger" (NGO Forum to the World Food Summit 1996).

A precedent had been set: when the Canadian government was preparing their submission to the World Food Summit: Five Years Later (to be held in Rome in early November 2001), government officials realized that they needed once again to include civil society in this report. In March of that year I joined a group of people, representing non-profit organizations from every province and territory, in a teleconference to discuss ways in which we could ensure civil society input into this submission. Within government, the Global Affairs Bureau of Agriculture and Agri-Food Canada offered some support for this idea. Within a few months, in June 2001, the Centre for Studies in Food Security (CSFS) at Ryerson University in Toronto organized a conference called "Working Together," which included representatives from various civil society organizations, as well as networks from every province and territory and financial support from several federal government agencies (Koç and MacRae 2001). This conference was a significant step in the formation of what became Food Secure Canada. The goals of the conference were to: (1) develop a working plan for a civil-society-based national action plan for food security; (2) assess the contributions of the Canadian government to food security nationally and internationally; and (3) make practical policy proposals to provincial and federal governments on achieving the goals of Canada's Action Plan for Food Security.

As participants examined the goals of the government's Action Plan and compared them to the food security situation in Canada as we had experienced it, we developed a long list of concerns and recommendations: these ranged from immediate action to address hunger in Canada to support for research in agro-ecological food systems. We also called for a comprehensive federal-government food policy. The final report defined food security broadly, including not only access to food but also the ability to produce food, protection of the environment, security of income and access to traditional territories and resources for Indigenous people. The conference thus recommended that the Canadian NGO delegates to the World Food Summit: Five

Years Later insist on the inclusion of the cultural, social and ecological — not just physiological and biological — dimensions of food security and the right to food. To effect agrarian reform domestically, the conference report said that we must apply the approach recommended for international rural development in the official FAO (Food and Agriculture Organization 1996) World Food Summit documents here in Canada. This means providing infrastructure, ensuring access to the means of production and protecting the sustainability of the future resource base (including stewardship and full-cost accounting). It also means recognizing farmers' priority to provide food for themselves, their communities and their country, before any consideration of export, a view that stands in marked contrast to the "Canada feeds the world" approach.

The World Food Summit: Five Years Later was postponed to the following June because of the fallout from the events of September 11, 2001. At this summit, representatives of La Vía Campesina insisted that the concept of food sovereignty (that they had introduced and which was reflected in the NGO Statement at the WFS in 1996) be paramount in any strategies for global food security. Their vision of food sovereignty was based on control of food systems by food providers and their communities. In Canada, however, when the term was used in the food movement, it was frequently limited to a matter of national control over staple foods. This was certainly the case in the discussions at the 2004 Canadian Food Security Assembly in Winnipeg entitled "Growing Together," hosted by the Canadian Foodgrains Bank and Winnipeg Harvest.

It was in Winnipeg that the defining concept of Food Secure Canada was framed, as the participants (again, a wide range of food activists from across the country) defined the three interlocking commitments for the new organization broadly as:

(1) *Zero Hunger*: All people at all times must be able to acquire, in a dignified manner, adequate quantity and quality of culturally and personally acceptable food. This is essential to the health of our population, and requires cooperation among many different sectors, including housing, social policy, transportation, agriculture, education, and community, cultural, voluntary and charitable groups, and businesses.

(2) *A sustainable food system*: Food in Canada must be produced, harvested (including fishing and other wild food harvest), processed, distributed and consumed in a manner which maintains and enhances the quality of land, air and water for future generations, and in which people are able to earn a living wage in a safe and healthy working environment by harvesting, growing,

producing, processing, handling, retailing and serving food.

(3) *Healthy and safe food*: Safe and nourishing foods must be readily at hand (and less nourishing ones restricted); food (including wild foods) must not be contaminated with pathogens or industrial chemicals; and no novel food can be allowed to enter the environment or food chain without rigorous independent testing and the existence of an ongoing tracking and surveillance system, to ensure its safety for human consumption. (Canadian Centre for Policy Alternatives, Manitoba 2004)

A committee made up of representatives from various national and regional organizations held extensive consultations in preparation for the next conference; they also drafted a constitution for the new organization. At the Food Security Assembly held in Waterloo in 2005, Food Secure Canada was formed with Mustafa Koç, a sociology professor at Ryerson University, as its interim chair. At this meeting about two hundred people wrestled through an intense three days to develop an Action Agenda for the new organization that focused on research and policy development, strategic alliances and capacity building, education and outreach, and advocacy (Desjardins and Govindaraj 2005). Among other things, the Action Agenda called for the development of several working papers (on child hunger and nutrition, food localism and the right to food in Canada) and the re-establishment of the People's Food Commission (PFC – which I discuss later on in this chapter). Over the next year, a set of by-laws and a constitution were thrashed out, and a fourth assembly was held in Vancouver in conjunction with the Community Food Security Coalition (CFS) of the U.S. This conference, entitled "Bridging Borders Towards Food Security," attracted more than nine hundred participants and provided a powerful opportunity for people from each country to gain insight into the initiatives, perspectives and challenges of the other. Here, for the first time, the key concepts of food sovereignty were presented to the Canadian movement by farmers from the Global South and North America; these included representations from the U.S.'s National Family Farm Coalition (NFFC) and the Canadian National Farmers Union (NFU). There were also presentations about Indigenous food sovereignty as it was being developed in the Interior of British Columbia.

At the first AGM of Food Secure Canada, members agreed to continue focusing on building relationships with Indigenous peoples and with Québec, with a plan to hold the next assembly in Montréal (although it eventually took place in Ottawa). Food Secure Canada/Sécurité Alimentaire Canada was chartered as a non-profit organization with an elected steering committee in October, 2006.

Food Secure Canada: Issues and Challenges

The fledgling organization faced — indeed, continues to face — a number of predictable challenges: geography, diversity and funding. Geography is always a huge challenge for any organization that tries to be effective at a national level in Canada. Travel between many communities, particularly in the North, is only feasible by air — even where ground transportation is available, it is expensive and time-consuming.

Recognizing the contribution of air travel to global warming, one of the first decisions of the new steering committee was to limit the national assemblies to every other year. Food Secure Canada has thus become something of a virtual organization conducting most of its business and communications on the Internet and through teleconferences. Even in the current digital era, this poses a real contradiction for people whose work is deeply grounded in local relationships with people and the land; some of these people do not even own computers. Only a fraction of FSC's constituency can afford to attend the biennial assemblies, so much of the essential face-to-face relationship building is carried out through local and regional meetings. All the provincial networks hold annual gatherings, and great efforts are made to ensure that steering committee or active members from other regions are able to attend such meetings to build links. The steering committee itself — twenty-two members from every province and one of the Territories — meets by teleconference every month. Food Secure Canada also continues to work on electronic communications with its website, webinars and e-mail lists. Important decisions are made electronically, as is the annual election of steering committee members.

Part of the struggle around geography is the desire to be inclusive. For Food Secure Canada there are several aspects of inclusion that are considered vital. The most obvious is the issue of language. Canada is officially bilingual, but most French speakers are clustered in Manitoba, eastern Ontario, Québec (where French is the official language) and New Brunswick, which is officially bilingual. Despite the teaching of French in schools, most Canadians in other parts of the country do not speak French. Québec, as the centre of *la francophonie*, has a long history of self-understanding as a nation, and a strong sovereigntist political movement. If Food Secure Canada is to really be Food Secure Canada /Sécurité Alimentaire Canada, it needs to find a way to be effectively bilingual without alienating the Prairie and coastal English speakers for whom French Canada is far away and for whom engaging with its culture and politics is at best a low priority.

Despite the efforts of church and state to assimilate (or destroy) them, more than six hundred First Nations (Statistics Canada 2006), not including the Inuit or Métis, reside in Canada The appalling state of many reserves, the skyrocketing prevalence of chronic disease and suicide, particularly among youth, have also prompted governments and health departments in some provinces, particularly in British Columbia, to pay more attention to the particular needs of Indigenous peoples. At the same time there are growing movements to reclaim culture and traditional foods and food practices (foodways) among some Indigenous peoples in Canada.

In B.C., home to twenty-seven major First Nations groups (including 197 recognized governments or "bands"), Indigenous peoples have provided leadership in the development of place-based food consciousness in the B.C. Food Systems Network. In turn, the Network sponsored the formation of the Indigenous Food Sovereignty Working Group (see www.indigenousfoodsystem.org and Chapter 6 for more information and discussion). In Ontario, a coalition between the Ardoch Algonquin First Nation and a group self-identified as "settlers" came together to fight uranium mining in their area. So partnerships are beginning to emerge which see colonization as a critical issue for both Indigenous people and settlers. This is, however, by no means widespread, even in Food Secure Canada's constituency, and, as a result, the organization has insisted on ensuring that Indigenous perspectives are well-represented at its assemblies. The 2008 assembly in Ottawa featured First Nations speakers on every plenary panel, as well as in several workshops. A panelist, speaking in the tradition of Indigenous storytellers, was awarded an enthusiastic standing ovation despite having used up all the discussion time by going well over his allotted time.

Inclusivity and diversity play out a bit differently in the larger cities that are home to substantial immigrant populations. In Toronto, for example, there are more than 140 languages spoken; in Greater Vancouver, visible minorities, of which the largest ethnic group is of Chinese descent, represent over 41 percent of the population (Statistics Canada 2006). While the Asian foodways are highly visible in the Vancouver area, there has been little integration of the Chinese community into the food movement, although other immigrant groups, particularly Punjabis, are starting to play a more significant role. In Toronto, FoodShare is one of several organizations that have been working to engage the immigrant populations for years, with programs ranging from the Good Food Box and collective kitchens preparing baby food, to community gardens, often involving people who arrived in Canada with their seeds braided into their hair. One of the programs Food Share has fostered is the Afri-Can Food Basket, which is now an independent organization. Greater inclusion of immigrant communities is a high current priority for Food Secure Canada.

Another element of diversity is, of course, political. From the beginning of Food Secure Canada there has been disagreement as to whether the organization is to be an umbrella — the "big tent," in which there is a place for everyone — or a platform from which members can act in solidarity with struggles of the deprived and marginalized. This diversity of perspectives can be seen clearly in the way in which the phrase "food sovereignty" has been used. Although the National Farmers Union, a founding member of La Vía Campesina, provides a lively discourse on food sovereignty, many other organizations in the food movement in Canada have generally preferred to use the terms "food security" or "community food security." Until very recently, use of the term "food sovereignty" implied state or national control of basic food staples (Centre for Policy Alternatives-Manitoba 2004). This has indeed been the effective policy in the province of Québec since the late 1970s.[3] A recent study noted that one Québec producer group, l'Union des Producteurs Agricoles, with a history of supporting industrial agriculture, supports the idea that the state is the principal agent through which people's sovereignty is expressed; meanwhile, l'Union Paysanne, a small group of autonomous farmers and food activists in Québec affiliated with La Vía Campesina, promotes a peasant agricultural farming model, built from the bottom up, that strives for social justice and sustainable development (Blouin et al. 2009).

Furthermore, as indicated above, among First Nations the concept of food sovereignty is related to sovereignty in general, and encompasses the key issues of access to traditional territories, harvesting and hunting, capacity to pass traditional foodways and skills to younger generations as well as protection of land, animals and water from industrial pollution and contamination or outright appropriation by outside entities (see Chapter 6). For First Nations people, sovereignty is often understood as encompassing the essential relationships between human beings and the other creatures with which they live: for them, all living creatures are deemed to be sacred, as they reflect the origins of the peoples themselves.

The federal government in Canada increasingly manifests a neoliberal position that includes an unwavering commitment to the market-driven productionist model of agriculture, with its dependence on fossil fuels and technology and its focus on commodity production for export. Given this attitude on the part of the federal government and its continuous drift to the political right, it is not surprising that the financial support which Food Secure Canada received from various government departments in its initial stages has since disappeared. The result is that the organization is largely dependent on the voluntary work of its steering committee, in particular the chair. Mustafa Koç, the chair of the initial steering committee which brought the idea of a national food security network to reality, devoted a huge amount of time to the project, and as the current chair I have followed suit. Clearly, this is not sustainable in the long term. In 2009, we were able to use membership fees and some surplus from grants obtained in support of the 2008 assembly to hire a part-time coordinator, part of whose role is fundraising. The goal is to hire a full-time executive director and to provide meaningful support to the provincial networks and organizational members of Food Secure Canada.

Food Secure Canada's Mandate and Food Sovereignty

From the beginning, the mandate of Food Secure Canada was to support the actions of its members, many of which are national organizations with their own agendas on food (e.g. Food Banks Canada, Dietitians of Canada, National Farmers Union, Canadian Foodgrains Bank, Beyond Factory Farming, Canadian Biotechnology Action Network, etc.). As an organization, it was to take action itself only when the members deemed it necessary. Nevertheless, the initial Action Agenda did include initiatives beyond research and networking. In particular, there was a proposal to advocate for a federal inter-departmental body to work on the development of a national food security policy, along with a proposal to explore the feasibility of repeating the People's Food Commission.

In February 2007, several members of Food Secure Canada, including me, were among a handful of Canadians to attend the Nyéléni Forum for Food Sovereignty in Sélingué, Mali, West Africa. This was an extraordinary worldwide gathering which brought together hundreds of peasants, artisanal-fisherpeople, nomadic pastoralists and forest dwellers, movements of the urban poor and other marginalized peoples in struggle to gain control over their access to food. On a specially built campus of mud-and-wattle huts and cinder-block meeting spaces on a hot and dusty field, and fed local food by a team of local women, the participants engaged in passionate debate about the nature and strategic directions for food sovereignty. The Canadians were inspired to come back home and share the analysis of food sovereignty with our communities and to further build the movement in Canada.

Over the next year, we pulled together a group of people representing organizations like Inter Pares, Unitarian Service Committee of Canada (USC), the National Farmers Union and other groups that had been involved with the People's Food Commission, to form a coordinating committee for a new project: we then worked to gain support and funding to make it a reality. With seed money from Heifer International Canada, consultations were held with groups in each province to clarify the scope and direction of the project. It was quickly agreed that there was no need of another commission to expose the reality of the industrial food system; its flaws were already quite evident. What was needed (as the Action Agenda from the assembly in Waterloo in 2005 had hinted) was a coherent policy framework for a different food system, one that was based in the principles of justice, equity, sustainable livelihoods and respect for the environment.

The coordinating committee therefore developed a proposal for a pan-

Canadian process, with animators from the food movement in every province, to engage people from every sector in developing a policy for food sovereignty — a policy based in, and supportive of, the needs and perspectives of the whole Canadian people, but particularly food providers and marginalized segments of the population. This proposal, named the People's Food Policy Project (PFPP), was supported by Heifer International, who provided funding for a part-time national coordinator and some operating expenses (see www.peoplesfoodpolicy.ca for more information).

While the project aims to achieve "a food sovereignty policy for Canada," there is still, as noted above, substantial discomfort within Food Secure Canada with the term "food sovereignty." As proposed by La Vía Campesina and adopted by others in the global movement, food sovereignty reflects the struggle of marginalized peoples to gain power over their food systems and their lives. Many Canadians, even those who have devoted their lives to precisely this project, are uncomfortable with the oppositional politics this implies. From a Food Secure Canada perspective, the People's Food Policy is clearly a "platform" project and some members felt this could seriously hinder the "big tent" goal of the organization. For this reason, and to facilitate support from other organizations, it was decided that the project would operate independently of Food Secure Canada. Nevertheless, at its assembly in November 2008 (entitled "Reclaiming Our Food System: A Call to Action"), Food Secure Canada heartily endorsed the People's Food Policy Project (Food Secure Canada 2008).

As a living concept, food sovereignty has spread across Canada and morphed into different and unexpected forms. There is a growing discourse on Indigenous Food Sovereignty as part of the struggle for justice for Aboriginal peoples. In Québec the concept of food sovereignty resonates with the general sovereigntist position of "*maîtres chez nous*." The recent food crisis, coupled with the ongoing collapse of farmer income, has also led to a more general call for a federal food policy even from more conservative elements (for example, the Canadian Federation of Agriculture (CFA) and the Liberal Party), and several representatives of mainstream farm organizations, who previously would have nothing to do with food security, have begun to talk about food sovereignty — however, their use of the term is open to different interpretations.

Since the People's Food Policy Project is clearly rooted in the global movement's understanding of food sovereignty, its first action was to collect and disseminate a series of Canadian stories to illustrate the six pillars of food sovereignty (see Box 5-1) which emerged from the Nyéléni conference (Nyéléni 2007). Like the project as a whole, this was a highly participatory and consultative process that took half a year to complete. In the process, the principle of international solidarity was re-emphasized and a whole new pillar emerged from the Indigenous Circle, established by the project to develop protocols for engagement with Indigenous Peoples. This seventh pillar of food sovereignty stresses that food is sacred, as it is part of the web of relationships with the natural world that define culture and community. A resulting series of seven colourful pamphlets were distributed by the project animators and published on the website.

In the development of the People's Food Policy Project, the seventh pillar has become foundational. If food is sacred, it cannot be treated as a mere commodity, manipulated into junk foods or taken from people's mouths to feed animals or vehicles. If the ways in which we get food are similarly sacred, Mother Earth cannot be enslaved and forced to produce what we want, when and where we want it, through our technological tools. And of course, if food is sacred, the role of those who provide food is respected and supported.

The principle of solidarity, implicit in the six pillars articulated at the Nyéléni Conference and highlighted in the discussions within the People's Food Policy Project, means that any assertion of food sovereignty cannot be at the expense of other people. Trade regimes and aid programs must be governed by this principle. A third implicit principle is gender and respect for the central role of women in food systems, which is also accepted as a core cross-cutting element of the People's Food Policy.

Peter Hallward (2007), speaking about a completely different context in his book on Haiti, gives an excellent description of the approach the People's

Box 5-1: Seven Pillars of Food Sovereignty — The People's Food Policy Project

1. Food sovereignty focuses on food for people, putting people's need for food at the centre of policies, and insisting that food is more than just a commodity.
2. Food sovereignty builds knowledge and skills. It builds on traditional knowledge, uses research to support and pass this knowledge to future generations and rejects technologies that undermine or contaminate local food systems.
3. Food sovereignty works with Nature, optimizing the contributions of ecosystems and improving resilience.
4. Food sovereignty values food providers, supporting sustainable livelihoods and respecting the work of all food providers.
5. Food sovereignty localizes food systems, reducing the distance between food providers and consumers. It rejects dumping and inappropriate food aid and resists dependency on remote and unaccountable corporations.
6. Food sovereignty puts control locally, placing control in the hands of local food providers. It recognizes the need to inhabit and share territories and rejects the privatization of natural elements.
7. Food sovereignty understands food as sacred, part of the web of relationships with the natural world that define culture and community.

Food Policy Project also takes:

> Politics doesn't concern things that make people different but things they hold in common... true political action is animated by collective principles that concern everyone by definition — principles of freedom, equality, solidarity, justice... the collective action required to apply such a principle requires the self-emancipation of the oppressed... [for] it is the oppressed who will "liberate themselves and their oppressors as well." (xxiv)

For nearly a year, ending in March 2010, the People's Food Policy Project engaged more than one thousand people: through kitchen table meetings and other gatherings across the country as well as through the website outreach it collected hundreds of proposals for the People's Food Policy. This mass of material was collated by yet another group of volunteers — people with research and policy experience — into a first draft that was circulated for even wider input. This entailed two daunting challenges. The first was to ensure that the draft policy reflected both the expressions and the concerns of all the proposals received, which contained many contradictory ideas. The second was to find ways to reflect the vision of food sovereignty based in the liberation of the oppressed and, at the same time, engage the mainstream of Canadians on the basis of the collective principles we all hold in common.

By the time the draft policy was presented at the Food Secure Canada Assembly in Montréal in November 2010, it had been sorted into ten Discussion Papers and more than 3,000 people had engaged with the project. After intense discussions on each of the ten papers during the Assembly, they were sent back to the volunteer writing teams who spent several months revising, refining and inserting further evidence for policy recommendations. Meanwhile, an overarching document was developed which summarizes the general approach of the papers as a whole, and lays out challenges, ways forward and key policy recommendations in the ten areas.

This document, entitled *Resetting the Table: A People's Food Policy for Canada*, was unveiled in April 2011, in the midst of a federal election campaign where, for the first time, the concept of food policy was an element in all the party campaign platforms. By this time the People's Food Policy Project process had come under the wing of Food Secure Canada, which had accepted its food sovereignty language as coherent with, and not necessarily replacing, other expressions of the organization's philosophy such as "food security" or "food democracy."

Resetting the Table, describing the deep flaws in the food system, notes:

> The root problem is that food is being treated as a commodity rather than as a necessity of life, and the foundation for healthy and strong

> communities and economies. The primary beneficiaries of the current system are the companies who trade in food and food-related products — global food and agri-business — and the international financial speculators who gamble on food commodities. What happened during the food price crisis that hit the news in 2008 is a clear example of how food systems are currently set up to benefit industry and the financial sector at the expense of the world's poor. (People's Food Policy Project 2011: 6)

To begin to change this system, the People's Food Policy proposes a long list of policy recommendations that include, among others:

- Ensuring that food is eaten as close as possible to where it is produced (for example, introducing domestic/regional purchasing policies for institutions and large food retailers, community-supported agriculture, local farmers' markets, etc.);
- Supporting food providers in a widespread shift to ecological production in both urban and rural settings (for example, supporting organic agriculture, community-managed fisheries, Indigenous food systems, etc.), including introducing effective policies for the entry of new farmers into agriculture;
- Enacting a strong federal poverty elimination and prevention program, with measurable targets and timelines, to ensure Canadians can better afford healthy food;
- Creating a nationally-funded Children and Food strategy (including school meal programs, school gardens and food literacy programs) to ensure that all children at all times have access to the food required for healthy lives; and
- Ensuring that the public, especially the most marginalized, are actively involved in decisions that affect the food system.

While organizations across the political spectrum are calling for food (or at least, "agri-food") policies, the People's Food Policy Project reflects the concerns and the language of ordinary people from coast to coast to coast: it proposes a framework that offers them a real voice. Through easily accessible "bite-size policies" focusing on specific issues in rural and urban communities, *Resetting the Table* offers a formal federal food policy proposal: the Discussion Papers are living documents subject to continual revision and expansion through public engagement. These mechanisms ensure that the People's Food Policy will be an ongoing process of engagement for Canadians in addressing the real and enormous problems in our food system. This marks a significant and potentially transformative moment for Food Secure Canada, as it gains in strength and credibility as the convener of the food movement in Canada, not only within the movement itself but also in broader social and political arenas.

Notes

1. Millstone et al. argue that "showing that a genetically modified food is chemically similar to its natural counterpart is not adequate evidence that it is safe for human consumption.... '[S]ubstantial equivalence'... means that if a GM food can be characterized as substantially equivalent to its 'natural' antecedent, it can be assumed to pose no new health risks and hence to be acceptable for commercial use. At first sight, the approach might seem plausible and attractively simple, but we believe that it is misguided, and should be abandoned in favour of one that includes biological, toxicological and immunological tests rather than merely chemical ones. The concept of substantial equivalence has never been properly defined; the degree of difference between a natural food and its GM alternative before its 'substance' ceases to be acceptably 'equivalent' is not defined anywhere, nor has an exact definition been agreed by legislators. It is exactly this vagueness that makes the concept useful to industry but unacceptable to the consumer" (Millstone et al. 1999).
2. For example, on May 11, 2004, CBC News reported the results of an Environics poll in 1999 which stated that 80 percent of Canadians wanted mandatory labelling of genetically engineered foods. A Decima Research poll in the fall of 2003 (Consumers Association of Canada 2003) showed that 91 percent wanted labelling and 88 percent wanted it to be mandatory.
3. I have some personal experience of this policy and its effects. When my husband and I were running a sheep farm in Nova Scotia, we found that our traditional markets in Montréal were becoming closed to us in favour of Québec farmers. The result was that we developed a cooperative for marketing our lamb within Nova Scotia — thus spreading the practice of local self-reliance, which is one foundation of food sovereignty.

References

Blouin, C., J.F. Lemay, K. Ashraf, J. Imai and L. Konforti. 2009. "Local Food Policies and Public Policy: A Review of the Literature." Report published by Equiterre and the Centre for Trade Policy and Law at Carlton University. At <bitsandbytes.ca/resources/Local_Food_Systems_and_Public_Policy_-_A_Review_of_the_Literature.pdf>.

Canadian Centre for Policy Alternatives-Manitoba. 2004. "Growing Together." Proceedings of the Second National Food Security Assembly.

CBC News. 2004. "Genetically Modified Foods: a Primer." *CBC Online News,* May 11. At <cbc.ca/news/background/genetics_modification/>.

Consumers Association of Canada. 2003. "Results of Decima Poll." At <consumer.ca/pdfs/2003.12.03-press_conference_slides.pdf>.

Desjardins, E., and S. Govindaraj. 2005. "Proceedings of the Third National Food Security Assembly." At <foodsecurecanada.org/sites/foodsecurecanada.itfor-

change.org/files/ASSEMBLY_PROCEEDINGS%20Waterloo.pdf>.

Food and Agriculture Organization of the United Nations. 1996. "Rome Declaration on World Food Security" and "World Food Summit Plan of Action" At <www.fao.org/wfs/index_en.htm>.

Food Banks Canada. 2009. "Hunger Count: A Comprehensive Report on Hunger and Food Bank Use in Canada, and Recommendations for Change." At <foodbankscanada.ca/documents/HungerCount2009NOV16.pdf>.

Food Secure Canada. 2008. "Reclaiming Our Food System: A Call to Action." Summary Report of the Fifth National Assembly. At <foodsecurecanada.org/sites/foodsecurecanada.org/files/2008%20Assembly%20report.pdf>.

Hallward, Peter. 2007. *Damming the Flood: Haiti, Aristide, and the Politics of Containment.* London: Verso.

Kneen, Brewster. 1989. *From Land to Mouth: Understanding the Food System.* Second edition. Toronto: NC Press. Updated version available at <ramshorn.ca> under the title *From Land to Mouth, Second Helping: Understanding the Food System.*

Koç, Mustafa, and Rod MacRae. 2001. "Working Together: Civil Society Working for Food Security in Canada." At <foodsecurecanada.org/sites/foodsecurecanada.itforchange.org/files/WorkingTogether.pdf>.

Millstone, E., E. Brunner and S. Mayer. 1999. "Beyond 'Substantial Equivalence.'" *Nature* 401, October.

NGO Forum to the World Food Summit. 1996. "Profit for Few or Food for All? Food Sovereignty and Security to Stop the Globalisation of Hunger." Statement of the NGO Forum to the World Food Summit. At <converge.org.nz/pirm/food-sum.htm#ngo>.

Nutrition and Food Security Network of Manitoba. 1992. *An Action Plan for Food Security for Manitobans.*

Nyéléni. 2007. "Forum for Food Sovereignty: A Synthesis Report." At <foodsovereignty.org/public/terrapreta/31Mar2007NyeleniSynthesisReport.pdf>.

People's Food Commission. 1980. "The Land of Milk and Money: The National Report of the People's Food Commission." At <foodsecurecanada.org/sites/foodsecure.openconcept.ca/files/The%20Land%20of%20Milk%20and%20Money.pdf>.

People's Food Policy Project. 2011. "Resetting the Table: A People's Food Policy for Canada." At <www.peoplesfoodpolicy.ca>.

Shore, R. 2010. "Cracks Are Showing in the Egg Market." *Vancouver Sun* April 10. At <forums.bcac.bc.ca/content.php?r=42-Cracks-are-showing-in-the-egg-market>.

Smith, Alisa, and J.B. MacKinnon. 2007. *The 100 Mile Diet: A Year of Local Eating.* Toronto: Random House.

Statistics Canada. 2006. *Census.* At <12.statcan.ca/census-recensement/2006/rt-td/index-eng.cfm>.

6. INDIGENOUS FOOD SOVEREIGNTY

A Model for Social Learning

Dawn Morrison

> "Food will be what brings the people together." (*Secwepemc* Elder, Jones Ignace)

While the language and concept of food sovereignty has only recently been introduced into communities and policy circles around the world, the living reality is not a new one in Indigenous communities. Over thousands of years, Indigenous peoples have developed a wide range of traditional harvesting strategies and practices, including hunting, fishing, gathering and cultivating a vast number of plants and animals in the fields, forests and waterways. These practices have shaped, supported and sustained our distinct cultures, economies and ecosystems. In turn, a wide range of cultural and biological diversity is reflected in the traditional harvesting strategies practised and maintained within our respective traditional territories, now referred to by settlers as Canada. Our traditional territories (ninety-eight nations in total) are defined by the major geographic regions, and our cultures are defined by eleven major language groups. Approximately one-third of all the cultural and biological diversity within our traditional territories exists within what is now known as the province of British Columbia (B.C.), where twenty-seven nations of Indigenous peoples (consisting of eight out of the eleven major language groups) have developed a tremendous abundance of localized Indigenous foods.

Indigenous cultures are shaped by our unique relationship to the land and food systems within our respective traditional territories. While there is no universal definition of food sovereignty that reflects all of the realities of the myriad of Indigenous communities around the world, the underlying principles of Indigenous food sovereignty are based on our responsibilities to uphold our distinct cultures and relationships to the land and food systems. To avoid the limitations imposed by definitions, the concept of Indigenous food sovereignty describes, rather than defines, the present day strategies that enable and support the ability of Indigenous communities to sustain traditional hunting, fishing, gathering, farming and distribution practices (Morrison 2006, 2008), the way we have done for thousands of years prior to contact with the first European settlers. Through a process of appreciative inquiry, Indigenous food sovereignty also provides a framework for exploring, transforming and rebuilding the industrial food system towards a more just and ecological model for all.

We have rejected a formal universal definition of sovereignty in favour of one that respects the sovereign rights and power of each distinct nation to identify the characteristics of our cultures and what it means to be Indigenous. Generally speaking, we are tribal peoples who are distinct from other sections of society: we are regulated, wholly or partially, by our own traditions, customs and laws. We descend from ancestors who originally inhabited our traditional territories at the time of colonization: irrespective of our "legal" status, we retain some or all of our own social, economic, cultural and political institutions (United Nations 2000). And while each nation is distinct in language and culture, it is important to note that we share similar worldviews, values and beliefs that underlie our relationships to the land and food systems that sustain us.

Since the time of colonization, traditional harvesters have witnessed the rapid erosion of the health and integrity of Indigenous cultures, ecosystems and social structures that are integral to maintaining Indigenous land and food systems. Environmental degradation, neoliberal trade agendas, lack of access to the land, breakdown of tribal social structures and socio-economic marginalization are only a few of the most serious issues that are negatively impacting our ability to respond to our own needs for healthy, culturally adapted Indigenous foods.

Supporting Indigenous food sovereignty requires a deepened cross-cultural understanding of the ways in which Indigenous knowledge, values, wisdom and practices can inform food-related action and policy reform. This chapter examines the main principles of Indigenous food sovereignty as well as current issues, concerns and strategies that have been identified in recent discussions, meetings and conferences in Indigenous communities towards building an Indigenous food sovereignty movement in B.C. and beyond.

Indigenous Eco-Philosophy

For thousands of years, watersheds, landforms, vegetation and climatic zones have worked together to shape and form Indigenous cultures and our respective land and food systems. Consisting of a multitude of natural communities, Indigenous food systems include all land, soil, water, air, plants and animals, as well as Indigenous knowledge, wisdom and values. These food systems are maintained through our active participation in cultural harvesting strategies and practices in the fields, forests and waterways, which represent the most intimate way in which we interact with our environment. Indigenous food systems ultimately support the transfer of energy, both directly and indirectly, to the current agriculture-based economy that was developed and subsequently industrialized by settlers through the process of colonization. The highest levels of agricultural production in the mainstream economy take place on areas that were once important traditional harvesting sites. For example, non-Indigenous agricultural settlements in B.C. are concentrated on fertile valley bottoms in the Fraser Valley and central interior regions, displacing traditional berry-picking and hunting grounds and decimating elk and other wildlife populations. Much of the agricultural and industrial activities in the mainstream economy have also contaminated waterways that are an important habitat for salmon: they have led to decreased water supplies for local communities as a result of the removal of native vegetation, modification of drainage and contamination by agricultural fertilizers and pesticides (Rosenau and Angelo 2009). A more sustainable and ecological approach to agriculture recognizes the ways in which the ability to grow healthy food is directly connected to maintaining the health and integrity of neighbouring Indigenous ecosystems, including land, air and water.

In contrast to the highly mechanistic, linear food production, distribution and consumption model applied in the industrialized food system, Indigenous food systems are best described in ecological rather than neoclassical economic terms. In this context, an Indigenous food is one that has been primarily cultivated, taken care of, harvested, prepared, preserved, shared or traded within the boundaries of our respective traditional territories based on values of interdependency, respect, reciprocity and responsibility (Morrison 2008).

The Indigenous eco-philosophy that underlies the ability of Indigenous peoples to maintain dignified relationships to the land and food system is in sharp contrast to the Eurocentric belief, inherent in the worldview proposed by European philosopher Rene Descartes, that humans are to dominate and control nature, and therefore seek to "manage" the land that provides us with our food. Indigenous eco-philosophy reinforces the belief that humans do not manage the land, but instead can only manage our behaviours in relation to it. Transformation of the Cartesian worldview that dominates the global food system will require recognition and inclusion of an Indigenous eco-philosophy in laws, policies and institutions rather than continuing the colonial legacy of asserting full "control with no soul" over Indigenous land and food systems (First Principles Protocol for Building Cross Cultural Relationships 2009).

Principles of Indigenous Food Sovereignty

Indigenous food sovereignty is the newest and most innovative approach to achieving the end goal of long-term food security in Indigenous communities. The Indigenous food sovereignty approach provides a model for social learning and thereby promotes the application of traditional knowledge, values, wisdom and practices in the present day context. In an approach that people of all cultures can relate to, Indigenous food sovereignty provides a restorative framework for health and community development and appreciates the ways in which we can work together cross-culturally to heal our relationships with one another and the land, plants and animals that provide us with our food.

There are four main principles that guide Indigenous communities who are striving to achieve food sovereignty. These principles have been identified by Elders, traditional harvesters and community members (often in various meetings, conferences and discussions that have been facilitated by the B.C. Food Systems Network (BCFSN) Working Group on Indigenous Food Sovereignty).

Sacred or Divine Sovereignty

Food is a gift from the Creator. In this respect, the right to food is sacred and cannot be constrained or recalled by colonial laws, policies or institutions. Indigenous food sovereignty is ultimately achieved by upholding our long-standing sacred responsibilities to nurture healthy, interdependent relationships with the land, plants and animals that provide us with our food.

Participation

Indigenous food sovereignty is fundamentally based on "action," or the day-to-day practice of nurturing healthy relationships with the land, plants and animals that provide us with our food. Continued participation in Indigenous food-related action at all of the individual, family, community and regional levels is fundamental to maintaining Indigenous food sovereignty as a living reality for both present and future generations.

Self-Determination

Self-determination in this context refers to the freedom and ability to respond to our own needs for healthy, culturally-adapted Indigenous foods. It represents the freedom and ability to make decisions over the amount and quality of food we hunt, fish, gather, grow and eat. Indigenous food sovereignty thus promotes freedom from dependence on grocery stores or corporately-controlled food production, consumption and distribution in the industrialized food system.

Legislation and Policy

Indigenous food sovereignty attempts to reconcile Indigenous food and cultural values with colonial laws, policies and mainstream economic activities. It thereby provides a restorative framework for a coordinated, cross-sectoral approach to policy reform in forestry, fisheries, rangeland, environmental conservation, health, agriculture as well as rural and community development.

History of the Indigenous Food Sovereignty Movement in B.C.

The Working Group on Indigenous Food Sovereignty (WGIFS) was born in March of 2006 out of a recognized need to carry Indigenous perspectives into various meetings, conferences and discussions that have taken place within the food security movement. Through participation in the B.C. Food Systems Network Annual Gathering and strategic planning meetings, the WGIFS was created to promote an understanding of the concept of food sovereignty and the underlying issues affecting Indigenous peoples' ability to respond to our own needs for healthy, culturally-adapted foods. The WGIFS seeks to apply culturally appropriate protocols and ancient ways of knowing through a consensus-based approach to critically analyzing issues, concerns and strategies as they relate to Indigenous food, land, culture, health, economics and sustainability.

The WGIFS consists of members who provide input and leadership on ways to increase awareness and mobilize communities around the topic of Indigenous food sovereignty. The WGIFS strives to ensure that Indigenous voices are given given strong and balanced representation: the group currently consists of participants from key communities and groups in each of the major regions around the province of B.C. The working group is comprised of, but not limited to, traditional harvesters (including hunters, fishers and gatherers), farmers/gardeners, Aboriginal community members (on/off reserve, urban/rural, Métis), academics/researchers, grassroots organizations, non-governmental organizations and political advocates. The group includes non-Indigenous advocates from settler communities, and it promotes cross-cultural participation that is representative and balanced, based on geography, community group and cultures.

The Indigenous Food Systems Network

The WGIFS facilitates relationship building by organizing the time and space for regular meetings and discussions to promote a better understanding of the needs and interests of each group, and of our unique relationship to land and food systems. With respect to the leadership and administrative support provided by the WGIFS and the B.C. Food Systems Network, a rapidly expanding Indigenous Food Systems Network (IFSN) has been born. Through electronic communications, including the Indigenous Food Systems Network website (www.indigenousfoodsystems.org/) and the Indigenous Food Sovereignty email list-serve, we network and share relevant information that helps to build capacity within the Indigenous food sovereignty movement by linking individuals and communities with regional, provincial, national and international networks.

Current Situations and Challenges for Indigenous Food Sovereignty

Even though Canada is recognized as having one of the highest standards of living in the world, Indigenous communities experience high rates of poverty and socio-economic marginalization, thereby being forced to live in conditions that lead to high levels of stress, economic uncertainty and loss of control. Major stressors include threats to food supply and declining access to adequate quantities of high-quality, culturally-adapted food. Such factors not only lead to high rates of disease, but they also ultimately shatter the illusion of control. In combination with the obvious impacts of widely known food-related diseases such as diabetes, stress is linked with many of the most serious autoimmune and cardiovascular diseases that are disproportionately evident in our communities. While acute stress is a physiological mechanism that is vital to life, chronic stress without resolution produces high amounts of the stress hormone cortisol which destroys tissues, raises blood pressure, damages the heart and inhibits the immune system (Mate 2004). This situation in turn has led to the declining health of our communities in the broadest sense of the term.

According to the National Collaborating Centre for Aboriginal Health (NCCAH), "Poverty has clear outcomes on health because in part, it determines what kinds of foods people have available to them and what they can afford to purchase" (Reading and Wien 2009: 14). Thus, persons with lower incomes are subject to the stress of food insecurity from a compromised diet when sufficient quantities and varieties of food are no longer available. From 1998 to 1999, Aboriginal people living off reserve were almost three times more likely to be living in households experiencing food insecurity than were all other Canadians — a ratio of 27 percent to 10 percent (Reading and Wien 2009: 14). Yet, rather than dwelling on the many statistics that offer a glimpse into the health disparities that exist between Indigenous communities in Canadian society and attempting to quantify negative situations, Indigenous food sovereignty provides a more solution-oriented strategy for improving the health of Aboriginal peoples.

In addition to the high levels of stress experienced from the threat of not being able to meet our most basic and profound need for food, the health of Aboriginal peoples has been severely impacted by emotional stressors triggered by the oppressive colonial government structures and processes instituted within the elected band council system. The system is divisive and adversarial in nature, lacking the ability to reconcile intra-tribal differences in decision making matters that impact Indigenous land and food systems. This system enables governments and corporations to take advantage of the differences that exist within the community between proponents of large-scale industrial development and proponents for the re-establishment of an ecological economic model based on Indigenous food and cultural values.

Neoclassic economic influences from mainstream culture and society continue to challenge Indigenous individuals and families to find a balance between the amount of time and energy spent in mainstream economic activities with the amount of time and energy spent harvesting, preparing and preserving traditional foods, as well as passing Indigenous food-related knowledge onto present and future generations. Due to the lack of intergenerational transmission of Indigenous food-related knowledge in the home and education system, Indigenous food-related knowledge systems are being rapidly eroded. Furthermore, losses of cultural values have led to the breakdown of tribal social structures and a disconnection of extended family and community networks, which in turn has resulted in fewer hands to do the work of harvesting and preserving enough food for the family.

The techno-bureaucratic approach to food production in the corporately-controlled global food system reinforces a sedentary lifestyle detrimental to the health of Indigenous communities who, until relatively recently, were participating on a day-to-day basis in Indigenous food-related activities. Reliance on food in the global market economy and displacement from many of the most culturally and spiritually significant traditional harvesting sites in the fields, forests and waterways has removed communities from the act of growing, harvesting, preparing and preserving food for their families and communities and has placed billions of dollars of profits in the pockets of a handful of some of the highest paid executives in the corporate world.

The concept of development instituted in the global economy assumes that Indigenous land and food systems are void of any value other than those held by governments and corporate stakeholders from foreign countries that are moving in to grab some of the last remaining fragments of Indigenous land and food systems. One of the most blatant examples of this neocolonialist agenda can be found in the interior of B.C. where a Japanese investor from Nippon Cable, in cooperation with Delta Hotels, has invested millions of dollars to develop an invasive, large-scale ski resort known as Sun Peaks, in the most culturally and spiritually significant hunting, fishing and gathering area in the *Neskonlith Secwepemc* traditional territory.

Multiple development practices continue to threaten the health and integrity of traditional harvesting sites, including the wave of recent mining proposals, the licensing of individual power projects in B.C. waterways and widespread pesticide use in forest- and range-management practices. Indigenous communities are witnessing the rapid depletion of salmon populations and of other important sources of protein in marine ecosystems due to environmental contamination, the licensing of open-net cage fish farms and the issuance of individual transferable quotas to wealthy corporate investors. High levels of carbon emissions and rapid climatic changes are challenging the most persistent traditional harvesters to adapt to changes outside of the historical range of variability, thereby adding to uncertainty as a characteristic of food insecurity in Indigenous communities. Movements of culturally important plant and animal species in and out of areas, changes to water levels and temperatures, as well as extreme storms and weather conditions are some of the most critical effects of climate change on Indigenous food systems.

Social Learning and Adapting Cultural Techniques

The food sovereignty approach provides a restorative framework for identifying ways that social and political advocates from the settler communities can work to support Indigenous food sovereignty in a bottom-up approach to influencing policy, driven by traditional practice and adaptive management. The practices of Indigenous peoples have been shown to be crucial in the maintenance of the world's biological diversity, as described in Toledo's (2001) extensive study that maps a "remarkable overlap between Indigenous territories and the world's remaining areas of highest biodiversity" (451). The study also highlights the importance of Indigenous views, knowledge and practices in biodiversity conservation. The ability of Indigenous peoples to sustain the land and food system for thousands of years can be attributed to a dynamic view of the land and food system, which assumes that nature cannot be controlled nor yields predicted. The uncertainty that has come to characterize the current food system calls for humans to adapt our strategies and cultural techniques to an equally dynamic system — one of learning by doing, of acquiring knowledge through trial and error (feedback learning) and of engaging in social learning with Elders and traditional harvesters (Berkes 1999: 126).

Adaptive management thereby provides a methodological framework for working across cultures to redesign the global food system through the creation of local and informal institutions that restore traditional harvesting and management strategies to the present day context. In contrast to the western, science-based resource management system, which relies solely on quantitative yield assessment to measure food-system productivity, adaptive management is a more flexible, process-oriented approach. It treats land, environment and health-related policies as experiments from which we can learn how to better manage human behavior in relation to the land and food system.

Many Elders and traditional harvesters offer stories that speak of the historical contributions made by Indigenous peoples to the food security of the first European settlers throughout the period of colonization. *Secwepemc* Elder Irene Billy talks about her experiences throughout the Great Depression in the 1930s:

> We [the *Secwepemc*] were not hungry, because we knew how to grow, gather, hunt and fish to put food on the table and we knew how to work together as a community to make it happen. It was the non-native people from across town who were knocking on our doors asking for food because they were hungry and lacked the knowledge and skills necessary to feed themselves by living on the land. (Personal communication)

The Sir Wilfred Laurier Memorial (George Manuel Institute 2010) outlines the history of the relationship between the *Secwepemc* (original inhabitants of the Shuswap geographic region in the southern interior of B.C.) and the European settlers up to the period of 1910. The memorial describes how the colonial relationship that was once based on values of respect, hospitality and sharing with the newcomers had devolved into one that displaced the *Secwepemc* from our land and food systems and that led to the near extinction and/or extirpation of culturally important animal species from traditional harvesting sites. Despite the increasingly adversarial nature of the colonial relationship between settlers and indigenous communities, many Elders and traditional harvesters maintain that Indigenous and non-Indigenous peoples alike must work together to reinforce positive behaviours that build resiliency in ecosystems and communities (Billy 2006).

Permaculture — Finding the Junction between Sustainable Agriculture and Traditional Harvesting and Management Strategies

Permaculture is an example of an informal institution that is built from alternate social ideals which are fundamental to the process of working cross-culturally to decolonize the land and food system and re-design human settlements towards a more sustainable, ecological model. The concept of permaculture, a set of farming and food production practices that involves the use of perennial crops and patterns to create a regenerative relationship between people and the earth, was co-originated by two Australians, Bill Mollison and David Holmgren, who accredited Indigenous peoples as inspiration for their work on understanding "how to live in place" (Fox 2009). In contrast to the Cartesian worldview and techno-bureaucratic approach that dominates the global food system, permaculture is a system of design that is inspired by an Indigenous eco-philosophy and thereby seeks to mimic relationships found in nature. For this reason, many of the most dedicated Indigenous harvesters, farmers and scholars agree that it promotes a deeper understanding of the ways to design highly productive, sustainable agriculture systems that are connected to the health of the neighbouring Indigenous land and food systems in the broadest sense of the term.

Furthermore, permaculture applies a method that integrates Indigenous "ways of knowing" by attempting to find solutions to contemporary problems through local and traditional ecological knowledge. Permaculture also provides a framework for understanding complex processes through lateral thinking and questioning natural phenomena. In contrast to the cognitive imperialism that exists in the mindset of western science (Battiste 2000), permaculture recognizes spirituality and intuition as valid forms of intelligence. It promotes self-determination and active participation in a process of analytical observation that is not just another formula taught by an outside "expert" (Fox 2009).

According to Rosemary Morrow in *The Earth User's Guide to Permaculture*, "the success of a bioregion lies in the way people work and it will fail unless societies move towards cooperation, not competition, as the prevailing mode of interaction and communication" (1993: 135). Permaculture provides an opportunity for cross-cultural learning, activism and the healing of colonial relationships by building bridges between Indigenous and non-Indigenous cultures and their traditional harvesting and farming techniques. It is a system of design that affirms Indigenous cultural and social values, and promotes healthy associations between all people, plants and animals living in a natural, definable bioregion.

Indigenous Food Sovereignty — Whose Responsibility Is It?

Indigenous food sovereignty provides a framework for exploring and appreciating the optimum conditions and possibilities that exist for reclaiming the social, political and personal health we once experienced prior to colonization. But the framework itself does not resolve where the responsibility for it lies. As Indigenous peoples, we clearly accept our responsibility and the need to balance the amount of time and energy spent reacting to the hundreds of "developments" that are threatening our land and food, with the amount of time and energy spent on activities integral to the preservation of Indigenous food sovereignty. These activities include (1) participating on a day-to-day basis in traditional harvesting strategies that promote and maintain cultural values, ethics and principles; (2) building meaningful and respectful cross-cultural coalitions with friends and allies from non-Indigenous society; and (3) asserting our values, ethics and principles in decision making matters relating to forest and rangeland, fisheries, environment, agriculture, community development and health.

However, the Cartesian worldview, which underlies mainstream society, promotes values of individualism, materialism and mass consumerism that have led to environmental degradation and destructive social phenomena such as neoliberal globalization, privatization, polarization and amenity-based migration to Indigenous territories. Global economic activities and the resulting in-migration to traditional Indigenous territories thereby perpetuates a system that results in the disconnection of humans from their ancestral lands, families and communities, and that continues to erode the tribal social structures that promote an ethic of cooperation, health, balance as well as social and environmental justice. One of the most significant ways in which these destructive social phenomena are playing out in our daily lives is through the global food system in the mainstream culture and economy.

Moving towards cooperative modes of interaction between Indigenous and non-Indigenous communities will require a shared understanding that "everyone is to blame, and everyone is responsible" for reconciling past social and environmental injustices that have impacted Indigenous peoples and the land and food systems. This shift will require evening out power imbalances that exist in the oppressive land regimes imposed by colonial governments by counteracting the tyranny of an imperialistic, rights-based strategy (discussed further immediately below) with a strategy that promotes corporate, social and environmental responsibility and respectful relationships between Indigenous peoples, settler communities and their governments.

Aboriginal Rights and Title Decisions: Implications for Food Sovereignty

The Rights-Based Strategy and its Failure

The "business as usual" actions taken by corporations and governments demonstrate the blatant non-recognition of Aboriginal title and rights. In turn, this situation presents many legal challenges for traditional harvesters, who, in most cases, have no other option than to try to stop harmful developments through direct action. The legalistic and individualistic disposition of the court system's rights-based strategy fails to recognize the sovereignty and jurisdiction of Indigenous peoples. Further, it has not led to best practices or the implementation of court decisions "on the ground" (Kneen 2009).

Traditional harvesters who assert their inherent jurisdiction through direct action often face civil and criminal charges in a court system that is adversarial in nature and has demonstrated a culturally biased tendency to make judgements in favour of corporate interests. For example, between 1998 and 2004, over fifty-four arrests were made of those participating in the *Skwelkwek'welt* Protection Centre established in opposition to the continued development of the Sun Peaks ski resort on traditional *Secwepemc*, *Neskonlith* and Adams Lake territory (McCreary 2005). Especially when considering applications for interim relief, such as injunctions, the test is one of balancing the interests of the corporation on one side and Indigenous peoples on the other. Judges often point to the mainstream economic interests, such as employment opportunities and potential profits from the development, but fail to take into account the interests of Indigenous food economies. From the perspective of the traditional harvesters, the courts fail to balance Indigenous economic values (including traditional food harvesting strategies and practices): instead, they favour the highly destructive industrial economic activities of mainstream society.

There are a few significant Aboriginal Title and Rights decisions recently handed down by the Supreme Courts of Canada and B.C. These cases have had important implications for Indigenous peoples and our ability to protect, conserve and maintain Indigenous land and food systems. At the same time, it is important to recognize that these court cases were extremely burdensome for the nations involved: as well, numerous barriers still exist to ensuring implementation of policy that will support Indigenous food sovereignty in B.C. A detailed analysis and discussion of the relevance of each decision is far beyond the scope of this chapter. We hope that all Canadian citizens will take responsibility to learn more about the underlying issues and outcomes of each case, as well as ways they can advocate for the protection, conservation and restoration of Indigenous land and food systems.

Nuu chah nulth Fisheries (2009)

After more than a decade of legal preparations and proceedings that challenged Department of Fisheries and Oceans (DFO) restrictions on aboriginal commercial fisheries, the Supreme Court of British Columbia ruled on November 3, 2009 that the *Nuu-chah-nulth* nation has the right to commercially harvest and sell all species of fish within its traditional territorial waters. This decision had important implications for Indigenous food sovereignty in the region, particularly in terms of self-determination, in that it affirmed the nation's right to implement fishing and harvesting strategies according to its own unique cultural, economic and ecological considerations. Cliff Atleo Sr., president of the recent Tribal Council, noted, "We have been stewards of our ocean resources for hundreds of generations. And the government of Canada was wrong to push us aside in their attempts to prohibit our access to the sea resources our people depend upon" (cited in Dolha 2009).

Xeni Gwet'in Ts'ilqotin Rights and Title (2007)

On November 30, 2007, based on findings that the provincial government's land use planning and forestry activities have "unjustifiably infringed" upon their Aboriginal title and rights (Porter et al. 2008), the Supreme Court of British Columbia ruled that *Tsilhqot'in* Aboriginal title "does exist" within approximately half of its claim area, and that the *Tsilhqot'in* people have inherent rights throughout their entire claim area. These entitlements include the right to trade in skins and pelts as a means of securing a moderate livelihood as well as the right to hunt and trap birds and animals for various purposes. This ruling removed some significant barriers to Indigenous food sovereignty by allowing the *Tsilhqot'in* to engage in traditional and adapted harvesting strategies throughout their territory and to respond to their own needs for healthy, culturally-adapted Indigenous foods. Further, following this victory, First Nations leaders from across B.C. issued the *All Our Relations Declaration*, which affirmed that negotiations with the Crown shall only proceed "on the basis of a full and complete recognition of the existence of our title and rights throughout our entire lands, waters, territories and resources" (Porter et al. 2008). Thus, the *Tsilhqot'in* ruling had, and will continue to have, important implications for the assertion of Indigenous food sovereignty across B.C.

The Haida Logging Case (2004)
On November 18, 2004, the Supreme Court of Canada ruled in favour of the *Haida* Nation's claim against B.C. and Weyerhaeuser, an American logging giant that was being permitted to extract a large portion of natural resources on *Haida Gwaii* (the homeland of the *Haida* Nation), including large tracts of old growth cedar. Logging by the company was not only exceeding sustainable rates for old growth cedar, but was also significantly harming the streams that support salmon and other fish. As a result of this landmark case, Weyerhaeuser was forced to abandon its operations on *Haida Gwaii*, giving the Haida Nation more power to implement sustainable systems of forest and stream management and to ensure the continuation of traditional harvesting practices that are important to sustaining Haida culture, livelihoods and ecosystems (*Haida* Nation 2010).

Delgamuukw Ruling (1997)
In the longest-running First Nations land claim court case in Canadian history, on December 11, 1997, the Supreme Court of Canada ruled in favour of the *Delgamuukw* land title and rights claim, recognizing that "the exclusive right to use the land is not restricted to the right to engage in activities which are aspects of aboriginal practices, customs and traditions integral to the claimant group's distinctive Aboriginal culture" (Chief Justice Antonio Lamer, cited in *Gitxsan* Nation 2010). This decision signifies that when First Nations groups exert their land rights under Aboriginal title, these rights are not restricted to traditional Aboriginal practices (such as berry picking and traditional hunting) but they can also include "modern" strategies. "This means that Aboriginal title is not 'frozen in time,' applying only to those rights practiced at the time of contact" (*Gitxsan* Nation 2010). In the context of Indigenous food sovereignty, this case removes some barriers to the implementation of adaptive management strategies by allowing the *Delgamuukw* to restore traditional harvesting strategies in a present-day context and to

manage land, environment, food and health-related policies in a more holistic manner. The *Delgamuukw* case was also instrumental in instituting the legal recognition of oral histories as valid evidence in the assertion of Aboriginal land titles and rights.

The Sparrow Case (1990)

On May 31, 1990, the *Musqueam* nation succeeded in appealing to the Supreme Court of Canada a previous decision that had charged Ronald Edward Sparrow, a member of the *Musqueam* nation, of fishing with instruments longer than permitted by the band's fishing license under the *Fisheries Act*. While Sparrow admitted to the charge, he justified his practices in the Supreme Court appeal on the grounds that he was exercising his Aboriginal right to fish under section 35(1) of the Constitution Act, 1982. Through the appeal process, the Court found that, based on historical records of the nation's fishing practices, the *Musqueam* nation had a clear right to fish for food. The ruling of the Supreme Court of Canada thus represented a groundbreaking decision regarding the application of Indigenous rights (particularly under section 35(1) of the *Constitution Act*, 1982) given that it affirmed that Aboriginal rights, such as fishing, (that had been in existence prior to 1982) are protected under the Constitution of Canada and cannot be infringed without justification. This case was also significant in changing the provincial government's policy of refusing to participate in treaty negotiations for the settlement of Aboriginal rights and title in B.C. (*Musqueam* Band 2010).

Policy Interventions

Building cross-cultural coalitions and social networks offers a platform for strengthening collaborative capacities for researching and influencing policy as well as informing widespread, systemic change. Participation in the South Africa Learning Exchange in November of 2009 (hosted by the Masifundise Development Trust and sponsored by the Canadian International Development Agency) provided an opportunity to link the B.C. Food Systems' Network Working Group on Indigenous Food Sovereignty with the Coastal Learning Communities' Network in Canada and the Coastal Links Network in South Africa. The learning exchange shed light on the many similarities of the socio-political challenges faced by Indigenous peoples in both Canada and South Africa, as well as presenting some interventions or ways in which Indigenous peoples are striving to enter into policy discussions that will promote food sovereignty.

As a result of the learning exchange, the following framework for action was adapted by the WGIFS from the key entry points and interventions developed by Masifundise Development Trust (2009) to guide policy and management in small-scale fisheries in South Africa:

- Legislation and policy
- Participation
- Knowledge of natural resources and human dimensions in the land and food system
- Integrated assessment
- Governance and co-management approaches
- Cross-sectoral coordination
- Making markets work for sustenance harvesters
- Developing human capacity
- Information and communication

Widespread systemic change that will serve to protect, conserve and restore the remaining fragments of Indigenous land and food system in B.C. and Canada will require adequate funding for network development and community mobilization.

Further, the enacting and implementation of Aboriginal Title and Rights legislation and policies, encoded in recent court decisions, will require comprehensive land reform and redistribution. Such reform will need to involve setting aside adequate tracts of land reserves for the exclusive purpose of hunting, fishing and gathering Indigenous foods. Furthermore, governments must take the responsibility to regulate neoliberal trade and promote corporate social and environmental responsibility, as well as the integration of Indigenous food and cultural values in land and resource management.

Sovereignty from the Ground Up

There is a wealth of knowledge, values and wisdom to share: we hope to engage in activities and policy creation that is not "about" Indigenous peoples' food systems but learns from and is informed by the experiences and expertise gained through many millennia of practice (*First Principles Protocol for Building Cross Cultural Relationships* 2009). At a grassroots level, the Indigenous food sovereignty approach seeks to reconcile Indigenous environmental ethics and cultural protocols with the re-establishment of community-based economies. Indigenous food sovereignty provides a framework for a specific policy approach to addressing the underlying issues impacting long-term food security in Indigenous communities: it serves to support Indigenous peoples and our efforts to uphold our sacred responsibilities to nurture relationships with our land, culture, spirituality and future generations. Through discussion, analysis and community mobilization, Indigenous food sovereignty seeks to inform and influence colonial "policy driven by practice" and promotes reconciliation of past social and environmental injustices.

From 2007 to 2008 the WGIFS met with more than four hundred people in more than sixteen communities across B.C. to explore and identify ways the WGIFS could support individuals and groups working on increasing food security in Indigenous communities. At the National Food Secure Canada meeting held in Ottawa in November of 2008, a Canada-Wide Working Group on Indigenous Food Sovereignty was designated as a priority. Much of the Indigenous food-related action, research and policy reform was spawned within this rapidly expanding Indigenous sovereignty movement that was formed within the colonial boundaries set out by the province of B.C. With respect for the boundaries of traditional territories defined by Indigenous peoples long before the provinces and Dominion of Canada was established, the Indigenous Food Systems Network reaches far beyond to link individuals, organizations, families and nations working across Canada and the U.S.

The strength of this movement lies in the relationships built within these extended networks: partnerships between the B.C. Food Systems Network, the Working Group for Indigenous Food Sovereignty, the Coastal Learning Communities Network (CLCN), Food Secure Canada (FSC), the Peoples Food Policy Project (PFPP), Coastal Links Network (South Africa) and several universities have emerged. We believe that these extended networks of Indigenous peoples and allies working to promote and protect Indigenous foods systems across the country will be able to influence a vast and diverse audience to recognize the complexity of colonial history and the destructive impacts of the global food system. As the original inhabitants of the land, we offer guidance in changing human behaviour and ending destructive relationships to Mother Earth and the land and food systems that sustain all human beings.

References

Battiste, Marie. 2000. *Reclaiming Indigenous Voice and Vision.* Vancouver, BC: UBC Press.

Berkes, Fikret. 1999. *Sacred Ecology: Traditional Ecological Knowledge and Resource Management.* Philadelphia, PA: Taylor and Francis.

Billy, J.R. 2006. "Cultural Survival and Environmental Degradation in the Mountains of the Secwepemc." In L.A.G. Moss (ed.), *The Amenity Migrants: Seeking and Sustaining Mountains and their Cultures.* Cambridge, MA: CABI Publishing.

Dolha, L. 2009. "Nuu-Chah-Nulth Celebrate Landmark Fisheries Decision." *First Nations Drum* 19, 11 (November). At <firstnationsdrum.com/2009/11/nuu-chah-nulth-celebrate-landmark-fisheries-decision/>.

First Principles Protocol for Building Cross Cultural Relationships. 2009. "People's Food Policy Project." At <peoplesfoodpolicy.ca/protocol>.

Fox, J.B. 2009. "Indigenous Science." *Cultural Survival Quarterly* 33, 1. At <culturalsurvival.org/publications/cultural-survival-quarterly/australia/indigenous-science>.

George Manuel Institute. 2010. "Memorial to Sir Wilfred Laurier, Premier of the

Dominion of Canada." At <andoftheshuswap.com/msite/laurier.php>.

Gitxsan Nation. 2010. "Gitxsan Chiefs: Delgamuukw, Aboriginal Rights and Title." At <gitxsan.com/html/delga.htm>.

Haida Nation. 2010. "Legal Cases." At <haidanation.ca/Pages/Legal/Legal.html>.

Kneen, Brewster. 2009. "The Tyranny of Rights." *The Ramshorn* (September). At <ramshorn.ca/node/180>.

Masifundise Development Trust. 2009. *A Draft Handbook Towards Sustainable Small-Scale Fisheries in South Africa: Promoting Poverty Alleviation, Food Security and Gender Equity in Small-Scale Fisheries.* Cape Town, South Africa: Masifundise Development Trust.

Mate, Gabor. 2004. *When the Body Says No: The Cost of Hidden Stress.* Toronto, Ontario: Vintage Canada.

McCreary, Tyler. 2005. "No Indians Allowed on Aboriginal Territory at Sun Peaks." *Canadian Dimension.* At <canadiandimension.com/articles/1940/>.

Morrison, Dawn. 2008. "BC Food Systems Network Working Group on Indigenous Food Sovereignty Final Activity Report. Unpublished report." At <indigenous-foodsystems.org/resources/all-resources>.

___. 2006. "First Annual Interior of BC Indigenous Food Sovereignty Conference Report. Unpublished Report." B.C. Food Systems Network. Available at <food-democracy.org/links.php>.

Morrow, R. 1993. *Earth User's Guide to Permaculture.* Kenthurst, Australia: Kangaroo Press.

Musqueam Band. 2010. "Legal Cases." At <musqueam.bc.ca/Cases.html>.

Porter, D., Chief J. Sayers and Chief E. John. 2008. "New Day for BC Native Claims: 'Xeni Decision' Casts Doubt on Provincial Authority over First Nations Land Dealings." *The Tyee.* February 12. At <thetyee.ca/Views/2008/02/12/NativeClaims>.

Reading, C., and F. Wien. 2009. *Health Inequalities and Social Determinants of Aboriginal Peoples' Health.* National Collaborating Centre of Aboriginal Health.

Rosenau, Marvin L., and Mark Angelo. 2009. *Landscape-Level Impacts to Salmon and Steel head Stream Habitats in British Columbia.* Vancouver, BC: Pacific Fisheries Resource Conservation Council.

Toledo, Victor. 2001. "Indigenous People and Biodiversity." In S.A. Levin (ed.), *Encyclopedia of Biodiversity.* San Diego, CA: Academic Press.

United Nations. 2000. "The Concept of Indigenous Peoples. Background Paper Prepared by the Secretariat of the Permanent Forum on Indigenous Issues." Department of Economic and Social Affairs; Division of Social Policy and Development.

7. THE LIMITS OF FARMER-CONTROL

Food Sovereignty and Conflicts over the Canadian Wheat Board

André Magnan

Founded in 1935, the Canadian Wheat Board (CWB) is a government-sponsored, farmer-controlled, collective marketing agency for Western Canadian wheat and barley. The CWB's jurisdiction covers the prairie provinces of Alberta, Saskatchewan and Manitoba, as well as the northeastern, grain-growing region of British Columbia. The CWB markets all wheat and barley produced in these areas, with the exception of wheat and barley used domestically as animal feed. The CWB thus serves as the single-desk (i.e., monopoly) seller of prairie wheat and barley, returning all proceeds of its sales, minus administrative costs, back to farmers. In turn, all prairie farmers must market these grains through the CWB single-desk. Based on the principles of grain pooling first articulated by agrarian movements in the early twentieth century, the Canadian government implemented collective marketing in response to the collapse of the private grain trade during the Great Depression. For several decades afterwards, the CWB served as a consensus instrument of Canada's agricultural policy, providing farmers with greater stability and market power in highly unequal world markets. Because it intersects with issues of market power and self-determination for prairie farmers, the survival of the CWB is a vital matter of food sovereignty in Canada.

In the early decades of the twentieth century, state actors and farmers struggled over the grain marketing question, as farmers demanded collective marketing through a wheat board, and governments resisted. Through collective marketing, farmers sought protection from the vagaries of unpredictable markets and the powerful private interests that organized the grain trade. The grain marketing question was eventually resolved when, under conditions of market collapse during the Depression, farmers and state actors coalesced around monopoly state-marketing, which was implemented under the CWB in 1943. In the postwar era, the CWB became a key mechanism for linking a relatively prosperous prairie farm economy to expanding world markets.

By the 1970s, however, as neoliberal restructuring redefined the role of governments in agriculture and farmers became increasingly split along lines of farm size, ideology and commodity, the consensus around collective marketing came undone. These changes led to the politicization of the CWB, with a particularly intense period of conflict occurring in the 1990s. In response to these conflicts, the CWB adopted a new governance model that established formal farmer-control over the organization and a mechanism by which farmers could democratically decide its fate. These governance changes, implemented in 1998, resulted in organizational renewal and greater accountability. This model seemed to offer a solution to the controversy over the CWB: farmers would ultimately decide whether or not to maintain the single-desk system.

The most recent round of conflict over the CWB has severely tested the principle of farmer-control. In 2006, the newly elected Conservative government began a concerted effort to end the CWB's grain marketing monopoly. In doing so, it has consistently challenged the CWB's autonomy from government and undermined farmer-control in principle and practice. This struggle over collective marketing and farmer-control has had significant implications for food sovereignty In terms of food sovereignty ideals, the farmer-controlled CWB is subject to both external and internal contradictions. The former relate to the tension between the CWB's dependence on a government statute for its monopoly powers and the organization's bid for independence. The latter relate to the CWB's exercise of farmer-control, which, in the political vacuum created by the decline of the prairie cooperative movement, has framed farmer cooperation in terms of economic goals. In my analysis of the impact of this struggle on principles of food sovereignty, I draw upon field interviews conducted with key CWB officials between January and June 2007.

Conflicts Over the CWB: Food Sovereignty, Collective Marketing and Farmer-Control

Food sovereignty embodies the principle of self-determination in its defence of the "right of peoples to define their agricultural and food policy" (La Vía Campesina, cited in Desmarais 2007: 34). Aside from affirming the cultural and political self-determination of diverse food-producing groups, food sovereignty also refers to the rights of governments, via genuinely democratic channels, to implement agricultural and food policies that benefit domestic food producers and consumers. Food sovereignty thus upholds the legitimacy of government regulation of markets, including supply-management and state-marketing bodies, which are seen as vehicles of self-determination and social protection for food producers (Desmarais 2007: 36). Contrary to the ideals of the corporate food regime (McMichael 2005), food sovereignty thus relegitimizes state regulation of agriculture.

Current conflicts over the CWB intersect with the question of food sovereignty in two ways. First, the conflict revolves around the role of the

CWB in collective marketing, anchored on the three pillars of its operation: the single-desk, grain pooling and government guarantees. The CWB's single-desk structure is enshrined by law in the *Canadian Wheat Board Act*, and is the basis for the agency's monopoly over wheat and barley sales. Under the second pillar, pooling, grain of the same end-use and quality (e.g., high-quality milling wheat) is pooled and sold by the CWB in a coordinated way over the crop year, helping to minimize market risks for individual farmers. All farmers delivering a given class and quality of grain receive the same payment, based on prices received for the pooled grain over the entire crop year. Under the third pillar, the federal government provides a set of financial guarantees to the CWB, allowing it to access credit at government rates and protecting farmers in the event of a catastrophic drop in prices. If the CWB faces a deficit in one of the pool accounts because of severe price depression, the government absorbs the difference. Pool account deficits for wheat have only occurred four times in the CWB's history: in 1968–69, 1985–86, 1990–91, and 2002–03 (Furtan 2005: 98).

Each pillar provides farmers with a distinct advantage in the highly uneven world grain trade: the single-desk providing market-power; grain pooling, affordable risk management and equity; and government guarantees, a basic public safety net. The single-desk also eliminates competition among farmers, allowing them to achieve greater economic clout in the global grain trade, 80 percent of which is controlled by just five giant transnational corporations (Measner 2007). Because the CWB is the sole seller of Canadian wheat and barley, it can extract price premiums for its product, especially from markets for high-quality wheat (Kraft et al. 1996; Furtan et al. 1999). The estimated net benefit of CWB price premiums to the prairie farm economy is $300 million per year (Pugh and McLaughlin 2007: 113).[2] The CWB is also an integral part of the unique set of prairie institutions (along with the Canadian Grain Commission or CGC) regulating grain quality and securing Canada's global reputation as a supplier of high-quality grain (Sinclair and Grieshaber-Otto 2009).

The debate over the CWB intersects with food sovereignty by pitting collective marketing against neoliberal ideals of market efficiency, free enterprise and free trade. In Canada, the most strident opposition to the CWB's monopoly powers has come from commodity organizations such as the Western Canadian Wheat Growers' Association (WCWGA), the government of Alberta and right-wing federal political parties (the Conservative Party and its predecessor, the Reform Party) (Skogstad 2005: 539). These groups view the CWB's monopoly mandate as an illegitimate infringement on the right of farmers to market their grain independently. Whereas these opponents once argued for the total elimination of the CWB, today the focus is on achieving "dual marketing." Under this scenario, the CWB would lose its monopoly powers and compete against other grain handling companies (i.e., transnational firms) for farmer deliveries. Whether or not the CWB could survive under a system of dual marketing is hotly debated: this issue has become a focal point of controversy in recent conflicts over the future of the CWB (see below).

Pressure to eliminate the CWB's single-desk has also come from foreign commodity groups, transnational grain companies and their state sponsors (especially the U.S.). Beginning in the late 1980s, North American free-trade policies made the U.S. market more attractive to the CWB, prompting increased Canadian exports that have angered American commodity organizations. At the behest of these organizations, the U.S. federal government has pursued unsuccessfully a continuous series of trade challenges against the CWB (fourteen to date) (CWB 2008b). In 2003, it imposed a steep tariff on Canadian wheat, which effectively shut out Canadian exports until 2006, when a North American Free Trade Agreement (NAFTA) dispute resolution panel ruled in Canada's favour (CWB 2008a). The U.S. has also sought to weaken or eliminate the CWB in World Trade Organization (WTO) negotiations (CWB 2008c). Although state-trading enterprises (STEs) are currently allowed under WTO rules as long as they can be shown to operate without distorting trade (Schmitz and Furtan 2000), the most recent negotiating text for a new WTO agreement contains language that would prohibit them altogether (CWB 2008c). Although Canada has not agreed to this text, if it were adopted, the CWB would cease to exist as a single-desk agency.

The second way in which recent conflicts over the CWB intersect with the question of food sovereignty is over the principle of farmer-control. Since 1998, the CWB has been governed by a board of directors composed of ten elected farmer representatives and five government appointees. According to the then Minister Responsible for the CWB, Ralph Goodale, this structure was designed to improve the CWB's accountability and transcend divisive battles over the agency's marketing mandate. Overall, the new governance structure has improved the CWB's legitimacy among farmers, as the CWB and its allies have succeeded in turning farmer-control into a powerful argument in its favour. The new structure has not, however, prevented the anti-CWB coalition — given new life by the election of a minority Conservative government in 2006 — from undermining farmer-control in principle and in practice. While conflicts over farmer-control suggest a real threat to the self-determination of prairie farmers, they also reveal contradictions in the model of farmer empowerment embodied in the CWB's governance structure.

The Struggle for Collective Marketing

Current conflicts over collective marketing must be understood in light of changing state-farmer relations over time. The history of the CWB highlights the search among farmers, governments and the grain trade with sometimes overlapping, sometimes contradictory interests for solutions to the problems of grain marketing in the prairie west. The various solutions proposed have involved a tension between the ideals of economic power and democracy, each combining them in imperfect ways. The solution eventually adopted — the modern CWB — implemented monopoly marketing (economic power) without any formal mechanism of farmer representation (democracy). Yet, the tension between economic compulsion (the monopoly powers of the single-desk) and the lack of direct farmer-control did not pose a problem of legitimacy for the CWB. On the one hand, this was because prairie farmers — from the 1920s onward — supported collective marketing nearly unanimously. On the other hand, the issue of governance lay dormant for decades because of the symbiotic relationship between the CWB and the prairie cooperative movement, led by farmer-owned grain-handling companies, known as the prairie Pools. In total, there were four original grain-handling cooperatives, the Saskatchewan Wheat Pool, the United Grain Growers (UGG), Manitoba Pool Elevators (MPE) and the Alberta Wheat Pool (AWP). While the CWB engaged in collective marketing, the Pools provided farmer-ownership of grain handling infrastructure and served as the vehicle through which farmers pursued cooperative principles of social development and democracy.

The Origins of Collective Marketing

Early farmers' movements embodied the principles of food sovereignty in their struggle for market power and self-determination in the prairie grain trade. In the early twentieth century, these movements came to see "orderly marketing," the principle of coordinated collective marketing, as a key component of their struggle (Irwin 2001). Prairie farmers faced a number of problems in the early grain trade, including local monopolies in grain handling, poorly coordinated transportation and sometimes fraudulent grain handling practices (Wilson 1978: 25–46). Each of these derived in some way from the structural inequalities of the wheat economy, with farmers up against the near-monopoly powers of the private interests that organized the trade (banks, railways and grain handlers). In grain marketing, farmers were at the mercy of seasonal price variations and the power of the grain trade (Irwin 2001: 90-91). Although the federal government was prepared to regulate the grain trade, as it did through the *Canada Grain Act* of 1912 (Wilson 1978: 42–45), it left grain marketing in private hands.

The basic principles of grain pooling, which became the foundation of the wheat pools and eventually the CWB, were expressed by the prairie farm movement in 1908 (Irwin 2001: 93). The idea was elegant in its simplicity. Farmers would "pool" their grain together, sell it collectively, and return the sales proceeds to individual farmers on the basis of the volume and quality of the grain each delivered. Pooling appealed to farmers as a means of evening out the highs and lows of the market and matching supply to demand, thereby achieving orderly marketing (Irwin 2001: 92). From the beginning, pooling proponents debated the question of democracy as it related both to governance and to the merits of voluntary versus compulsory pooling. The principles of orderly marketing were given their first practical expression when the federal government experimented with monopoly control in the immediate aftermath of World War I (Morriss 1987: 14). The first CWB (1919–1920) combined centralized marketing and grain pooling under government control and proved the success of orderly marketing in stabilizing farmer income. The operation was overseen by a government appointed "board" composed of leading figures of the prairie wheat industry, but without formal democratic representation for farmers. The government understood the first CWB to be only a temporary measure, and was eager to reinstate the open market, which it did in 1920 (Wilson 1978: 170). When prices fell steeply in the aftermath, farmers demanded the reinstatement of the compulsory board (Irwin 2001: 94).

Pressure from the farmers' movement led, in 1922, to federal legislation that would have reinstated the wheat board on a temporary basis. When the plan failed, farmers' organizations abandoned the goal of reviving the wheat board and turned instead towards establishing their own voluntary, cooperative wheat marketing institutions (Wilson 1978: 181). Organizers mounted a massive recruitment drive encouraging farmers to sign contracts with farmer-owned "wheat pools," which would market the grain collectively and distribute returns via the pooling principle (Fairbairn 1984: 26–35). The prairie Pools quickly attracted a significant share of farmers' grain deliveries. By the mid-1920s, prairie Pools in each of Alberta, Saskatchewan and Manitoba marketed, on average, over 50 percent of the prairie wheat crop (Wilson 1978: 219– 25). The practices of price-pooling and collective marketing, pioneered by the first CWB, were thus translated, in the 1920s, into new forms of economic cooperation organized by the agrarian movement.

The significance of the Pools went beyond strictly economic cooperation, however, as they came to play a major role in the social empowerment of prairie farmers. The Pools operated on principles of democratic accountability to farmer-members, with an extensive structure for electing farmer delegates to Pool meetings and for electing Pool directors from among the delegates (Fairbairn 1984: 40–41). They also established elected advisory committees to oversee local grain deliveries at country elevators. Pool delegates, directors and advisory committee members served as a valuable network of local organizers and promoters of cooperative grain marketing (Fairbairn 1984: 45–46). Likewise, the Pools organized outreach, extension and education initiatives aimed at spreading cooperative principles. The Saskatchewan

Wheat Pool (SWP), for instance, employed fieldmen in each of the province's pooling districts: they were responsible for organizing local meetings, meeting with individual farmers and selling subscriptions to *The Western Producer*, the Pool-owned agricultural newspaper (Fairbairn 1984: 70). The Pools lent human and organizational resources towards the development of other co-operatives on the prairies (e.g., credit unions) and lobbied governments on behalf of farmers. In the 1920s and 1930s, the Pools contributed to prairie culture through travelling movie nights, a mailing library and weekly radio broadcasts (Fairbairn 1984: 119–21, 131–32).

In this way, the Pools embodied the ideals both of economic and social empowerment. However, without the statutory monopoly powers and government financial guarantees of the CWB, the collapse of grain prices in 1929 pushed the Pools — dependent on private loans to finance advance wheat purchases — to near insolvency. With the threat of huge financial losses (large enough to destabilize the whole Canadian economy), banks demanded that the federal government guarantee loans advanced to the Pools for the 1930 crop year (Morriss 1987: 32). In 1931, the government assumed control of the Pools' common sales arm, the Central Selling Agency, and its wheat stocks, in a stabilization operation lasting until 1935. This marked the end of the Pools' role in grain marketing. From this point onward, they would exist only as cooperative grain handling businesses. Between 1935 and 1943, the government experimented with voluntary pooling, where farmers chose to deliver to either the reinstated CWB or to the private trade. Under this system, the CWB only received a large share of wheat deliveries when open market prices dropped below the CWB's floor price, with losses incurred by the state treasury (Irwin 2001: 97). Unsatisfied by the inability of the voluntary CWB to provide a sufficient degree of orderly marketing, farmers' movements continued to press for monopoly control. Only under war-time conditions did the government finally intervene to reinstate the CWB's marketing monopoly. The pressure from war-time shortages caused wheat prices on the open market to rise, with the result that in 1943 the CWB received virtually no deliveries, threatening Canada's ability to continue provisioning the U.K. In response, the government suspended private wheat trading and made deliveries to the CWB compulsory (Wilson 1978: 782; Irwin 2001).

Collective Marketing in the Post-War Period

The single-desk CWB became the centrepiece of Canada's agricultural policy in the post-war era, playing two key roles. First, the CWB negotiated and administered large multi-year grain deals (Morriss 1987: 170). In the 1950s and 1960s, the CWB was very successful at establishing new markets and negotiating major wheat agreements with state-importers, especially China and the U.S.S.R. Second, the CWB assumed a key role in maintaining Western farm income. It did so not through the mechanism of floor prices (pool deficits were rare), but rather through the exercise of market power. In this period, Canada dominated the high-quality segment of the wheat trade, allowing it to withhold stocks from the market in order to support world prices. In the absence of any other comprehensive government income support, the CWB's ability to support world prices served to guarantee a minimum Western farm income (Oleson 1979: 94).

During this period, the CWB enjoyed widespread farmer support, prompting the expansion of its marketing authority to oats and barley in the 1950s (Morriss 1987: 199–200). Given the high level of support by farmers and the state, the question of CWB governance was moot. Charged with a single, unambiguous mandate — marketing prairie grain to the best advantage of farmers — the CWB's appointed government commissioners were largely considered to be working in the interests of the prairie wheat economy. Meanwhile, the prairie Pools remained a key vehicle of farmer-controlled economic cooperation and social development. Having ceded their role in grain marketing to the CWB, the Pools operated an extensive network of grain elevators serving farmer-members, to which they added other agri-business ventures after World War II (Fairbairn 1984: 165–96). The Pools lobbied governments on behalf of prairie farmers and vigorously supported the CWB, whose role they considered complementary to their own.

1970s: The Decline of State-Marketing

The prairie wheat economy entered the 1970s facing a number of serious challenges. The end of international cooperation on wheat prices — largely the result of U.S. attempts to increase its market share (Morriss 1987: 254) — and the E.U.'s transition from the world's largest importer to a net exporter made for a much more competitive international environment. Canada's dominance in markets for high-quality milling wheat ended when the U.K., seeking to decrease its dependence on imports, introduced new baking technology, which allowed for the substitution of Canadian wheat with British varieties (Oleson 1979). Under these conditions, the CWB could no longer count on its market power to support prices. Meanwhile, wheat began to lose its pre-eminent place in prairie agriculture, as Canadian farmers expanded livestock production and shifted towards other crops, especially those marketed outside of the authority of the CWB (See Figure 7-1). In 1974, the question of canola marketing was put to a farmer plebiscite in which farmers voted overwhelmingly to continue to market canola outside of the CWB's monopoly (Morriss 2000: 124). The shift away from wheat made the CWB progressively less central as an instrument of domestic agricultural policy.

The 1970s also ushered in an era of increasing price volatility for farmers as structural changes in world grain markets sowed the seeds of a decades-long farm crisis (see Friedmann 1993). World prices soared when, in 1972, the U.S.S.R. entered the world market with a massive demand for grain. Governments encouraged farmers to expand production, but the boom ended in the late 1970s, and surpluses returned. The subsequent price collapse, combined with higher interest rates beginning in the 1980s, spelled financial crisis for many farmers who had borrowed to expand production. Caught between increasingly powerful agri-business corporations on both the input and output sides of agriculture, farmers increasingly faced the "cost-price squeeze" of depressed prices and increasing input costs (Mitchell 1975: 18–21): this precipitated a prolonged income crisis (see Chapter 2).

These financial pressures coincided with growing social, economic and ideological cleavages among farmers. Although government marketing boards such as the CWB provided farmers with market power and greater income stability, they did not fundamentally change the long-term trends whereby larger, more efficient farm operations squeezed out smaller ones in a process referred to as "rationalization" (Troughton 1989: 373). Farm land became consolidated into fewer hands, as farm sizes increased from an average of 432 acres to 845 acres between 1941 and 1971, and farm numbers declined from nearly 139,000 to 77,000 over the same period (Figure 7-2). This process of

Figure 7-1 Seeded Area, Wheat and Canola, Prairie Provinces, 1945–1970

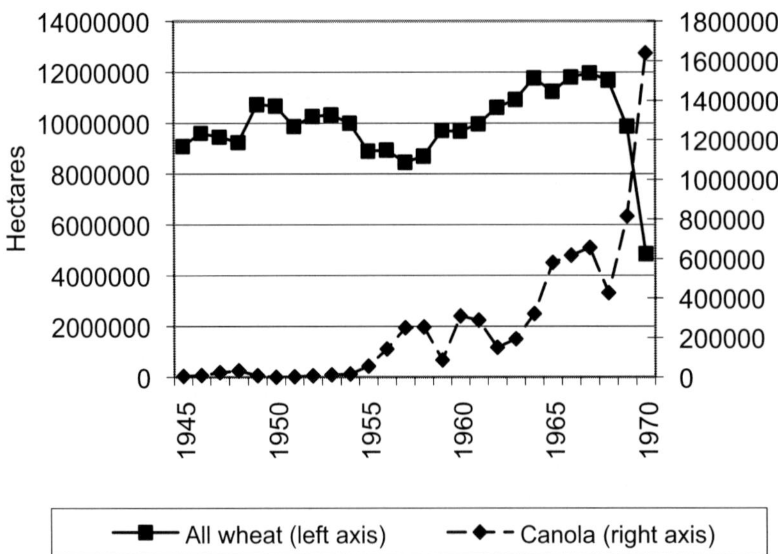

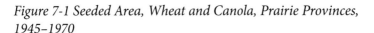

Source: Statistics Canada, Table 001-0010: Estimated areas, yield, production and average farm price of principal field crops, in metric units, annual (Statistics Canada 2011a).

differentiation between large and small farms eroded the political effectiveness and solidarity of family farms as a class (Winson 1992: 92). In turn, declining farm numbers undermined the democratic vibrancy of the Pools, as it became increasingly difficult to fill delegate positions among the membership (Fairbairn 1984: 205). Growing ideological differences among prairie farmers also undermined the Pools' political leadership, as some farmers abandoned cooperation for free-market principles (Fairbairn 1984: 197–98).

Just as farmers faced price volatility, increased international competition and farm rationalization, governments began to re-imagine their role in agriculture. The landmark Task Force on Agriculture (TFA) of 1970 reframed the problems of agriculture as questions of efficiency and competitiveness (Department of Agriculture 1970). Governments embraced this brand of neoliberalism with cuts to farm programs, and, eventually, the deregulation of key aspects of the prairie grains sector (Knuttila 2003). All of these factors placed increasing strain on the postwar consensus linking the state and a relatively united farm lobby in a set of institutions, of which the CWB was the centrepiece, regulating prairie agriculture.

The first organized opposition to the CWB emerged during this tumultuous period. In 1970, a group of prairie farmers founded the Palliser Wheat Growers Association (PWGA), a commodity organization devoted to transportation reform and the abolition of the CWB (Fairbairn 1984: 214-5). Later

Figure 7-2 Farm Size and Total Number of Farms, Saskatchewan, 1941–1971

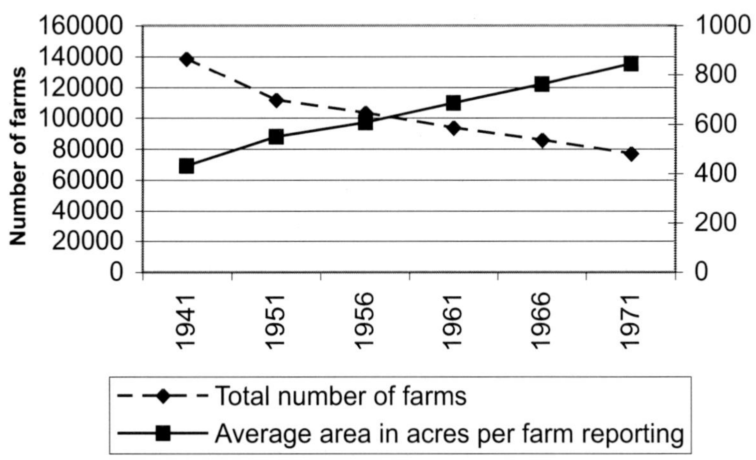

Source: Statistics Canada, Census of Agriculture, Historical Data. Table 1.1: Selected agricultural data, number and area of farms, land in crops and selected crop data, Canada and provinces, census years 1921 to 2006 (Statistics Canada 2011b).

to become the Western Canadian Wheat Growers Association (WCWGA), the organization found support among business-oriented farmers who embraced neoliberal ideals of market efficiency and distrust of government intervention. Despite these early manifestations of farmer discontent, the real test for the CWB would not emerge until the severe crisis of legitimacy of the 1990s.

The 1990s: Crisis of Legitimacy and Organizational Change

In the 1990s, latent conflicts over the CWB turned into overt confrontation, as deepening divisions among farmers, augmented by agricultural restructuring at the global scale, eroded the legitimacy of the single-desk. For example, new conflicts arose when Canada's transportation subsidy on exported grains (the Crow Rate) was eliminated to comply with the North American Free Trade Agreement (NAFTA): this created an incentive for prairie farmers to sell into markets closer to home (Schmitz and Furtan 2000: 117). Meanwhile, the U.S.'s use of export subsidies artificially inflated domestic U.S. prices in relation to the world market price (Schmitz and Furtan 2000: 73). This made the U.S. market more attractive to western Canadian farmers, leading some farmers to lobby strenuously for the right to deliver grain directly to U.S. elevators, where, depending on market conditions, spot prices were sometimes higher. In 1993, the Conservative federal government of the day attempted to end the CWB's monopoly on barley exports by executive order, but was thwarted by a legal challenge sponsored by the prairie Pools (Skogstad 2005: 538). When the Liberals won the 1993 federal election, they inherited the divisive question of the CWB's future. In the mid-1990s, the most strident CWB opponents engaged in illegal border running operations in protest of CWB control over grain export licenses (Skogstad 2005: 539). Calling themselves the Farmers for Justice, this group consisted of a small number of highly committed anti-CWB activists. In a form of civil disobedience, the group coordinated several convoys of prairie trucks that crossed into the U.S. to make grain deliveries directly to local elevators. Dozens of farmers involved in these deliveries were arrested for violating the law governing the CWB's monopoly powers: thirteen were subsequently jailed after refusing to pay court-imposed fines related to their conviction (Walton and Brethour 2002).

In order to address the impasse, the Liberal Minister responsible for the Canadian Wheat Board, Ralph Goodale, devised a two-pronged strategy. First, he called a plebiscite on the question of the single-desk for barley. Goodale insisted on a clear-cut question based on two options: retain the CWB's monopoly on barley, or remove the CWB's monopoly. The question as to whether a third alternative — "dual marketing" — could be viable was the subject of controversy between pro- and anti-CWB activists. Prairie grain farmers voted by a two-thirds majority to retain the CWB's monopoly powers. Second, he introduced sweeping reforms to CWB governance and operations by rewriting the agency's governing legislation, the *CWB Act*. During this period, the Pools still served as key allies of the CWB, and played an important role in sponsoring the legislative changes establishing farmer-control.

The new *CWB Act*, passed into law in 1998, established the CWB's current governance model, with a board of directors comprised of ten elected farmers and five government appointees. It also formalized the process for changing the CWB's marketing mandate, requiring that any change to the CWB's powers be decided by a farmer plebiscite, conducted in consultation with the CWB and subsequently ratified by a vote in the House of Commons.

Just as the CWB became, for the first time, directly accountable to elected farmer-directors, the Pools entered a period of terminal decline brought on by declining membership and financial pressures. For the Saskatchewan Wheat Pool (SWP), the impending retirement of a large portion of its members, whose accumulated equity they were obligated to pay out, combined with ambitious expansion plans posed a capital shortage problem (Painter 2004: 73). The SWP's solution was to raise money by offering, for the first time, a class of publicly traded shares, effectively transforming the company into a publicly traded cooperative in 1996 (Painter 2004: 73–74). This began the process of its eventual full privatization. A wave of consolidation and subsequent privatizations among the other prairie grain handling cooperatives followed. In 1998, Manitoba Pool Elevators merged with the Alberta Wheat Pool to form Agricore; in 2001, Agricore merged with the United Grain Growers to form Agricore United (Painter 2004: 78–79). To complete the process, Agricore United was absorbed into SWP in the fall of 2007, forming Viterra (Briere 2007). Viterra, the last remaining vestige of the once formidable prairie cooperative movement, is now a large, publicly-traded agri-business corporation (2007 revenues were $4 billion), accountable to shareholders, not farmer-members.

In the wake of the spectacular decline of the Pools, debates over farmer-control of the CWB became all the more significant. According to a former CWB official, the farmer-controlled CWB was considered by many to be the last chance to achieve meaningful "producer presence in the supply chain." However, with the demise of the Pools, the link between economic cooperation and social empowerment became uncoupled in the collective imagination of prairie farmers.

The CWB under Farmer-Control

The 1998 changes to the *CWB Act* precipitated rapid organizational and operational changes at the CWB. In an interview, Ralph Goodale — the key political architect of the changes — said the shift to direct farmer-control had led to a period of innovation and renewal:

> You had producer-directors around that table that came not from the Grain Exchange down the street in Winnipeg, or the Chamber of Commerce, or the Business Club, they came from the farm. And they had an anticipation — personal experience of what farmers needed and wanted — and I think that innovation is a direct result of ten farmers being elected and sitting around the table and identifying the problems, identifying the way to solve the problems.

One result of direct farmer-control has been an improvement, according to annual CWB producer surveys, in farmers' perceptions of the CWB (Gandalf Group 2007: 15). While farmer opposition to the CWB remains, a senior CWB official believes that, overall, the governance changes have helped democratize the CWB and improve farmer "buy-in" for the organization.

According to one CWB farmer-director, in the political vacuum left by the demise of the prairie Pools, the farmer-controlled CWB has given prairie farmers a new voice on important issues facing the prairie grains sector. One important example was the CWB's vocal opposition to Roundup Ready (RR) wheat, developed by Monsanto, the first genetically modified (GM) wheat to be proposed for introduction to the prairies. Arguing that RR wheat would jeopardize premium markets in GM-wary countries (especially the U.K. and Japan), the CWB played the leading role in a coalition of social movements, farmers and industry actors that succeeded in stopping GM wheat (Magnan 2007). In the realm of transportation, the CWB has won significant concessions from Canada's rail duopoly over freight rates and level of service complaints (Measner 2007). On the international scene, the CWB has defended the legitimacy of state marketing as a matter of market power and self-determination for prairie farmers. The agency has lobbied strenuously against attempts to weaken or eliminate its single-desk powers in WTO negotiations. Given that single-desk selling is not trade distorting, the CWB insists that the fate of the organization must rest with prairie farmers and not international trade bodies (CWB 2008d). The new governance structure has therefore allowed the CWB to take on a more politicized role as a farmer advocate.

In these ways, the 1998 governance changes have increased farmer-control over the organization, mitigated farmer discontent and provided a new vehicle of farmer advocacy. Through the farmer-elected board of directors, prairie farmers now have a direct hand in running the organization, and, through the plebiscite requirement, they have ultimate say over the fate of single-desk selling. As a result, conflicts over collective marketing have partially been reframed as questions of self-determination and accountability for prairie grain producers. Despite the persistence of entrenched anti-CWB views among a segment of prairie farmers, there is strong consensus among prairie farmers that they themselves should decide the CWB's fate (Wilson 2006a).

The Limits of Farmer-Control

Despite the successes outlined above, the model of farmer-control contains tensions in the way that it has combined accountability to farmers and collective marketing. The key contradiction lies in a conflict between the principle of farmer-control and the CWB's dependence on government statute for its monopoly powers. The combination of statutory monopoly and farmer-control instituted by the 1998 changes allowed the government to retain some powers over the CWB. One of these is the government's prerogative to appoint five of the fifteen directors of the CWB. The federal government also retained a "power to direct" (*CWB Act,* Section 18) over the CWB, which, as Ralph Goodale said, was intended as a means of safeguarding the government's financial stake in guaranteeing CWB initial payments and its broad powers over the design and execution of farmer plebiscites for changes to the CWB's marketing mandate (*CWB Act,* Section 47.1). Under the condition of statutory authority, these government powers place limits on complete farmer-control and independence. The contradictions inherent in the model only became apparent, however, in the context of the hostile political environment resulting from the change in federal government in 2006.

Following through on its longstanding platform policy, in the spring of 2006, the Conservative government announced its intention to end the CWB's marketing monopoly (first on barley and later on wheat). The ensuing period of conflict pitted this government policy against the wishes of the CWB board of directors, controlled by a majority of farmer-elected single-desk supporters. Traditional opponents of the CWB, including commodity groups such as WCWGA and the government of Alberta, have supported the Conservative agenda. Having lost important allies in the prairie Pools, CWB supporters have formed new organizations devoted to defending the single-desk. The group Real Voice for Choice (RVFC) was formed in the fall of 2006 with the principle goal of persuading the government to hold a plebiscite on the question of barley marketing. Another new group, the Friends of the Canadian Wheat Board (FCWB) has pursued legal challenges to government actions, on behalf of prairie farmers (FCWB 2010). Among existing farmers' organizations, the National Farmers Union (NFU) and the Canadian Federation of Agriculture (CFA) both took a strong stand in favour of the single-desk and the principle of farmer-control.

For its part, the Conservative government used its powers, as set out in the *CWB Act*, to attempt to push through its agenda, thus severely testing the principle of farmer-control. Acute conflicts occurred over the interpretation and practice of the government's "power to direct," its power to appoint CWB directors and its power to design and conduct farmer plebiscites. Though these powers had been intended only to provide residual oversight over the CWB, each became a test-case for the legal limits of farmer-control as enshrined in the CWB *Act*. The conflicts revealed not only weaknesses in the *Act*, but more fundamental contradictions in the principle of farmer-control. In late 2006, the government replaced four of the CWB's five government appointed directors with new appointees sympathetic to "marketing choice" (Ewins 2006a; Ewins 2006c). The power to appoint directors had been intended to allow the government to appoint non-farmer directors with expertise (for example, in finance or governance) deemed complementary to the strengths of the farmer-directors. However, the Conservative government has used this power to change the balance of pro-single-desk and anti-single-desk directors of the CWB. With two farmer-elected directors committed to ending the CWB's barley monopoly, the current board of directors is divided eight to seven in favour of retaining the CWB's single-desk. Further, during farmer-director elections in October 2006, the government arbitrarily changed the voters' list, reducing the number of eligible voters by 16,000 (Wilson 2006b: 5). When then CWB President and CEO Adrian Measner began to publicly challenge the government's tactics, he was summarily fired, despite the board of directors' unanimous expression of confidence in his leadership (Ewins and Wilson 2006).

The most controversial set of actions taken by the government was in relation to the farmer-plebiscite it conducted in February 2007, which presented farmers with three ballot options, including the "marketing choice" option favoured by the government and long-standing opponents of the CWB. It is questionable whether or not the CWB could survive under "marketing choice" — a situation in which it would compete with private grain companies for the ability to sell farmers' grain. Because the CWB does not own any grain handling facilities, it would be entirely reliant on private grain companies to source grain for its sales (Fulton 2006). As its direct competitors, grain companies would obviously give priority to their own sales over the CWB's contracts. Because the CWB would be unlikely to survive without its monopoly powers, industry analysts have argued that this option presented a false choice. Following this logic, critics of the plebiscite contended that the only fair wording would have been to present a clear-cut choice between retaining and eliminating the CWB's single-desk authority (as had previously been done in 1996).

In the 2006 plebiscite, 38 percent of farmers voted to retain the single-desk, 14 percent to eliminate the single-desk and 48 percent for "choice" (AAFC 2007a). Combining the tallies for the last two options, the government concluded that 62 percent of the farmers polled desired "marketing choice" (AAFC 2007b). On this basis, the government attempted to eliminate the CWB's monopoly on barley, effective August 1, 2007, through an Order-in-Council (executive order) (AAFC 2007c). The FCWB immediately launched a legal challenge of the government's action. On July 31, 2007, the Federal Court ruled against the government, insisting that the change could only be made through legislation, as specified in the *CWB Act* (Hansen 2007). The Conservative government's gambit had failed. The incident marked the high-point of the government's repeated challenges to the principle of farmer-control.

Market Power and Democratic Control as Food Sovereignty

Since it provides market power and democratic control over farmers' own marketing arm, the existence of the CWB is vital to the question of food sovereignty on the prairies. As conflicts over the CWB since 2006 have shown, the fate of the single-desk also hinges on the question of self-determination. In its ideological campaign against the CWB, the federal government has sought to impose its grain marketing policy on prairie farmers. Meanwhile, the U.S. continues to target the CWB, expressing the ability of powerful states and social actors to impose restructuring on others under a neoliberal regime. The irony is that the U.S. pursues its continual trade harassment of prairie wheat producers while it continues to subsidize its own wheat producers at more than three times the rate Canada does (CWB 2003).

I have argued that the exercise of farmer-control in the CWB has been subject to contradictions arising from the agency's latent ties to the state. Specifically, the principle of farmer-control has been eroded by the re-politicization of the CWB via government interference. The experience over 2006-2008 suggests that, with a government intent on dismantling the CWB's marketing monopoly, the current governance structure is not enough to guarantee democratic farmer-control over the agency. Aside from the blow to the CWB's morale, some of the Conservative government's actions have substantively reduced the agency's autonomy. For many farmer-directors, these events revealed weaknesses in the current model. As one CWB farmer-director said, "the current government has in a sense been putting the lie to the fact that farmers are in control."

Ultimately, it was the government's legislative minority that prevented it from seeing through its desire to dismantle the CWB. Without the support of other political parties, it was forced to try to remove the CWB's single-desk for barley by executive order rather than by legislation. This action was thwarted by the Federal Court's 2007 ruling, thus granting the beleaguered CWB a reprieve. Having survived this test, it is clear that farmer-control needs to be further solidified. Some farmer directors see the need to amend the *CWB Act*: this was indicated by another farmer director, who stated,

> The governance structure has not changed enough yet.... we are not completely independent from the government and they are still able to exert a significant degree of control over the organization... I think we need to make sure that... we do become fully independent of the government and fully farmer-controlled.

These sorts of changes are proposed in the CWB's plan for corporate evolution, *Harvesting Opportunity*, released in the summer of 2006. It calls for the elimination of ties to the government through its financial guarantees. In turn, full independence from the government would require more formalized farmer-control, including a CWB Electoral Commission authorized to oversee farmer-director elections, and the power of farmer-directors to appoint external directors (CWB 2006: 24–25). These changes would go a long way towards assuring the self-determination of prairie farmers on the perennial question of grain marketing.

Although the survival of the CWB as a vehicle of farmer cooperation is important, something has been irretrievably lost with the demise of the prairie Pools. In the CWB's exercise of farmer-control, the value of the single-desk has been framed primarily in terms of economic rationality — i.e., as a way of obtaining greater economic rents from an uneven global market. Although the CWB advocates on behalf of prairie farmers on some issues directly related to grain marketing, it has not adopted the broader role of social empowerment and political representation once held by the Pools. Meanwhile, farmers' organizations are more divided than ever over the question of grain marketing. While many of the CWB's farmer-directors believe that a narrower focus on the economic value of the CWB strengthens the organization in the eyes of increasingly business-oriented farmers, it may leave the organization more vulnerable. Opponents of the CWB continue to argue that plebiscites related to the future of the CWB should be decided by ballots weighted according to the volume of production (reflecting the economic stakes involved for different farm operations), rather than assigning one vote per farming operation. Some CWB opponents argue that it is altogether illegitimate for matters of individual economic rights to be decided by majority rule (Ewins 2006b). Perhaps more importantly, framing the question purely as a matter of dollars and cents severs the link between collective marketing and social empowerment, contrary to the original vision of early agrarian movements for food sovereignty on the Canadian prairies.

Notes

1. All interviews were conducted as part of my dissertation research at the University of Toronto, ethics protocol #21707, "Conflicts over Canadian Wheat Board in Food Regime History." In order to protect the confidentiality of some interviewees, I have used a generic reference instead of their names (e.g., CWB farmer-director). Where I have not provided a citation, all quotations are from these interviews.
2. This figure is based on an estimated price premium of $10–13 per tonne and recent annual prairie production of wheat and barley. The range of calculated price premiums is drawn from several agricultural economic studies (Kraft et al. 1996, Schmitz et al. 1997, Gray 2001, and Schmitz et al. 2005).

References

AAFC (Agriculture and Agrifood Canada). 2007a. "Backgrounder. Plebiscite Results." At <agr.gc.ca/cb/index_e.php?s1=ip&page=ip60908a_bg1>.

AAFC (Agriculture and Agrifood Canada). 2007b. "Barley Producers Choose Marketing Choice." News release, March 28. At <agr.gc.ca/cb/index_e.php?s1=n&s2=2007&page=n70328>.

AAFC (Agriculture and Agrifood Canada). 2007c. "Marketing Choice for Barley to Start August 1, 2007." News release, June 11. At <agr.gc.ca/cb/index_e.php?s1=n&s2=2007&page=n70611>.

Briere, Karen. 2007. "Pool Slides into History; Viterra Comes to Life." *Western Producer* September 6.

CWB (Canadian Wheat Board). 2008a. "A History of US Trade Challenges: US Challenges and Canadian Wheat Imports." At <cwb.ca/public/en/hot/trade/popups/trade_history.jsp>.

CWB (Canadian Wheat Board). 2008b. "Backgrounder: Canada-US Wheat Relations." At <cwb.ca/public/en/hot/trade/relations/>.

CWB (Canadian Wheat Board). 2008c. "Backgrounder: WTO Issues for Western Canadian Wheat and Barley Producers." At <cwb.ca/public/en/hot/trade/issues/>.

CWB (Canadian Wheat Board). 2008d. "The WTO and You." At <cwb.ca/public/en/hot/trade/pdf/wto_and_you.pdf>.

CWB (Canadian Wheat Board). 2006. *Harvesting Opportunity.* Winnipeg: Canadian Wheat Board.

CWB (Canadian Wheat Board). 2003. "US Tariffs Unfair to Western Canadian Wheat Farmers." News release, March 4. At <cwb.ca/en/newsroom/releases/2003/030403.jsp>.

Department of Agriculture (Canada). 1970. *Canadian Agriculture in the Seventies: Report of the Federal Task Force on Agriculture.* Ottawa: Queen's Printer.

Desmarais, Annette Aurélie. 2007. *La Vía Campesina: Globalization and the Power of Peasants.* Black Point, NS: Fernwood Publishing.

Ewins, Adrian. 2006a. "Appointments Shift Power on CWB Board." *Western Producer* November 9.

Ewins, Adrian. 2006b. "Call for Vote Raises Issue of Questions." *Western Producer* November 9.

Ewins, Adrian. 2006c. "New CWB Director Favours Open Market." *Western Producer* December 7.

Ewins, Adrian, and Barry Wilson. 2006. "Turmoil Around CWB Costly: Experts." *Western Producer* December 7.

Fairbairn, Garry. 1984. *From Prairie Roots: The Remarkable Story of Saskatchewan Wheat Pool.* Saskatoon: Western Producer Prairie Books.

FCWB. 2010. "About Us." At <friendsofcwb.ca/about/>.

Friedmann, Harriet. 1993. "The Political Economy of Food: A Global Crisis." *New Left Review* 197.

Fulton, M. 2006. "The Canadian Wheat Board in an Open Market: The Impact of Removing the Single-Desk Selling Powers." Saskatoon: Knowledge Impact in Society Project, University of Saskatchewan. At <kis.usask.ca/publications/

pub-cwbliterature.html>.

Furtan, W. H. 2005. "Transformative Change in Agriculture: The Canadian Wheat Board." *Estey Centre Journal of International Law and Trade Policy* 6, 2.

Furtan, W.H., D.F. Kraft, and E.W. Tyrchniewicz. 1999. "Can the Canadian Wheat Board Extract Monopoly Rents? The Case of the Spring Wheat Market." *International Journal of the Economics of Business* 6, 3.

Gandalf Group. 2007. *CWB 2007 Producer's Survey Results.* At <cwb.ca/public/en/farmers/surveys/producer/pdf/survey_full_062107.pdf>.

Gray, R. June 2001. "Benchmarks to Measure CWB Performance — Recommendations. A Report Submitted to the Canadian Wheat Board." Knowledge Impact Society. At <kis.usask.ca/publications/pub-cwbliterature.html>.

Hansen, D. 2007. Federal Court of Canada Decision, Docket T-1124-07. At <decisions.fct-cf.gc.ca/en/2007/2007fc807/2007fc807.html>.

Irwin, Robert. 2001. "Farmers and 'Orderly Marketing': The Making of the Canadian Wheat Board." *Prairie Forum* 26, 1.

Knuttila, Murray. 2003. "Globalization, Economic Development and Canadian Agricultural Policy." In H. Diaz, J. Jaffe, and R. Stirling, (eds.), *Farm Communities at the Crossroads: Challenge and Resistance.* Regina: Canadian Plains Research Centre.

Kraft, D.F., W.H. Furtan, and W.E. Tyrchniewicz. 1996. "Performance Evaluation of the Canadian Wheat Board." Winnipeg: Canadian Wheat Board.

Magnan, André. 2007. "Strange Bedfellows: Contentious Coalitions and the Politics of Genetically Modified Wheat." *Canadian Review of Sociology* 44, 3.

McMichael, Philip. 2005. "Global Development and the Corporate Food Regime." In F.H. Buttel and P. McMichael (eds.), *New Directions in the Sociology of Global Development.* Oxford: Elsevier.

Measner, Adrian. 2007. "The Global Grain Trade and the Canadian Wheat Board." In T. Pugh and D. McLaughlin (eds.), *Our Board, Our Business: Why Farmers Support the Canadian Wheat Board.* Black Point, NS: Fernwood Publishing.

Mitchell, Don. 1975. *The Politics of Food.* Toronto: James Lorimer.

Morriss, William E. 2000. *Chosen Instrument, Volume 2.* Winnipeg: The Canadian Wheat Board.

Morriss, William E. 1987. *Chosen Instrument.* Winnipeg: The Canadian Wheat Board.

Oleson, Brian. 1979. "Price Determination and Market Share Formation in the International Wheat Market." PhD dissertation, Agricultural economics: University of Minnesota.

Painter, Marv. 2004. "Saskatchewan Wheat Pool." *International Food and Agribusiness Management Review* 7, 3.

Pugh, Terry, and Darrell McLaughlin (eds.). 2007. *Our Board, Our Business: Why Farmers Support the Canadian Wheat Board.* Black Point, NS: Fernwood Publishing.

Schmitz, Andrew, and Hartley Furtan. 2000. *The Canadian Wheat Board: Marketing in the New Millennium.* Regina: Canadian Plains Research Centre.

Schmitz, A., R. Gray, T.G. Schmitz and G. Storey. 1997. "The CWB and Barley Marketing: Price Pooling and Single-Desk Selling." Winnipeg: Canadian Wheat Board.

Schmitz, A., T.G. Schmitz and R. Gray. 2005. "The Canadian Wheat Board and Barley

Marketing." February. At <kis.usask.ca/publications/pub-cwbliterature.html>.
Sinclair, Scott, and Jim Grieshaber-Otto. 2009. *Threatened Harvest: Protecting Canada's World-Class Grain System.* Ottawa: Canadian Centre for Policy Alternatives.
Skogstad, Grace. 2005. "The Dynamics of Institutional Transformation: The Case of the Canadian Wheat Board." *Canadian Journal of Political Science* 38, 3.
Troughton, Michael. 1989. "The Role of Marketing Boards in the Industrialization of the Canadian Agricultural System." *Journal of Rural Studies* 5, 4.
Walton, Dawn, and Patrick Brethour. 2002. "Growing Defiance on Western Farms." *Globe and Mail* November 1.
Wilson, Barry. 2006a. "Producers Want Way on CWB: Poll." *Western Producer* November 9.
Wilson, Barry. 2006b. "Witnesses Question Voters List Changes." *Western Producer* November 2.
Wilson, C.F. 1978. *A Century of Canadian Grain.* Saskatoon, SK: Western Producer Books.
Winson, Anthony. 1992. *The Intimate Commodity: Food and the Development of the Agro-Industrial Complex in Canada.* Toronto: Garamond Press.

8. COMMUNITY NUTRITION PRACTICE AND RESEARCH

Integrating a Food Sovereignty Approach[1]

Rachel Engler-Stringer

In 2009, in an average month, 794,738 individuals in Canada received food from a food bank, an increase of 18 percent from 2008: and families with children constituted about half of all households assisted by food banks (Food Banks Canada 2009). The number of people accessing food banks in Canada has grown every year since data has been collected. While these statistics alone demonstrate the existence of a serious problem, it is important to note that food-bank usage statistics significantly under-represent the number of food insecure households in Canada because, among other issues, using a food bank is socially unacceptable for many people. Often, in order to make their food resources stretch, people will compromise on the quality of food they consume and use many other strategies that can cause significant emotional, financial and psychological stress before resorting to charitable food donations. The issue of food insecurity in Canada is thus complex, requiring solutions from various, often disparate, sectors. In order to better address the complexities of ending food insecurity, we need new interdisciplinary paradigms which can go beyond a "food security" approach. Community nutrition and food sovereignty approaches together can broaden research and practice possibilities to address the complex intersecting issues of hunger and ecological and social (in)justice associated with today's food system.

Community nutrition, also known as "community dietetics" and "public health nutrition," is a branch of nutrition research and practice that focuses on improving the nutritional health of individuals and groups of people within communities (Boyle and Morris 1999). Community nutrition professionals are trained in, for example, nutrition education, nutrition program planning and evaluation, nutritional counselling and work within policy making institutions. Community nutritionists are most often employed by government-run health regions, the private sector and other organizations such as community clinics and tribal councils.

Many working within the field now argue that community nutrition should be most concerned with the "big picture" of how public policy and income inequalities impact the nutritional health of communities. In fact, a major critique of community nutrition has arisen from its lack of action on the root causes of nutritional problems such as poverty (Tarasuk and Reynolds 1999; Travers 1996). While social constructs such as gender, class, commerce, policy and discourse entrench nutritional health disparities, these are rarely acted upon or even discussed in significant depth (Travers 1996; Dietitians of Canada 2009). For example, Michael Pollan (2008) describes what he calls "nutritionism," as a reductionist ideology that focuses on individual nutrients rather than foods as a whole. According to Pollan, when the focus of eating rests on individual nutrients, the social and environmental relations around food are ignored: foods are deemed "good" or "bad" based purely on the nutrients contained within them.

Given these patterns within the profession, an explicit focus on the principles of food sovereignty could help community nutritionists refocus their efforts to improve community nutrition by considering the root causes of nutritional problems. Even a brief history of the evolution of thought about issues of hunger, poverty and environment as they impact on community nutrition and public health shows this thinking has already begun to intersect with food sovereignty principles, albeit largely unknowingly. However, community nutrition could benefit from a more conscious adoption of food sovereignty principles, as some examples of current practice and research already demonstrate.

Evolving Discourse in Community Nutrition and Public Health Practice and Research

From Food Poverty to Household Food Insecurity

Beginning in the latter half of the 1980s, community nutrition researchers and practitioners working with low-income people in North America began to conceptualize household food insecurity as an alternative to the narrower concept of hunger, which is focused simply on the amount of food a person has to eat. As poverty in Canada and the United States was increasing, due in large part to neoliberal reforms introduced in the 1980s, it became clear that the narrow concept of hunger masked the complexities inherent in the experience of food poverty in a wealthy country. For example, according to Riches (1986), the establishment of food banks in Canada in the early 1980s and their rapid entrenchment were a result of government cutbacks that led to the deterioration of unemployment insurance and social assistance programs. Thus, to understand the growing prevalence of food poverty, one had to look beyond food. This led to a new conceptualization of food poverty: "household food insecurity" became the term used to describe the limited or uncertain availability of nutritionally adequate and safe foods, or the limited or uncertain ability to acquire acceptable foods in socially acceptable ways (Radimer et al. 1990). Household food insecurity also became and continues to be key to community nutrition practice and research, largely due to its measurability through survey research.

Food insecurity and food security came to be seen as including four dimensions that are quantitative, qualitative, social and psychological in nature (Radimer et al. 1990; Frongillo 1999). The quantitative dimension is similar to assessments of hunger: it means having sufficient food to meet basic needs. The qualitative aspect focuses on access to food that is safe (no dented cans, for example) and sufficiently diverse. Dietary monotony and consumption of a narrow range of inexpensive foods are also examples of quality issues that are associated with food insecurity. The third dimension, social acceptability, emphasizes how food is acquired; for example, charitable sources such as food banks are associated with feelings of humiliation. Linked to the social is the psychological aspect that highlights issues such as anxiety about running out of food and other psychological distress. According to this conceptualization, the path from food security to household food insecurity tends to follow a predictable sequence: from worrying about not having enough money to buy food, to compromising on quality, and then finally to compromising on the quantity of food eaten (Chen and Che 2001).

Recent analyses have put national rates of household food insecurity (based on the conceptualization described above) in Canada at 9.2 percent (Health Canada 2007). Certain populations, such as Aboriginal people and single women with children, are at higher risk of experiencing food insecurity. For example, 33 percent of Aboriginal households in Canada experience food insecurity versus 9 percent of non-Aboriginal households (Willows et al. 2008). Thus, food insecurity is clearly linked to social and economic inequalities, even though how these connections are played out is not necessarily well-understood within the field.

Community Food Security

In the latter part of the 1990s, the term "community food security" began to be used in North American nutrition and public health discussions and literature (Allen 1999), partly due to dissatisfaction with the limited nature of the concept of household food security. The emergence of a community food security framework developed independently from the discussions about food sovereignty, which were being developed at about the same time (personal communication, Andy Fisher, executive director of the Community Food Security Coalition). The transition from a focus on households to a consideration of community food security broadened considerably the scope of areas for research and action (Dietitians of Canada 2007; OPHA Food Security Work Group November 2002). According to Hamm and Bellows (2003: 37) "Community food security is... a situation in which all community residents obtain a safe, culturally acceptable, nutritionally adequate diet through a sustainable food system that maximizes community self-reliance and social justice." Community food security enhanced the concept of household food security by explicitly emphasizing issues of human rights, community empowerment and self-reliance, and the importance of food-system environmental sustainability. It is important to note that this definition includes linking agricultural sustainability to food security at the household and community levels.

Community food security initiatives attempted to reintegrate production and consumption issues, albeit usually with a local or regional focus (Allen 1999). The consumption element of community food security was concerned with the needs of low-income people, while initially the production side focused on the promotion of local and regional food systems. Allen (1999) argued that there were problems inherent in the early focus on local and regional food systems within a community food-security framework, because the emphasis on "local" assumed that communities made up of people with disparate power will inherently make better decisions about the food system. In addition, Allen stressed that a focus on the "local" distracted attention from macro-level economic and political structures that actually caused food insecurity. In part because of this critique, proponents of community food security shifted their concern to a broader consideration of sustainable agriculture, rather than looking primarily at local or regional food systems (Hamm and Bellows 2003). While community food security emerged as an approach to thinking about food systems in North America, nutritionists and other researchers also began to rethink the role of nutrition as a science.

New Nutrition Science

This new direction in thinking about nutrition is reflected in the Giessen Declaration (2005): formulated by representatives of the International Union of Nutritional Sciences (IUNS) and the World Health Policy Forum (WHPF) and representing nutrition experts from around the globe, it made a case for a "new nutrition science." The Declaration was critical of the traditional role that nutrition science has played in society:

> The application of the principles that have explicitly or implicitly governed nutrition science, has created food systems that have greatly contributed to the six-fold increase of the global human population in the last 150 years. During this time non-renewable energy use, material consumption and waste generation have increased enormously. This has resulted in the depletion of many living and physical resources and changes to ecosystems, and also has heightened the contrast between and within rich and poor regions and countries in access to material and other resources. (2005: 2)

These principles of nutrition science are largely the same ones that Pollan (2008) refers to in his critique of "nutritionism." For example, by focusing heavily on individual nutrients within foods and reducing nutrition to how to get the "correct" amount of the nutrients our bodies need, nutrition science has generally ignored the environmental and social relations that comprise global food systems.

The Giessen Declaration argues that it is critical for the nutrition sciences to begin to incorporate a comprehensive understanding of the global industrial food system and its role in the health of individuals, populations and the planet — an understanding that a group of nutrition and dietetics professionals are now referring to as "critical dietetics" (Dietitians of Canada 2009). The Declaration lists a series of consequences of the industrialized food system, which have also often been discussed by proponents of food sovereignty: loss of amenities and skills; loss of traditional farming, food cultures, land, property and independence; vulnerability to unemployment, dislocation and other impoverishments; rapid urbanization; increased social, economic and political inequities; as well as poor governance, conflicts and wars (Giessen Declaration 2005). Thus, the critical dietetics' reorientation towards a new nutrition science goes beyond community food security and is more consistent with food sovereignty.

Community Nutrition Practice and Research — Moving Towards Food Sovereignty?

Recent position statements and other writing in community nutrition and public health have emphasized the need for a combined focus on agriculture, food systems and sustainability. Statements and documents issued by organizations such as the Dietitians of Canada (2007), the Ontario Public Health Association (OPHA Food Security Work Group November 2002), the American Public Health Association (APHA 2007) and the British Columbia Provincial Health Services Authority (BCPHSA 2008), discuss issues, such as market concentration, and goals, such as the need to strengthen local and regional food systems, as well as the need to promote good working conditions and sustainable livelihoods for farmers and other workers within the food system. These are all issues associated with the food sovereignty framework (La Vía Campesina 2007; 1996). Nutrition researchers have also begun to recommend that nutrition and public health officials educate themselves about food systems in order to facilitate the promotion of healthy and sustainable food choices (Webber and Dollahite 2008; Muller et al. 2009). Community nutritionists and public health experts, along with sustainable agriculture advocates and environmentalists, have begun to recognize the links between a healthy, sustainable food system, a healthy environment and healthy people. Those working in community nutrition and public health are urged to become more involved in discussions about food system equity and justice and to take a leadership role in educating people — especially policy makers and other health professionals, as well as the general public — on food-system sustainability. The discourse about ecological approaches to food and food systems amongst health professionals points to an emerging openness to the principles of food sovereignty and a new role for community nutrition professionals in advocating for a sustainable and socially just food system.

One Québec-based research group, the Groupe d'Études en Nutrition Publique (GENUP, Public Nutrition Research Group), has taken a cue from the idea of a new nutrition science and is promoting what they refer to as "public nutrition" (Beaudry et al. 2004; Beaudry and Delisle 2005). GENUP argues that "[i]t is unusual in nutrition courses to address the impact of Western food systems on local and global food security, on equity of access to food resources in low-income countries, and on environmental sustainability" (Beaudry and Delisle 2005: 375). Again, these are all issues integral to the concept of food sovereignty. They also argue that "[t]he major share of the nutrition problems of concern in society require action outside of the health sector, particularly with regard to food systems" 2005: 375). This group sees the concept of public nutrition as encompassing community nutrition, public-health nutrition and international nutrition, as well as extending beyond all of these areas to include a stronger focus on the food system as a whole. These researchers recommend establishing new divisions between the various subfields of nutrition, so that students can train in either basic nutrition, clinical nutrition or, for those who wish to integrate the social and environmental dimensions, public nutrition (Beaudry and Delisle 2005).

Recent discourse about obesity in community nutrition and public health has also been moving towards more systems-based approaches, with a focus on what are being called "upstream" causes of food insecurity and other nutritional problems, including the social, economic and political structures that impact food and nutrition (Sturm 2009; Glanz et al. 2005). For example, Adam Drewnowski, an expert on the economics of poor nutrition and its link with obesity, writes that "obesity is a toxic consequence of economic insecurity and a failing economic environment" (Drewnowski 2009: S36). Similarly, a recent report from the Canadian Agri-Food Policy Institute entitled *Building Convergence: Toward an Integrated Health and Agri-Food Strategy for Canada* (Dube et al. 2009) links rising obesity rates in Canada with globalization and the increased consumption of processed foods. While the report does not call for systemic changes, it certainly argues for making a connection between current Canadian agricultural policies and ill health.

In addition, nutritionists have been saying more about the benefits of eating a predominantly local or regional diet (Rose et al. 2008). They also exhibit changing attitudes towards food-system sustainability concepts

(Webber and Dollahite 2008). Preliminary research in North America has shown the health benefits of eating primarily locally produced foods, largely due to increased reliance on vegetables and fruit, at least during the summer and fall, and decreased consumption of heavily processed foods (Rose et al. 2008). In fact, according to Hamm (2008), it is increasingly clear that public health dietary guidelines cannot be met without a simultaneous focus on sustainable agriculture and food production. He stresses the importance of diverse family farms, sustainable farming practices and the linking of viable rural and urban communities. He explains that food choice needs to be triaged using three questions: "(1) Can it be sourced locally? (2) If not, can a local substitute suffice? (3) If not, can a more distant source be used that incorporates the same environmental, social and economic traits desired in the local?" (Hamm 2008: 174). What is most fascinating and unusual about Hamm's argument is the link he makes between the development of sustainable agriculture, as well as sustainable rural communities, and diets that meet dietary guidelines for public health. In other words, shifting from a focus on the food supply to an emphasis on enhancing the sustainability of the food system with greater localization provides opportunities to link public health/community nutrition, sustainable agriculture, environmental stewardship and economic development.

Community Nutrition: Contributions to Advancing Food Sovereignty

A strength of community nutrition is its ability to educate the public about issues related to nutrition and health. But, while the community health curriculum has been expanded to include material on the food system in some instances (Story et al. 2009; Klitzke 1997), few Canadians know about the conditions under which the food they consume has been produced (Jaffe and Gertler 2006). They have little knowledge of the effects of factory farming of animals and the general industrialization of agriculture, for example, on surrounding communities, small producers, waterways, biodiversity, antibiotic resistance, animal welfare and farm workers' rights and safety. Few understand the impact of the globalized food system on agricultural communities around the world, as well as its links to global warming and diminishing fossil fuel resources. According to Jaffe and Gertler (2006), this lack of awareness represents a "deskilling": they argue that food and cooking skills include the ability to make informed choices, not simply about the nutritional quality of food, but also about how food choices affect society as a whole — from the people who produce it locally and abroad, to the land and non-renewable resources that are exploited in the process.

While people may be interested in food issues, it can be difficult to sort through the information available (as well as disinformation and lack of information). There is a growing gap between what people need to know in order to make healthy food choices (in both narrow and broad senses), and information that is available and readily assimilated. While knowledge about cooking, food preservation and food production (especially gardening) is being reproduced and expanded in some circles (such as among well-educated "foodies" and other relatively privileged groups), for the majority of Canadians, such food knowledge is elusive and increasingly fragmented and partial.

In response, community nutrition is very much concerned with cooking and with the changes in food and cooking practices, especially in the North American context. For example, a 2005 report entitled "Canadian Food Trends to 2020: A Long Range Consumer Outlook" prepared for Agriculture and Agri-Food Canada describes one of the major trends in Canadians' relationship to food: "Consumers will become even more disconnected from food preparation. Shopping and eating habits will be sporadic; meal planning cycles will be shorter, snacking will replace courses, as well as whole meals, and food will become even more portable" (Serecon Management Consulting 2005: i). Based on these predictions, unless significant changes occur, the food system will continue to become progressively dominated by food industry corporations, selling food that is further transformed into highly processed meal "components." Food will thus be bought and consumed with varying but limited levels of preparation or transformation in the home before it is eaten. This process will contribute to a further disconnect between what ordinary people receive as information about food and the food system, and what they need to know to make fully informed decisions regarding environmental sustainability and social justice. It will also likely lead to ever worsening health outcomes for the general population. Community nutrition practice, education and skill building could make a significant contribution to avoiding these outcomes by advancing the principles of food sovereignty. In particular, community nutrition practice is well-positioned to educate people about the food system, and to advocate from a public health perspective for access to healthy food that is produced in a manner that is socially just and environmentally sustainable.

Agrarian reform, for example, is a key principle of food sovereignty. Land reform generally is an issue that has relevance to the fields of community nutrition and public health because it can be framed with a socio-health focus in which greater control over land and other resources can translate into improved health for communities and populations. The problem is that much of the discussion on agrarian reform originates in the agricultural and social sciences, and, while it can be used to make community health arguments, health experts rarely interact with this area of research. One obvious exception is the research on the health impacts of access to and control over traditional lands for Indigenous peoples. Nutrition researchers in Canada have studied Indigenous land, food systems and access to traditional foods as they relate to nutritional health (Kuhnlein and Receveur 1996; Kuhnlein et al. 2004). For example, researchers at the Centre for Indigenous Peoples' Nutrition and Environment (CINE) at McGill University have made numerous recommendations that are consistent with demands for agrarian reform and food sovereignty, such as increased access to land for the purposes of traditional hunting and gathering, training in agricultural methods (especially traditional forms of agriculture) and preparing traditional foods (Kuhnlein et al. 2006; see also Chapter 6 in this volume on Indigenous food sovereignty). While the work of CINE is focused on nutrition, it also considers environmental and agricultural or land use issues. It is also informed by a consideration of Indigenous sovereignty, as well as related issues of control over resources, including education. There is no explicit focus on food sovereignty for Indigenous peoples in CINE research; however, it is implicit in many of the recommendations they present.

Finally, opposition to genetically modified organisms (GMOs) and concerns about Intellectual Property Rights (IPRs) are two other issues that are often raised in key food sovereignty documents (La Vía Campesina 2007; 1996) but rarely examined by community nutrition researchers. Social science and agriculture researchers who are critical of mainstream corporate views on GMOs have rarely focused their work on educating nutritionists, yet nutritionists are consistently targeted by corporations with pro-GMO information through, for example, conference sponsorship, trade shows and advertising in nutrition journals. Relatively recently, community nutrition/public health researchers began to write about problems with GMOs, including how they relate to intellectual property rights (McCullum et al. 2003). To date, research in community nutrition has focused primarily on the contribution of GMOs to global food insecurity and to loss of crop diversity. Overall, however, similar to other issues related to corporate control in agriculture, there is little published in the field of community nutrition on this topic.

Community Nutrition Programs and Initiatives

Several current programs and initiatives related to community nutrition are examples of food sovereignty in practice, including promotion and support for community or collective kitchens, food hubs, farmers' markets and urban agriculture. "Community kitchens" encompass a variety of community-based cooking programs where people cook and sometimes eat together on a regular basis (often monthly or bi-weekly). They include groups that meet monthly to cook and eat one meal together and groups that cook food received through charitable donation. "Collective kitchens," on the other hand, are community kitchens that focus on bringing small groups of people (usually four to eight) together to produce large quantities of food in bulk to take home to their families (Tarasuk and Reynolds 1999). Collective and community kitchens began largely as grassroots initiatives in Québec and then grew and evolved across Canada. There are at least 2,500 individual collective and community kitchens across the country: many have significant support from community organizations and occasionally from health authorities or other government bodies (Engler-Stringer and Berenbaum 2005; Engler-Stringer 2005). In some places, such as Québec, members have well-developed networks that voice a strong anti-poverty, feminist analysis, and are active in discussions around food system sustainability.

Collective kitchens, which have both formal and informal aspects, are extremely diverse. They sometimes have financial and/or organizational support, yet they are also spaces where women (and to a lesser degree, men) socialize, make friends and find a place in their community. They have also been shown to have many different impacts on the lives of participants, ranging from social impacts, such as developing community, to educational impacts, such as learning about food security and other nutritional concerns (Tarasuk and Reynolds 1999; Engler-Stringer 2005). For many participants who are socially isolated, a collective kitchen is a place where they develop friendships, where they find support to cope with poverty and where they sometimes begin to examine the root causes of that poverty (Engler-Stringer 2005). Collective kitchens can be places where members control what they cook, when they cook, how much they cook, whether or not they eat together and whether or not they have a strong educational or community-organization focus. They also have a role to play in food sovereignty: they focus on self-sufficiency, active engagement and education about the food system; as well they emphasize linking with other initiatives, particularly alternative food networks and community/urban gardening programs.[2]

One of the key ways collective kitchens reflect a food sovereignty approach is when they meet the specific needs of those who participate in each individual group, whether that group is young mothers or homeless or under-housed men or seniors living in various degrees of isolation. For example, a collective kitchen group in Toronto for homeless or under-housed men found ways to meet the special needs of that particular group. Usually participants meet and spend most of a day cooking four to five dishes in large enough quantity so that each participant can take four or more portions of each dish home. However, in this case, the host organization knew that the men in the group did not have access to adequate kitchen facilities. They decided to create their own model in which participants cooked enough food for six portions each of five or so dishes and then froze the portions individually in containers in a freezer provided by the host community centre. This centre provided various services, as well as a meeting space for the homeless and under-housed. Since, one of those services was access to kitchen facilities, the participants could come in whenever they needed to heat up one of their meals. Participants were therefore in a position to eat home-cooked food despite not having access to their own cooking facilities.

This approach allowed people who are extremely marginalized in Canadian society (homeless men) to take control of a very basic and intimate aspect of human existence — eating. The men I interviewed in that group contrasted it to their previous experiences, attending soup kitchen after soup kitchen, eating food they often did not like, at times and in places that they did not get to control: they were grateful not to be in that position anymore. This small program is an example of how food sovereignty can work in practice. Of course it was done on a small scale and focused on only one aspect of the approach, but it illustrates how attitudes towards food can change, and how even the most marginalized can gain some control over an important aspect of their lives.

Food Hubs

Another community-led initiative that illustrates a food sovereignty policy approach is the proposed Station 20 West in Saskatoon. Station 20 West is a "Community Enterprise Centre" that emerged as a partnership between community members and community-based organizations, the local health region and the University of Saskatchewan <www.station20west.org/>. Saskatoon, like many cities across Canada, has an inner core of neighbourhoods that are low-income, and experience significant health disparities in comparison to more affluent neighbourhoods (Lemstra et al. 2006). The Station 20 West project was born from a need for improved access to quality food. Large areas of Saskatoon's low-income neighbourhoods do not have access to a full-service grocery store within walking distance. In the Station 20 West area, there has not been a full-service grocery store in the area for over ten years (though not for lack of trying to entice the private sector to fill the gap). Much of the food that is available comes from convenience stores and is heavily processed and often expensive.

At the time of writing this chapter, fundraising and other forms of organizing for Station 20 West had been underway for over two years (since its original funding was cut by an incoming conservative — Saskatchewan Party — government). When the project is finally completed the lowest income neighbourhood in Saskatoon will have a full-service grocery store called the Good Food Junction that emphasizes local, sustainably-produced food, an incubator kitchen, a community café, office space for community-based organizations, health region programs, university researchers and space for community gatherings. A library and an affordable housing project have already been built on the site, both of which will be integrated into Station 20 West.

Station 20 West meets food sovereignty objectives at the local level where most nutrition practitioners work. It focuses on the right to high-quality, healthy and affordable food; on issues of access and community control over programs and services; on the right of poor people to sustainably-produced food; on supporting local producers to have places to sell their food in their community; and on issues of social justice, especially as these relate to health inequities. Reflecting these diverse foci, the board of directors of Station 20 West includes local residents, a nutrition expert from the University of Saskatchewan, a community development worker and representatives from community-based organizations, amongst others. Also, the board of directors of the food store component of Station 20 West includes local farmers.

From its early stages, various researchers and practitioners in community nutrition supported Station 20 West, in part because the project has clear public health objectives, such as access to healthy food and health services. It has also been exciting for community health practitioners who take a food sovereignty approach, especially as discussion about food environments and their importance for health has become an important area of research and action in the field (Glanz et al. 2005; Hemphill et al. 2008).

Farmers' Markets and Urban Agriculture

Farmers' markets and various forms of urban agriculture are also initiatives where community nutritionists can take a leadership role in advancing food sovereignty. Farmers' markets, which have grown exponentially in the last two decades, visibly link rural producers and urban eaters (consumers). One example of a farmers' market initiative that benefited from the support of community nutritionists is the British Columbia Farmers' Market Nutrition and Coupon Project (FMNCP), which was piloted in 2007–2008 and then renewed in 2009 (B.C. Association of Farmers' Markets 2010).[3] The FMNCP was developed based on the United States Farmers' Market Nutrition Program, in which food stamp recipients received coupons that could be redeemed at farmers' markets for produce, meats and other foods. That program had two major impacts: increasing the dietary quality of nutritionally vulnerable people, as well as increasing the revenues of farmers who participated in the program (Dollahite et al. 2005; Joshi et al. 2008). In British Columbia the FMNCP was seen as "an innovative project — the first of its kind in Canada," and one that "provided low-income families with children and low-income pregnant women coupons to access fresh fruits, vegetables, meats, eggs, dairy or fresh cut herbs at participating farmers' markets across B.C." (B.C. Association of Farmers' Markets 2010).

The FMNCP, which had a coupon redemption rate of almost 100 percent, started with five communities that grew to sixteen over its three first years of operation; it was generally viewed as a success by both producers and coupon recipients. The project enabled people on limited incomes to access high quality nutritious food and choose which products to buy based on their personal preferences. It also provided an extra source of income for producers — often more than the coupons were worth, because some recipients chose to spend a portion of their normal food budget at farmers' markets.

Community gardens, which are often supported by community nutritionists, are another important urban agriculture initiative consistent with food sovereignty (see Chapter 9 for a detailed discussion of community gardens.) Related to community gardens, but with an explicit educational focus, are school gardens. These too are supported by community nutritionists and are consistent with food sovereignty principles. They are part of a strategy for improving nutritional and educational outcomes, which has not been evaluated extensively: they have, however, shown benefits for the schools and children who participate in them (Joshi et al. 2008). These gardens are usually set up in schoolyards and are integrated into the curriculum and food services of participating schools. They allow students to become familiar with the challenges and rewards of growing food as well as the flavours of home-grown vegetables or fruit. In many cases students also learn how to prepare the products of their labour into nutritious and tasty meals.

Where to From Here?

By integrating theory with practices such as community kitchens, food hubs and urban agriculture, we can begin to integrate a food sovereignty approach with community nutrition. By advancing programs such as collective kitchens and community gardens and initiatives such as Station 20 West — all familiar to the vast majority of practitioners and researchers within the field of community nutrition — we are making the discussion of food sovereignty real; it is also being empirically tested. Discussion about principles such as autonomy, human rights and community control over resources are more real when they flow out of actual experience. And, given the current "buzz" around sustainable agriculture and food systems in the field of nutrition, those who are already familiar with these different areas are broadening the discussion by concentrating on how they are intimately linked. Even though this is occurring in pockets all over the country with passionate and dedicated practitioners and researchers, we still need more ways to communicate with each other and more opportunities to share what has and has not worked with our peers. The Canadian Association for Food Studies (CAFS) and Food Secure Canada (FSC) (see Chapter 5) are obvious networks to tap into, but there is a need for venues within these organizations where people working in nutrition and public health can come together to discuss food sovereignty with others who understand the challenges of our field. Nutrition and public health working groups within these organizations, as well as within the Dieticians of Canada and the Canadian Public Health Association (two key professional bodies within our field) are certainly places to pursue the discussion.

Food Sovereignty = Community Nutrition

If we integrate food sovereignty principles into community nutrition practice and research, the focus of our field will expand to include the systemic factors that lead to many of the nutritional health disparities we currently encounter. Food sovereignty has an important role to play in moving beyond the individual nature of most community nutrition practices towards challenging the social and political structures that create poverty, health inequalities and environmental destruction. Much of the emphasis in community nutrition practice to date has been dominated by an individualistic ideology that has led to a focus on increasing food skills and on changing food choice patterns through education rather than on addressing the root causes of poverty (McCullum et al. 2004). Food sovereignty also points towards solutions that are consistent with human and natural systems' health.

Of course, taking a food sovereignty approach would also entail changes in how researchers and practitioners in community nutrition approach and work with communities (McCullum et al. 2004). A more equitable relationship that acknowledges communities' assets is inherent in a food sovereignty approach to community nutrition. It would support the work of some nutrition researchers and practitioners working to bring a stronger focus on the rights of communities and individuals to control resources.

I agree with Hamm (2008) that there is an urgent need to focus, at the same time, on the goals of sustainable agriculture and population-wide adoption of public-health dietary guidelines, because only when agricultural policy is focused on growing healthy food for people to eat over the long term, rather than on commodities for trade, will the population as a whole be in a position to eat recommended foods. Moreover, it is only when the fields of nutrition and public health as a whole understand the intimate links between human health and social and environmental justice within food systems, that they will be in a position to take their place in working towards food sovereignty for all.

Notes

1. Sections of this chapter appear in an unpublished draft report, entitled "Food Sovereignty in Canada: Issues, Initiatives and Opportunities," by Rachel Engler-Stringer, Michael Gertler and Daniel DeLury, prepared in 2009 for Heifer International and the Community-University Institute for Social Research.
2. The remainder of this chapter, unless otherwise noted, is based on the doctoral research I conducted in 2001 and 2002. The dissertation is entitled *Collective*

Kitchens in Three Canadian Cities: Impacts on the Lives of Participants (Engler-Stringer 2005).

3. As this book went to print the program was halted due to nonrenewal of funding.

References

Allen, Patricia. 1999. "Reweaving the Food Security Safety Net: Mediating Entitlement and Entrepreneurship." *Agriculture and Human Values* 16.

American Public Health Association. 2007. *Toward a Healthy, Sustainable Food System.* Washington, DC: American Public Health Association.

B.C. Association of Farmers' Markets. 2010. "The Farmers' Market Nutrition and Coupon Project." At <bcfarmersmarket.org/ind/fmncp.htm>.

Beaudry, M., and H. Delisle. 2005. "Public('s) Nutrition." *Public Health Nutrition* 8, 6A.

Beaudry, M., A.M. Hamelin and H. Delisle. 2004. "Public Nutrition: An Emerging Paradigm." *Canadian Journal of Public Health* 95, 5.

BCPHSA (British Columbia Provincial Health Services Authority). 2008. *A Seat at the Table: Resource Guide for Local Governments to Promote Food Secure Communities.* June.

Boyle, M.A., and D.H. Morris. 1999. *Community Nutrition in Action: An Entrepreneurial Approach* second ed. Belmont, CA: Wadsworth Publishing.

Chen, J., and J. Che. 2001. "Food Insecurity in Canadian Households." *Health Reports* 12, 4.

Dietitians of Canada. 2009. "Beyond Nutritionism — An Invitation to Critical Dietetics Dialogue." At <practiceblog.dietitians.ca/2009/12/beyond-nutritionism-invitation-to.html>.

____. 2007. *Community Food Security: Position of Dietitians of Canada.* Dietitians of Canada.

Dollahite, J.S., J.A. Nelson, E.A Frongillo and M.R. Griffin. 2005. "Building Community Capacity Through Enhanced Collaboration in the Farmers Market Nutrition Program." *Agriculture and Human Values* 22.

Drewnowski, A. 2009. "Obesity, Diets, and Social Inequalities." *Nutrition Reviews* 67, Suppl 1.

Dube, L.P., P. Thomassin and P. Beauvais. 2009. *Building Convergence: Toward an Integrated Health and Agri-Food Strategy for Canada.* Canadian Agri-Food Policy Institute.

Engler-Stringer, Rachel. 2005. "Collective Kitchens in Three Canadian Cities: Impacts on the Lives of Participants." PhD Dissertation, College of Pharmacy and Nutrition, University of Saskatchewan.

Engler-Stringer, Rachel, and Shawna Berenbaum. 2005. "Collective Kitchens in Canada: A Review of the Literature." *Canadian Journal of Dietetic Practice and Research* 66, 4.

Fisher, Andy, 2011. Executive Director, Community Food Security Coalition, U.S. Personal communication, March 25.

Food Banks Canada. 2009. "HungerCount 2009." At <http://www.foodbankscanada.ca/HungerCount.htm>.

Frongillo, Edward A. 1999. "Validation of Measures of Food Insecurity and Hunger."

Journal of Nutrition 129, 2.

Giessen Declaration. 2005. At <www.iuns.org/features/05-09%20NNS%20 Declaration.pdf>.

Glanz, K., J.F. Sallis, B.E. Saelens and L.D. Frank. 2005. "Healthy Nutrition Environments: Concepts and Measures." *American Journal of Health Promotion* 19 (5).

Hamm, M.W. 2008. "Linking Sustainable Agriculture and Public Health: Opportunities for Realizing Multiple Goals." *Journal of Hunger and Environmental Nutrition* 3, 2–3.

Hamm, M.W., and A.C. Bellows. 2003. "Community Food Security and Nutrition Educators." *Journal of Nutrition Education and Behavior* 35.

Health Canada. 2007. *Canadian Community Health Survey, Cycle 2.2, Nutrition (2004): Income-Related Household Food Security in Canada*. Ottawa, ON: Health Canada.

Hemphill, E., K. Raine, J.C. Spence and K.E. Smoyer-Tomic. 2008. "Exploring Obesogenic Food Environments in Edmonton, Canada: The Association Between Socioeconomic Factors and Fast-Food Outlet Access." *American Journal of Health Promotion* 22, 6.

Jaffe, JoAnn, and Michael Gertler. 2006. "Victual Vicissitudes: Consumer Deskilling and the Transformation of Food Systems." *Agriculture and Human Values* 23, 2.

Joshi, A., A.M. Azuma and G. Feenstra. 2008. "Do Farm-to-School Programs Make a Difference? Findings and Future Research Needs." *Journal of Hunger and Environmental Nutrition* 3, 2–3.

Klitzke, C. 1997. "Dietitians: Experts about Food Systems?" *Journal of the American Dietetic Association* 97, 10 Suppl 2 (Oct).

Kuhnlein, H.V., B. Erasmus, H. Creed-Kanashiro, L. Englberger, C. Okeke, N. Turner, L. Allen and L. Bhattacharjee. 2006. "Indigenous Peoples' Food Systems for Health: Finding Interventions that Work." *Public Health Nutrition* 9, 8.

Kuhnlein, H.V. and O. Receveur. 1996. "Dietary Change and Traditional Food Systems of Indigenous Peoples." *Annual Review of Nutrition* 16.

Kuhnlein, H.V., O. Receveur, R. Souieda and G.M. Egeland. 2004. "Arctic Indigenous Peoples Experience the Nutrition Transition with Changing Dietary Patterns and Obesity." *Journal of Nutrition* 124, 6.

La Vía Campesina. 2007. "Declaration of Nyéléni." At <nyeleni2007.org>.

___. 1996. "Food Sovereignty: A Future Without Hunger." At <voiceoftheturtle.org/ library/1996%20Declaration%20of%20Food%20Sovereignty.pdf>.

Lemstra, M., C. Neudorf and J. Opondo. 2006. "Health Disparity by Neighbourhood Income." *Canadian Journal of Public Health* 97, 6.

McCullum, C., C. Benbrook, L. Knowles, S. Roberts and T. Schryver. 2003. "Application of Modern Biotechnology to Food and Agriculture: Food Systems Perspective." *Journal of Nutrition Education and Behavior* 35, 6 (Nov–Dec).

McCullum, C., D. Pelletier, D. Barr, J. Wilkins, and J.P. Habicht. 2004. "Mechanisms of Power Within a Community-Based Food Security Planning Process." *Health Education and Behavior* 31, 2.

Muller, M., A. Tagtow, S.L. Roberts and E. MacDougall. 2009. "Aligning Food Systems Policies to Advance Public Health." *Journal of Hunger & Environmental Nutrition* 4, 3.

OPHA Food Security Work Group. 2002. *A Systemic Approach to Community Food*

Security: A Role for Public Health. November. Ontario Public Health Association.
Pollan, M. 2008. *In Defense of Food: An Eater's Manifesto*. New York: Penguin Group.
Radimer, K.L., C.M. Olson and C.C. Campbell. 1990. "Development of Indicators to Assess Hunger." *Journal of Nutrition* 120.
Riches, Graham. 1986. *Food Banks and the Welfare Crisis*. Ottawa: Canadian Council on Social Development.
Rose, N., E. Serrano, K. Hosig, C. Haas, D. Reaves and S.M. Nickols-Richardson. 2008. "The 100-Mile Diet: A Community Approach to Promote Sustainable Food Systems Impacts Dietary Quality." *Journal of Hunger and Environmental Nutrition* 3, 2–3.
Serecon Management Consulting. 2005. *Canadian Food Trends to 2020: A Long Range Consumer Outlook*. Ottawa: Agriculture and Agri-Food Canada. At <www4.agr.gc.ca/resources/prod/doc/agr/pdf/ft-ta_eng.pdf>.
Story, Mary, Michael W. Hamm and David Wallinga. 2009. "Research and Action Priorities for Linking Public Health, Food Systems, and Sustainable Agriculture: Recommendations from the Airlie Conference." *Journal of Hunger & Environmental Nutrition* 4, 3.
Sturm, Roland. 2009. "Affordability and Obesity: Issues in the Multifunctionality of Agricultural/Food Systems." *Journal of Hunger & Environmental Nutrition* 4, 3.
Tarasuk, V., and R. Reynolds. 1999. "A Qualitative Study of Community Kitchens as a Response to Income-Related Food Insecurity." *Canadian Journal of Dietetic Practice and Research* 60, 1.
Travers, K. 1996. "The Social Organization of Nutritional Inequities." *Social Science and Medicine* 43, 4.
Webber, C.B., and J.S. Dollahite. 2008. "Attitudes and Behaviors of Low-Income Food Heads of Households Toward Sustainable Food System Concepts." *Journal of Hunger and Environmental Nutrition* 3, 2–3.
Willows, N.D., P. Veugelers, K. Raine and S. Kuhle. 2008. "Prevalence and Socio-demographic Risk Factors Related to Household Food Security in Aboriginal Peoples in Canada." *Public Health Nutrition* 12, 8.

9. GROWING COMMUNITY

Community Gardens as a Local Practice of Food Sovereignty

Yolanda Hansen

For over ten years, a tract of land along a busy Regina street bloomed every summer. It was one of Regina's best known community gardens and its patchwork of plots showcased a wide variety of vegetables. Throughout the summer, one could find men and women bent under the sun amidst the lush green plants. People of different ages and backgrounds were drawn to it from the surrounding neighbourhoods and buildings, even from within their cars as they drove by. This community garden was a sign of verdant life at the edge of the city's downtown core. I was also drawn to that garden, so when I drove past it in the spring of 2006 to discover it barren and lifeless, crowned by a for-sale sign, I too felt the loss of that space, although I did not garden there. At the time, that empty piece of land symbolized a sadness that I could not articulate.

Today, I understand that community garden and its eviction as symbolic of a much deeper dichotomy inherent in the idea and practice of community gardens. Community gardens are often applauded as positive endeavours, which are encouraged for a variety of reasons: fostering self-help, community building, food security and enjoyment and education for children and immigrants. Yet their establishment and practice are often temporary and transient, for most Canadian cities have yet to recognize these gardens as worthy permanent urban fixtures, despite their long history in North America, Europe and other parts of the world. This history demonstrates that community gardens, contrary to contemporary public opinion, are not a fleeting fancy but are a part of an important historical practice of urban food provisioning and community building.

Framed by their positive social, environmental and even political goals, community gardens can also be considered a local practice of food sovereignty. Three community gardens in Saskatchewan demonstrate how these urban spaces reconnect people to their sources of food and the natural environment, offer an empowering space for community building and participatory decision making, and spark personal politicization as a place of resistance to an industrialized and globalized food system. The experiences of gardeners in the Grow Regina Community Garden in Regina, City Park Community Garden in Saskatoon and the Yara Community Garden in Moose Jaw demonstrate that these gardens, envisioned as spaces for community building and food security, actually engage in food sovereignty. Their success may foster a positive future for this practice in the province and encourage further discussion of how food sovereignty is applicable to urban Canadian spaces.

A History of Community Gardening

To understand the importance of contemporary community gardening and its rich foundation of community self-provisioning, it is useful to delve into European and North American history. British allotment gardens have been a ubiquitous sight in Britain for the past two hundred years. Usually designated on "left over spaces," allotment gardens were provided by local authorities or railroad companies to the poor and working classes as spaces to grow vegetables on both public and private land. These gardens have always been underwritten with a strong theme of self-help for the working class. Drawn into the cities as a result of the enclosures, workers embraced the allotments not only as an extra source of food for their families, but also for the creation of a collective identity and culture, and for the politicization it brought to their lives. Key to this culture was land; both the authorities and workers recognized the importance for displaced peoples of having a parcel of earth. While governments and companies looked to these pieces of land to quell agitation, the allotment gardeners used the community that arose from these spaces to create a culture of self-help and to support each other in seeking greater empowerment and further rights for land ownership. Reformers loved the gardens, for they saw them as tools to help keep workers and their money out of the pubs and in the open air with their families. In the dirty, crowded environment of British cities during the early stages of the Industrial Revolution, these green spaces provided a much-needed refuge (Crouch and Ward 1988; Scott 2005).

European settlers to the Canadian prairies brought gardening habits with them as they sought food self-sufficiency in their new land. As towns and cities were settled and expanded in Saskatchewan, horticultural agendas emerged with the focus of gardening and beautifying these new landscapes. In 1913, the Regina Vacant Lot Gardening Association became Regina's first gardening organization to go beyond improving the city's appearance to identify a collective gardening agenda.

Although unrecorded, it is likely that urban growth, driven by immigration and a consequently high unemployment rate, was the impetus behind the Vacant Lot Gardening Association (VLGA). As an organization of local "public spirited" citizens, the VLGA managed fifty acres of city-owned land on which unemployed men could rent plots of one to five acres to for vegetable cultivation (Beach 1914a). The support of the municipal government, through its provision of vacant land as well as a monetary loan (Beach 1914b), was necessary for the success of the garden, although its control and supervision were the responsibility of the citizen organization (Beach 1915). At the rate of $1 per acre of broken land, and with a cooperative seed-buying scheme to assist gardeners, this was affordable for many: during its ten years of operations the VLGA had a membership exceeding one thousand gardeners (Macoun 1917; Sheard 1978). This project attracted attention in the larger social and economic context of World War I. Other prairie towns and cities requested information on the VLGA gardens, hoping to implement their own model as increased garden production was encouraged for the Dominion war effort.

Along with restricting household consumption, the promotion of community gardening was an important strategy for Canadian and American governments during World War I. By advocating this practice as patriotic, people were inspired to help with the war effort by growing their own food. In this context, Regina's vacant lot gardeners were implored to increase food production. In February 1917, the Federal Minister of Agriculture pleaded with Regina's city council to encourage its citizens to alleviate farm labour shortages and increase food supplies as a boost to the "great cause" (Burrell 1917). Agricultural pamphlets, sponsored by Dominion Experimental Farms and distributed to Canadian farmers and gardeners, promoted gardening at home and in vacant lots during this time; one even used the example of Regina's VLGA as an encouraging practice (Macoun 1914; 1917). The British Empire looked to Canada and the United States to supplement their besieged food stocks, which meant diverting a considerable amount of the domestic supply. Media and catchy slogans encouraged growing food; calls for "soldiers of the soil" to "hoe for liberty" and "plant for freedom" stirred U.S. and Canadian patriotic fever, and would serve as a model for a similar gardening campaign during World War II (Bassett 1981, Lawson 2005). During the 1920s, however, because it became too difficult to secure property for gardening within a reasonable distance from the city centre, the practice of vacant lot gardening ended (Sheard 1978).

With such a history of self-help operating as an alternative to charity, it is no surprise that community gardening re-emerged in Regina during the harsh times of the Great Depression. Elements of earlier allotment programs were evident in this new model: through the provision of land, and occasionally materials, instruction and supervision to the unemployed and working poor, the logic of providing access to healthy food, while bolstering the self-respect of "charity cases," was reborn. In Regina, a central community garden was created and administered by the army for unemployment-relief recipients during the 1930s, and others were established in different areas of the city, with land and seeds supplied through the local relief department (*Leader-Post* 1935). Local organizations and the provincial department of agriculture encouraged these gardens, the latter organizing competitions to encourage production and boost morale (Sheard 1978). The model of work relief rather than monetary charity was greatly preferred by governments and relief agencies, and work relief gardens flourished along with subsistence gardens during this period (Lawson 2005).

By the end of the Great Depression, community gardens found a purpose again as patriotic endeavours of World War II, remodelled as the victory gardening campaign. The Canadian and U.S. governments had not forgotten the success of earlier campaigns. Citizens were bombarded with the patriotic gardening campaign through many media forms, particularly mass periodicals. Gardeners in Regina were determined to take part in this campaign despite the lingering environmental effects of drought and strict wartime rationing. Local organizations like the Kiwanis Club supported these endeavours, awarding a number of cash prizes in 1943 for the best Victory Garden in different areas of the city. By 1944, however, Regina's program was struggling due to a lack of gardeners, thus dissolving at the war's end (SHA 1977).

After the victory gardening fever passed, those who continued to garden did so privately for food and leisure purposes. It was not until the 1970s and 1980s, when the growing environmental and urban green space movement blossomed, that community gardening re-emerged in Saskatchewan's cities. Today's practices began in this latest phase, based on efforts to increase beautiful, useful urban green spaces as well as to boost community food security.

These historical examples of community gardens denote practices born during periods of crisis, such as the two world wars and the Great Depression, to address pressing social and economic issues like unemployment, hunger and strained domestic food supplies. At the same time, community gardens encouraged values viewed as important for overcoming these crises, such as patriotism, self-help, cooperation and sharing. I argue that the growth in popularity of today's community garden movement is based on social, economic and environmental factors that have created a crisis in our food system. The re-emergence of community gardens in the late 1970s and 80s coincides with two major trends that are still present, even amplified, in 2011. These trends include the emergence of Canadian food banks in the early 1980s to provide emergency food supplies in the face of growing hunger and a burgeoning public environmental consciousness. Fears about the cost and availability of oil following the 1973 oil crisis may have been an influence on community gardening then, just as concerns about peak oil and long-distance food miles are present now. The current food crisis is yet another impetus for greater local food provisioning, including community gardens.

Themes and values evident in these historical examples of community gardening continue to be relevant today. The importance of British allotment gardens to the working class transcended a physical need for fresh food to speak to the gardeners' desire to build a community and a collective identity during a period of social and economic upheaval. The value of community and collective identity as well as food provisioning is also evident in vacant-lot gardening and depression-era community gardens. The participants of historical gardens were often marginalized people, primarily the working poor and immigrants, who used these gardens as empowering spaces. These principles continue to influence contemporary community gardens and demonstrate the applicability of food sovereignty to this urban practice. The personal experiences of men and women in three Saskatchewan community gardens confirm that self-help, food provisioning and community building remain strong influences on the practice of community gardens.

A Tale of Three Gardens

Grow Regina Garden in Regina, Saskatoon's City Park Community Garden and the Yara Community Garden in Moose Jaw[1] all offer important lessons in community gardening and social justice (see Table 9-1). All three gardens use the language and practices of food security and community building, which give them a common foundation from which to pursue positive social and environmental goals. Although these gardeners do not use the language of food sovereignty, theoretical elements of food sovereignty are evident in their gardening practices. The fact that their operations are led by a group of volunteer gardeners, rather than by government or business, offers them freedom within their agendas as well as an inherent sense of financial instability.

Table 9-1 Income and Population Levels in Community Gardens' Neighbourhood/ City

Community Garden	Location	Average income[2]	Neighbourhood/ City Population
Grow Regina Community Garden 1994-2005	Near downtown residential	$33,003	9,345
Yara-Grow Regina Community Garden 2005-present	Middle-class neighbourhood	$69,091	7,600
Yara Community Garden	Near downtown in an older neighbourhood	$45,860	34,156
City Park Community Garden	Near downtown residential	$55,552	4,305

Despite these similarities, each operates within distinct social, physical and historical contexts and has encountered different challenges along the way. The lessons learned from these gardens are valuable for understanding social justice within the larger food system as well as the potential role of community gardens in the food sovereignty movement. Food sovereignty has the ability to embrace community gardens due to its emphasis on active participation and control of citizens over their food system as well as the centrality of the right to produce culturally appropriate, healthy and affordable food.

Grow Regina

The Grow Regina Community Garden in Regina emerged as a food security initiative from the heightened awareness of hunger that followed Mayor Doug Archer's Hunger Report in 1988. In 1993, over twenty local organizations, including the Regina and District Food Bank, Regina Education and Action on Child Hunger (REACH) and the City of Regina, came together to organize the Grow Regina Community Garden on land (near Broad Street and College Avenue) temporarily leased from the provincial government. A search had been made for an appropriate location: this one was chosen as it was close to downtown's apartment residents and inner city neighbourhoods that struggled with hunger and poverty. It was one of the largest community gardens in Regina. Gardening began in 1994 on 127 irrigated plots; this number expanded to 275 plots within four years. At its inauguration in May 1994, it was estimated that 1,100 people could be fed by the food grown in the garden (*Regina Leader-Post* 1994). While gardeners from the surrounding neighbourhoods were given priority, residents from around the city flocked eagerly to this visible and vibrant community garden.

However, in recent years, Grow Regina has faced significant challenges. In 2005, the lease was terminated when the land was sold to new property owners. As an organization whose budget was based on minimal user fees, Grow Regina was financially unable to purchase the land. Politics and bitterness quickly entered into the fray as the previous landowner, the provincial government, sought to close a lucrative land deal. Left without a place to cultivate, the Grow Regina Community Garden moved temporarily to the Wascana Park tree nursery in 2006 before deciding to focus their energies on finding a permanent new location. After consultations and proposal discussions with the City of Regina, they found a new home in city-owned McLeod Park in south Regina. The process of finding a new home was rife with conflict between Grow Regina, the municipal government and previous landowners. Gardeners voiced feelings of frustration and impotence, during their struggle, about bureaucratic obstacles and the lack of transparency in decision making.

With their new garden location and recent sponsorship by Yara, a local nitrogen fertilizer company previously known as Saskferco, Grow Regina hopes to start a new chapter in their operations. Although board members are relieved that their land tenure struggle has been temporarily concluded with a five-year renewable lease from the City of Regina, expectations for their future in a new location are mixed. Some welcome the opportunity to cultivate their garden in a city park, which may mean more stable tenure and the opportunity to incorporate innovative features, while some fear that moving from an inner city location to a well-to-do subdivision may mean a worrisome shift in goals.

Since moving to McLeod Park, Grow Regina has been flourishing. In their first growing season in 2007, 191 plots (75 percent of the garden) were cultivated and 100 percent of the garden plots were occupied in 2008. While many previous tenants continue to garden, residents from the immediate neighbourhood have also joined the garden. In 2008, gardener and leadership morale was high; the board of directors had filled its twelve seats; and new infrastructure plans (including walking paths, fruit trees and a gazebo) have re-energized volunteers.

The volunteers' relationship with the municipal government has also improved; this could be reflective of their changed circumstances. The gardeners' fight to relocate has shown that this group of citizens are serious about the garden and not just following a fad. New gardeners and board members have also re-energized the group; people are focused on future tasks in the garden rather than a more basic fight for survival. The city is also the landowner, which necessitates a closer working relationship. This improvement is a positive sign, one that hopefully points to a municipal willingness to support and foster community gardens in Regina.

Although other community gardens were operating in Regina at the same time as Grow Regina, the goals of this project have set it apart. Their original goals of providing affordable gardening space for people to grow fresh food and working toward community food security have been important and continuous aims. As board member J. Fagan said, "[w]e want to have more than a landlord/tenant relationship — we want to think and plan around food security."[3] One way they do that is by offering a number of sponsored plots for low-income gardeners. Grow Regina also has a close relationship to the Regina and District Food Bank, which has operated as their "parent" organization, and gardeners donate 15 percent of their produce to the food bank annually.

The ability of community gardening to speak to all ages, incomes and backgrounds is demonstrated by the vibrant diversity among these gardeners. Its ranks include both young and old, immigrants, people of rural and urban backgrounds, low-income families and individuals, schools, single parents and people with disabilities. Yet some dominant trends are evident, including the heavy involvement of seniors, particularly in leadership roles, women and people from farms or rural communities who have moved to the city. These trends are shared by the other two community gardens.

Yara Community Garden

Of the three community gardens, the Yara Community Garden in Moose Jaw is the newcomer having begun operations in 2006. Its early success has fostered a high level of excitement and future anticipation among gardeners and steering committee members alike. Its birth followed a similar trajectory to Grow Regina; a coalition of community organizations concerned about food security, led by the non-profit cooperative Connecting as Neighbours, provided the impetus for the garden. Ideas for the creation of a community garden had been percolating a few years before its inauguration on Homes Street, located on city-owned land adjacent to the Canadian Pacific Railway (CPR) tracks. In line with its environmental goals, this land had been "re-claimed" from an industrial area across the tracks from the CPR diesel engine shop, where engines from Western Canada undergo repairs; it had been polluted with high levels of mercury and other heavy metals. By using the land for organic gardening, the gardeners hoped to have a positive impact on this environment. The garden's original area of approximately forty-three plots, servicing more than seventy gardeners and their families, was too small to accommodate all those interested and the garden had doubled in size for the 2008 growing season. Although the garden attracts participants from the adjacent older neighbourhoods, gardeners from any area of the city are welcomed.

This community garden has a unique relationship with its corporate sponsor, Yara. In 2005, Yara (then Saskferco) donated $30,000 to the project with more funding promised in the future. With this money, the community garden was able to invest in infrastructure as well as fund a seasonal gardening coordinator position. This relationship has benefits: not only does the garden rely on this financial and material support, but the company also appreciates being involved in the community and achieving positive media attention.

Yet a cautionary note must be sounded regarding the possibility of acquiring money with strings attached to the company's expectations. As an example, Yara challenged the garden's organic production and education practices when the garden tried to host a public workshop on organic composting. As title sponsor of the garden, the company felt the public promotion of such activities clashed with the company's image as a fertilizer company and therefore restricted the garden's public advocacy of organic gardening. The implications of such a demonstrated clash in values are troubling and should act as a caution for other gardens seeking sponsorship, for that money may be tied to the funder's image and values. Yet gardeners at the Yara Community

Garden accepted their sponsorship pragmatically, as many non-profits do, because it had struggled to operate without financial support and felt it was necessary to their survival.

This sponsorship influence may pose a contradiction to the goals of food sovereignty and raises an uncomfortable question: can sponsored community gardens like the Yara Community Garden still practise food sovereignty? I believe they can, given that control over the garden and its activities ultimately lies with the gardeners, who have demonstrated their commitment to the goals of food security, community building, empowerment, participatory decision making and the recognition of holistic sustainability. While sponsorship should be problematized and considered carefully by community gardens, it must be remembered that these gardens often have few other means of monetary support, which is important for infrastructure and upkeep. Gardeners may face financial sponsorship pragmatically as a means of supporting the positive work they are doing.

The Yara gardeners speak of food security as a primary goal of their garden. Affordable access to gardening space, and being able to grow healthy, nutritious food is important to this group of gardeners. Gardeners donate excess produce to the local food bank; for example, the Yara employees' plot donated all of its produce — 500 lbs of potatoes and carrots — to the Moose Jaw Food Bank in 2007. Education, particularly increasing environmental awareness, is also a stated goal of the garden, and one it enthusiastically pursues through various innovations. As the only community garden currently operating in Moose Jaw, it also strives to build a sense of community among gardeners. While this garden operates in a different context from Regina and Saskatoon through its unique funding situation, the language and practices of claiming physical and social spaces for growing food and building community speaks to its ability to pursue the goals of food sovereignty.

City Park Community Garden

This community garden in Saskatoon's City Park welcomed gardeners from the neighbourhood in 2003. Its creation was driven by a dedicated group of individuals and assisted by the Child Hunger and Education Program (CHEP), a local non-profit food security organization that acted as an advocate for the garden, and for the City of Saskatoon. The impetus behind the garden was a merger of community and environmental aspirations. Two of the original leaders had initiated a community compost pile that continues today in the garden, and environmentally conscious gardeners in City Park wholeheartedly endorse an organic focus. The ability to grow food under their own guidance and control is an important aspect for these gardeners. Supported by the local community association, the gardeners also seek to create a space of community building through daily interactions concerning the garden and special events. In 2007, the garden doubled in size to accommodate growing interest.

This community garden holds other important distinctions. It was the first to be cultivated in a public park, Wilson Park, in Saskatoon. Only residents of City Park neighbourhood are permitted to participate in this community garden, making it a source of envy from nearby areas. It also operates completely free of money: the City of Saskatoon has contributed the land and water supplies, while the infrastructure, including a new shed, was donated by individuals, with the result that gardeners do not have to pay a rental fee. From the start, the garden's design enabled the creation of a place of beauty for its participants. The gardeners' sense of ownership of the park through their gardening efforts and increased use of this public space by residents and their families are visible results of the success of this effort.

Paint Me a Picture: Perceptions of Community Gardens

Although each garden has emerged from different contexts and is driven by different people, these gardeners share common experiences. Community gardeners described three intersecting social spaces where people garden together, overcome challenges and build their own unique community. Gardeners are often driven by common motivations and reap similar benefits. For many participants, a love of gardening has been a lifelong passion and, although an enjoyment of food production is an obvious motivation, it is one that cannot be overemphasized. Community gardeners pursue this love of gardening in a social fashion; the interaction between diverse peoples, the creation of friendships and the sense of building a unique and satisfying community are powerful incentives. Sometimes, as gardener G. Androsoff said, "the social aspects are larger than the physical food benefits at the end of the day."

Along with food production and social outcomes, like meeting people, making friends and sharing produce and knowledge, positive environmental benefits were highlighted. Gardening allows people to reconcile their existing environmental beliefs and philosophies with practice. This includes the implementation of organic horticulture, interaction with nature and learning positive environmental practices such as composting. As mentioned by gardener L. Probert, there can be a strong educational aspect to gardening, particularly for children, since it teaches them that "everything has its place… that things aren't just bought, that it all comes from someplace."

Such a cultivation of positive environmental interaction is a key pillar of community gardens, for they offer ways of reconnecting people to their food and the natural world around them. The physical acts of working in a garden to grow our own food before preparing and eating it offers a deep and immediate reconnection to the food system. In this way, community gardens offer a solution to the ideological problem of "distancing," the physical and intellectual separation of people from their food (Kneen 1989). A renewed physical relationship also relates to a spiritual sense of interconnectedness: gardening physically and spiritually connects these men and women with the earth, soil and nature. These feelings are evident in the statement of the gardener L. Sauer who said "I enjoy working in the earth — I feel more human," while another gardener, B. Colenutt, explained that "I come from a culture where they believe they need to give back to the earth and we haven't been doing a good job of that." That community gardens facilitate this reconnection to nature offers an argument for their spiritual relevance.

Unsurprisingly, capable leaders, in both an individual and collective sense, are vital to the creation and sustainability of community gardens. What is perhaps less understood is that the necessary skills for leadership include political knowledge and the ability to manoeuvre within city hall, which is the political structure most relevant to the continuing existence of these gardens. The need for political savvy has resulted in a few gardeners shying away from leadership roles; however, it is clear that the structure of these gardens does require democratic decision making and committee operations, encouraging the development of these skills.

The creation of a unique community within these gardens requires effort from both leaders and gardeners, and its establishment is important to the gardens' success. Community is commonly conceived as people sharing and working toward common goals. The diversity of garden participants and interactions within the social space created are also considered as key aspects of community. A sense of shared goals and identity, and their residual positive energy, spills into the surrounding neighbourhood and/or larger city. A positive view of community, cultivated through these gardening activities, affected some residents' views of the neighbourhood: they experienced a greater feeling of personal safety when walking alone in the area or interacting with other residents. A sense of belonging and importance is also fostered through such participation: "I've become much more confident about my place in the community. I feel I'm involved and belong — the garden was a part of this," said City Park gardener T. Wolf.

Community Gardens as Sites of Political Resistance

Most gardeners are humble about the size and impact of their own local community garden, while recognizing the importance of people working on these collective projects and goals across Canada. Yet the idea of these community gardens as an alternative and a site for resistance to the global food system is accepted by some gardeners, but dismissed by others. There is skepticism about the size and scale of these community gardens; they are not seen as able to pose a true alternative to the industrial food system unless there is a dramatic increase in the size and number of gardens and participants.

The limits of the Saskatchewan growing climate and season, as well as our dependence on a wide variety of foods beyond locally-sourced vegetables, are also pointed out as limitations to their effectiveness as alternatives to the mainstream food system. There are similar doubts regarding these gardens as a form of resistance to the global food system. Many gardeners conceded that community gardening could be a form of resistance, although few were likely to personally identify with this sentiment. A. Swenson, a gardener involved in the Yara Community Garden says, "In talking to the gardeners, I don't think they see it as rebellion against grocery stores, they just enjoy it." When framed as a source of food production in a global system, these gardens are perceived as ineffectual against industrial food giants. For the gardeners, the language of "resistance" is also perceived as too negative, and therefore not reflective of the positive work that the community gardens are doing. Only a few gardeners, such as S. Gibson of Yara and F. Hunter of Grow Regina, framed their actions as resistance, stating that "the success [of this community garden] in this part of the world shows there can be resistance" and that "if people are gardening without chemicals, they're making a statement against megafarms, but it's a small gesture."

Can community gardens be a source of resistance to the global industrialized food system, even if most gardeners do not see their gardens in this way? While gardeners are able to situate themselves and their actions within the dominant food system, and agree that they could present an alternative to sourcing food from industrial giants, most do not see the gardens as a form of resistance. Resistance is interpreted as defiant and aggressive: this could be attributed in part to the vilification of current forms of resistance in the mainstream media, examples of which include isolated incidents of violent anti-globalization protest. This narrow portrayal blinds people from equating resistance with creating positive alternatives. As a result, few understand themselves as resisting the negative aspects of the global food system, just as only a few would consider themselves to be radical, politicized citizens. The example of the Yara Community Garden particularly supports this view of non-radical action, since the gardeners were willing to accept corporate sponsorship to achieve their goals.

Yet community gardens may be a form of resistance to the dominant industrial food system. Antonio Gramsci's theory of counter-hegemony, defined as resistance to powerful minority interests accepted by the majority of people through a balance of force and consent (1971), is applicable to the practice of community gardening. By creating an alternative space to produce local food, community gardens physically resist the dominant methods of producing and distributing food. They also provide a social space that fosters the exploration of new ideas and alternative ways of being, which can provide the intellectual basis of counter-hegemony.

This exploration of community gardens demonstrates that these spaces are much more than just places for cultivating food. A host of motivations, benefits and understandings lie beneath the simple rental of plots to grow vegetables. This complexity is encouraging, as is the ability of these gardens to emerge as local responses to specific concerns, for this points to flexibility in goals and agendas. These three community gardens can be viewed as more than just food producing ventures: their attention to building a community space, environmental education and participatory decision making speaks strongly to the principles of food sovereignty. Indeed, it is possible to frame these community gardens as food sovereignty practices. By doing so, community gardening may be a catalyst for local change in our food system.

Community Gardens as a Local Practice of Food Sovereignty

Community gardens fit well within the food sovereignty framework of active participation, control over the food system and the right to produce. As both producers and consumers, gardeners actively participate in the decision making and social structures of community gardens. Discussion and decision making take place in both informal gardeners' meetings to manage the garden operations and formal board or committee meetings. Being involved in decision making processes offers opportunities to all gardeners to learn skills needed for participation and leadership. Gardener involvement and leadership impart skills, confidence and sense of accomplishment and pride; it ensures a visible presence of diversity in the community gardens.

All community gardeners also have the opportunity to be involved in the physical spaces created. The participation of people of different abilities and income levels is aided through physical and financial assistance, including sponsored plots, raised garden beds and accessible locations. Because their physical involvement as gardeners is facilitated through these means, their ability to be involved in the resulting social space is also enabled. A strong sense of community can therefore include all participants.

Being community-minded is also linked with being civic-minded: gardener participation in policy making internal and external to the gardens is encouraged. Internal policy making is evident through input in gardener manuals and annual decision making. External policies, such as city policies dealing with community gardens, also bear the mark of gardener participation. As a result of the actions and leadership of two gardens, Saskatoon and Regina now have municipal policies to deal more effectively with future community gardens.

Intimately related to a discussion of participation is the possibility for greater access, power and control of people over their food system. These elements are vital for confirming the practice of food sovereignty. Participation in a community garden offers people important access to the food system.

In the dominant food system, the primary form of access for consumers is through the purchase of food items. The relationship of producers is also mediated through the sale of food items and the purchase of off-farm productive inputs. Although community gardens are often concerned about rent to operate infrastructure such as water, they have also found creative means of financial inclusion, including sponsored plots, participation through the plots of community-based organizations or operating exclusively by donation. By doing so, they encourage the involvement of people who may have been previously denied monetary access to full participation in the food system.

Greater power by gardeners over their lives is cultivated through the gardens' "culture of participation." Gardener D. Mitchell (Yara) pointed out that this culture is not emphasized or taught in mainstream institutions like schools, workplaces or even families; it is up to social spaces like these gardens to teach the skills necessary for participation. Within community gardens, this culture enables people's empowerment by helping them achieve greater control and ownership over their food production and its social spaces. All of these gardens are controlled and managed by the gardeners themselves, rather than by outside bodies like municipal authorities, corporations or non-profit organizations. The fact that gardeners make important decisions regarding the operation and future of the garden serves to incorporate an important aspect of autonomy. This theme of self-determination is also a principle food sovereignty.

Notions of ownership are also applicable to gardeners' lives. Rather than feeling like consumers buffeted by uncontrollable actions and events in the food system, they are empowered by their personal ownership of a plot of land and its produce. This sense of empowerment includes feelings about control: "the control you have over your life when you're able to grow your own food" (R. Forbes, Yara). Thus gardeners experience a greater sense of command over the food eaten and the manner in which it was produced. The responsibility of gardeners over their individual plot, and collective spaces like flowerbeds, compost heaps and gardening sheds also fosters a sense of ownership. That gardeners' control extends beyond their private plots demonstrates that these types of gardens are open to alternative notions of ownership. Many gardeners remarked on the significance of control and ownership, for it is prominently lacking in our dominant food system. Its local application can be very empowering. For example, gardener T. Wolf says, "An important observation I've made is the pride people took in their gardens. Maybe they hadn't owned land [before]. It's really a stewardship concept — this is my land and I'll take care of it."

Just as food sovereignty advocates for an alternative international space to discuss and determine food and agricultural policy — a central aspect of equitable participation — community gardens create a democratic space in their operations. Community gardens are also an alternative space to practice social and environmental ideas, and to hone the awareness and agency of participants. The lack of a rigid model of what community gardens are and how they should operate has meant that they flourish according to local conditions and are led by the passion and creativity of their gardeners. These conditions enable a great amount of autonomy and control in how community gardens operate as social spaces; they hold innumerable possibilities for affecting positive local change within the gardens and their surrounding communities. Although they are constrained by local land regulations, community gardeners' involvement in policy decisions can lead to the possibility of regulatory changes amenable to the gardens.

Any discussion of policy regarding community gardens must point out the centrality of secure land tenure for these gardens. A key demand of food sovereignty is that the people of a territory have the right to produce food in a way that works best for their sovereignty and environment. These community gardens address this right to produce food locally. Although exercising this practical human right through the production of food in a social space is rewarding, it also presents their greatest challenge due to development and political pressures, in both a contemporary and historical sense. The right to produce cannot be realized unless a community garden has the stability of affordable and secure lands; this is aptly demonstrated by Grow Regina's struggle to find a new gardening location. When community gardens have secure tenure, they are able to operate in ways that guarantee the right to produce food.

The importance of secure tenure in the urban landscape points to the pivotal role municipal governments could and should play in supporting community gardens. Urban green space and community gardening are linked as important elements of cities: the support for gardens in parks reflect this. Crafting and supporting municipal policies that encourages the creation and maintenance of these spaces is important. There is great potential for urban planners to incorporate these spaces into new urban or suburban developments as well as in downtown and inner-city neighbourhoods. Financial support and resources from cities can also be guarantors of success. This support would signal the recognition by municipal planners and authorities of these gardens as an important urban feature and practice.

As a space receptive to alternative ideas, different types of knowledge are respected and appreciated. Food sovereignty recognizes traditional or alternative knowledge as important contributors to food and agriculture, rather than dismissing it as non-scientific. Within the dominant food system, scientific experts have often scorned and dismissed the agricultural knowledge and practices of peasants and Indigenous peoples, which can be viewed as subjugated knowledge. Community gardens and other food sovereignty practices offer social and physical spaces that encourage and foster such alternative knowledge. The multi-faceted practice of organic gardening in these community gardens is an example of this, for it encompasses techniques and understandings of organic ranging from insect control based on family kitchen tips to the efficient management of compost piles.

Many of the social and physical practices of community gardens are based on holistic ideas of sustainability that incorporate social, economic and environmental goals. Economically, these community gardens encourage lessened seasonal dependence on grocery stores; they also make it possible for participants to save money. The creation of community and the pursuit of positive social goals, from supporting local food banks to encouraging diversity within the gardens, support social sustainability. Environmentally, these gardens encourage organic gardening by banning chemical pesticides and practicing composting. The Yara Community Garden is considered a local, even regional, environmental leader for its implementation of a green roof and a composting toilet. Practices within these gardens have encouraged deepened personal environmental convictions, as well as a change in attitudes and practices. This is seen in the recognition of the importance of urban green space, land reclamation and stewardship, based upon the gardeners' positive experiences. Another common theme, particularly for Saskatoon and Regina, where gardeners experienced the successful implementation of their community garden on park land is the use of public parks as a holistic and useful space. The tenure of these two gardens in public parks speaks to the possibility of preserving these parks as useful urban green spaces.

As spaces that encourage local food production and community building, community gardens have the potential to be a strong player within the food sovereignty movement in Canada, particularly within an urban context. Although they do not demonstrate a perfect practice of social justice or food sovereignty, they exhibit commendable social and environmental goals and practices. The food sovereignty movement can embrace the practice of community gardens due to its inclusive nature, its wide-reaching social, political and environmental goals, and its ability to give structure to projects that go beyond their original food-security goals. Perhaps recognition from the food sovereignty movement would enable community gardens to gain acceptance as permanent urban fixtures and would facilitate stable land tenure. By food sovereignty embracing community gardens, we can ensure that this practice and its benefits remain an important aspect of our food production within an increasingly urbanized global context.

Notes

1. Please note that in the remainder of this chapter the gardens are given agency as they refer to both the physical space and the collective of people engaged in this space.
2. For the Grow Regina Community Garden (1994-2005), the average income is taken from statistics on the neighbourhoods of Gladmer Park, Core and the Transitional Area, as those areas were targeted for potential community gardens (City of Regina 2004a, 2004b, 2004c, 2004d). The income shown for the Yara Community garden is the average city-wide income since gardeners participate from all city areas (Moose Jaw REDA 2008a, 2008b). All statistics, including those for the neighbourhoods of Lakeview (City of Regina 2004a, 2004b, 2004c, 2004d) and City Park (City of Saskatoon 2003). are based on 2001 census information.
3. Community gardeners were interviewed in 2007 and 2008. Permission to use names was granted.

References

Bassett, T.J. 1981. "Reaping on the Margins: A Century of Community Gardening in America." *Landscape* 25, 2.

Beach, G. 1915. Reply to Sgt. J.L. McCullough, Chairman of Assiniboia Board of Trade from City Clerk. City of Regina Archives. Unpublished correspondence. February 16.

____. 1914a. Letter to C.F. Lidster, City Auditor from City Clerk. City of Regina Archives. Unpublished correspondence. October 10.

____. 1914b. Letter to C.F. Lidster, City Auditor from City Clerk. City of Regina Archives. Unpublished correspondence. October 21.

Burrell, H.M. 1917, Letter to Regina Mayor and City Council from Minister of Agriculture. City of Regina Archives. February 13.

City of Regina. 2004a. "Core: 2001 Neighbourhood Profile." Community Services Department: Urban Planning Division. At <regina.ca/pdfs/Core.pdf>.

____. 2004b. "Gladmer Park: 2001 Neighbourhood Profile." Community Services Department: Urban Planning Division. At <regina.ca/pdfs/Gladmer%20Park.pdf>.

____. 2004c. "Lakeview: 2001 Neighbourhood Profile." Community Services Department: Urban Planning Division. At <regina.ca/pdfs/Lakeview.pdf>.

____. 2004d. "Transitional Area: 2001 Neighbourhood Profile." Community Services Department: Urban Planning Division. At <regina.ca/pdfs/Transitional.pdf>.

City of Saskatoon. 2003. "City Park: 2003 Neighbourhood Profile." City Planning Branch. At <saskatoon.ca/org/city_planning/resources/neighbourhood_demographics/2003/city_park.pdf>.

Crouch, D., and C. Ward. 1988. *The Allotment: Its Landscape and Culture*. London: Faber and Faber.

Gramsci, A. 1971. *Selections from the Prison Notebooks of Antonio Gramsci*. Q. Hoare and G.N. Smith (eds.). New York: International Publishers.

Kneen, B. 1989. *From Land to Mouth: Understanding the Food System*. Toronto: NC Press.

Lawson. L. 2005. *City Bountiful: A Century of Community Gardening in America*.

Berkeley: University of California Press.

Leader-Post. 1935. "Relief Plot Garden Seed Board Worry." March 18.

Macoun, W.T. 1917. "Garden Making on Vacant Lots and the Home Vegetable Garden." Pamphlet no. 13. Dominion of Canada, Department of Agriculture Experimental Farms.

___. 1914. "The Home Vegetable Garden and a Patriotic Gardening Competition." Pamphlet No. 13. Dominion of Canada, Department of Agriculture Experimental Farms.

Moose Jaw REDA Inc. 2008a. "2007 Covered Population Statistics." Sourced from Saskatchewan Health Covered Population Statistics, 2007. <At mjreda.com/>.

___. 2008b. "Average Salary and Incomes." At <mjreda.sasktelwebhosting.com/economic_profile/average_salary_incomes.html>.

Regina Leader-Post. 1994. "Campaign Begins." May 25.

Scott, E. 2005. "Cockney Plots: Working Class Politics and Garden Allotments in London's East End, 1890–1918." MA thesis. Saskatoon: University of Saskatchewan.

SHA. 1977. *History of the Saskatchewan Horticultural Association 1927–1977*. Regina: Self-published.

Sheard, K. 1978. *Regina Horticultural Society: Historical Notes from the Period 1901–1978*. Regina: Regina Horticultural Society.

10. FOOD SOVEREIGNTY IN THE GOLDEN HORSESHOE REGION OF ONTARIO

Harriet Friedmann

Southern Ontario is a highly urban region of ten million people. Just under 40 percent live in the dominant city, Toronto, while most of the rest live in and around smaller cities and towns which together constitute an almost continuous urbanized region stretching along Lake Ontario between Niagara Falls and Oshawa. In a dramatic reversal of immigration history, in which newcomers came mostly to farm, the arrival of the present generation of immigrants coincided with the development of global markets in food and agriculture. Immigrants have had little incentive or opportunity to connect with an older generation of European-origin farmers, while those farmers have often preferred to take advantage of opportunities to sell their land to companies building houses and shopping malls (or to reorient to export markets), rather than connect with the diverse, young, cosmopolitan newcomers.

Food sovereignty is a movement led by those who grow food, raise animals and capture fish in ways that are very different from those utilized in the industrial and trade-based system. It is a movement of peasants and farmers[1] that arose in response to trade agreements that favour the takeover by transnational corporate supply chains of farming systems that are embedded in particular social, cultural and ecological contexts. Furthermore, by most accounts, food sovereignty is an increasingly important issue in the North as well as the South (IAASTD 2009).

What, then, does food sovereignty mean for a largely urban region? How can a politics created by small farmers linked across North and South find a home in an urbanized region like the Golden Horseshoe region of Ontario? These questions are really about the relations between countryside and city, and between farmers and urban dwellers. As such, their answers are relevant across the North and much of the South.

In a highly urbanized region in which specialized industrial farms predominate, the paths towards food sovereignty are complex. For one thing, sustainable, mixed farming faces multiple obstacles: conversion of farmland to other uses, low farm incomes relative to many urban occupations and a mismatch between the types of crops appropriate to near-urban and urban agriculture (fresh vegetables, fruits, eggs, meat, etc.) and the single crop or livestock farms (mainly dairy, soy and maize) inherited from a time when these were located farther from cities. Despite excellent work by the National Farmers Union (NFU) in Ontario and organizations I describe below, the interests of industrial farmers, with little interest in food sovereignty goals, dominate in provincial policies. Second, many non-farmers support food sovereignty, but many of the people working towards a just and sustainable food system have little contact with farming or farmers. The good news is that city people and agro-ecological farmers, both actual and hopeful, have much in common.

A conference on food sovereignty was held in Toronto in 2009 to launch a conversation across food sectors, including farmers, urban growers, social enterprises, academics and justice and sustainability activists. The discussion was sparked by speakers from the National Farmers Union of Canada, Food Secure Canada (FSC), FoodShare, the Toronto Food Strategy (TFS), Sustain Ontario, the People's Food Policy Project (PFPP) and FoodNet Ontario; it was sponsored by FoodShare, FoodNet, Heifer International and the FoodShed Project, as a framework for understanding Southern Ontario as an ecological, social and political context.[2] The event generated over two hundred ideas that were summarized by a FoodShare staff writer into six categories:

1) Increase and focus support on localized food systems
2) Support farmers
3) Maintain, develop and redevelop food infrastructure
4) Educate people about food
5) Advance social inclusion
6) Create coordinated and enabling policy. (FoodShare 2009: 16)

This set of themes is reasonably comprehensive as a first step in a conversation between urban and rural interests about a just and sustainable food system. It points to some significant gaps — why do people need to be educated about food, and what do they need to know? How can social inclusion of people who cannot afford enough food of any kind be reconciled with support for farmers who need decent prices? The Toronto conference was also a first step at bridging the great gap that has arisen between town and farm, partly because of trade, but also because of changes in demography and culture. It is clear that the success of food sovereignty depends on overcoming the division between urban and rural lands and activities (Roberts 2008; Steel 2009a).

What is at stake in the region is, in part, a lost coherence as an agri-food region. Re-establishing this coherence requires a discussion of how to "scale up," or how to employ what Roberts (2008) calls the "fusion" way of doing food. According to Roberts, a "scaling up" of food system change involves "joining up" vibrant initiatives so that food sovereignty can shift from the margins to the centre of economy, policy and society. This use of the term, "scaling up," is becoming common, but should be distinguished from the "growth imperative" imposed on corporate farms and other food businesses; the food sovereignty idea of scaling up involves a networked agri-food economy composed of small private and social enterprises embedded in the natural, social and cultural features of a region (Day-Farnsworth et al. 2009; Nasr et al. 2010; Friedmann 2007). The idea of scaling up networks, rather than enterprises, is increasingly important to social innovation (Wheatley and Frieze 2006). While still in its infancy, some work has begun in the application of this idea to food sovereignty (usually without using the term "scaling up") in rural and urban parts of the region.

Historical Context

Historically, the economic and cultural connections between town and farm in southern Ontario were not only denser but also more fluid than today. As the wheat frontier moved west in the late 1800s (Fowke 1957), farms specialized in other products such as dairy, fruits, vegetables and livestock, while processing industries such as cheese factories multiplied to serve local markets (Menzies 1994). At the same time, there was a great deal of food production in the city of Toronto — even cows were kept for milk (Cohen 1988). Certainly the cultures of city and farm, however different they may have seemed at the time, were deeply connected culturally and demographically.

As food and agriculture became industrialized, however, many gaps began to appear: between genders, as dairy moved from women's work on the farm to men's work in factories, and between growers, artisans and eaters (Cohen 1988). As cities grew and farmers diminished in numbers and were located farther from the city, the groundwork was laid for prices to become the main connection between growers and eaters (Kneen 1989). Production of "cheap food," still the bane of farmers today, began with settlers, who were forced to exploit soils to export crops to Britain, and intensified during the deeper industrialization of farming in the past fifty years. However, for labour-intensive products such as fruits and vegetables and pasture-fed livestock, the push to "get big or get out" came from imports. These imports were increasingly organized directly by supermarkets, as they took control of the food system in the 1980s and especially the 1990s.

A capsule history of the dilemmas of food sovereignty in the region around Toronto, therefore, goes like this. Toronto was built on farmland which is the best in Canada and among the most fertile in North America. In the 1960s, specialized livestock farmers in Ontario (e.g., hogs, dairy) created marketing boards which succeeded in limiting vertical integration by processors[3] (McMurchy 1990). However, while farmers continue to this day to produce milk and other supply-managed products for Ontario markets, their farms became larger in size and fewer in number. A shift in field crops towards corn and soybeans for livestock feed eliminated much of the diversity of crops and livestock needed by urban eaters. During the period 1945–1980, Canada shared with governments all over the world a focus on basic agricultural commodities, designed to assure enough calories and proteins to populations, as well as to stabilize increasingly specialized farm sectors (Friedmann 1993).

Until the 1990s, international trade in fresh fruits and vegetables was very limited. As was the case in most of the world's cities, in 1950, the fruits and vegetables sold in Toronto and other Ontario cities still came from surrounding orchards and fields. Small farmers delivered their crops either to a network of shops, facilitated by the (still) publicly owned Ontario Food Terminal (which handles imports as well as local produce), or to a network of processors — the large tomato canneries and other vegetable operations southwest of the metropolis and a web of abattoirs serving local livestock farmers. Many growers formed marketing boards: today the newest agricultural entrants, greenhouses, continue to do so (OMAFRA 2005).

Meanwhile, increasing urbanization in Southern Ontario created an almost continual urbanized region called the "Golden Horseshoe." While the city of Toronto contains 2.6 million people, an additional 7.4 million live in rapidly growing suburbs, smaller cities and towns, from Oshawa in the east to Niagara Falls in the southwest. If regional agricultural markets for fresh produce and livestock had been able to grow in tandem with cities and towns, farmers might have found a vibrant regional market (Winne 2008). Farming might have had a chance to stay connected to urban consumers and be renewed, both economically and culturally, as consumer tastes changed and as new people with farming skills arrived in the region. Indeed, agriculture did grow in tandem with cities for decades, until cars made it possible for cities to sprawl and trucks made it easy to move food long distances for trade. The same roads that, together with cheap fossil fuel, made it seem more efficient to move fresh fruits and vegetables long distances to urban markets, also competed with farmland, as did housing estates and shopping centres designed around automobile use. Consequently, the very rich farmland, stretching from Niagara to the southwest and to the Holland Marsh to the northeast and beyond, came under increasing pressure for conversion to other uses. Growers were squeezed out of regional markets as cities expanded: by 1986 Ontario orchard acreage had already fallen by 30 percent from its level in 1941 (Gayler 1994: 284). Total farm area in Ontario, which had been 22.8 million acres in 1931, decreased to 13.3 million acres in 2006 (Statistics Canada 2006c). The rest is in danger of being paved over if present market rule continues — though there are some recent signs that this may not happen.

As retail and processing industries became centralized, regional food industries and traders were marginalized. In contrast to supply-managed sectors, notably dairy, where farms consolidated but still supplied regional markets, vegetable, fruit and small livestock operations suffered. When canneries, jam operations and other processing industries closed, for instance, Niagara orchards and market gardens lost their most stable buyers. At the same time, supermarket supply chains spread across the continent and even the world. The result has been that the Golden Horseshoe is left with a "missing infrastructure" for a regional food system (Baker et al. 2010) — one which applies disproportionately to fruit and vegetable processing (Carter-Whitney and Miller 2010: 12–13).

The other route for farmers was to shift from diverse crops for a growing regional population to specialized exports. The Holland Marsh, located at the northern edge of Toronto, is one of the most fertile regions in North America. It is still very productive farmland with 135 farmers producing more than $50 million worth of vegetables on ten thousand acres (Reinhart 2009). More than half of the produce from the Holland Marsh is exported. Farmers have concentrated on a small number of crops, especially carrots and onions, to achieve economies of scale suited to exports. Strangely, these same crops are also imported for local consumption, mainly through supermarket supply chains (Reinhart 2009).

Given the combined constraints of the consolidation of local agriculture to a reduced variety of crops, oriented to export, the increased trade and import of fruits and vegetables, and increased urbanization, the renewal of farming as part of a regional food system presents an enormous challenge. Both land and labour are difficult to find and protect in an integrated way (Roberts 2008). Although the Golden Horseshoe contains about a quarter of Canada's population and has, according to the official Canada Land Inventory (Ontario Farmland Trust 2010), more than half of Canada's best farmland, both this farmland and the farmers who have based their livelihoods on it are under great pressure from powerful urban interests to convert to urban uses. Not only do farmers disagree about whether to preserve or sell remaining farmland, but they are also faced with a huge problem of generational renewal. Many farmers' children have moved into other occupations, and those who do wish to inherit often intend to farm differently from their parents — moving towards sustainable, intensive crops and specialty livestock, often on smaller farms than the acres for corn and soybeans that are typical of the older generation.

Ontario farmers understandably respond to loss of markets and speculative land prices by sometimes wanting to cash out. They are aging — of all

Ontario farm operators counted by the Census of Agriculture in 2001, 37 percent were 55 years or older; of these, 16.9 percent were 65 or over and another 20.6 percent expected to turn 65 by 2011 (Statistics Canada 2003). Farmers who have worked for very little income during their lifetimes are tempted to sell farmland, where they can, to agents of urban sprawl to finance their retirement.

The challenge of turning this around is compounded by a deep cultural gap. In the past two decades, a vast social and cultural gap has grown up between young multicultural cities and aging farmers who are mainly of European descent. The whole region, not only Toronto, is the site of an intersection of transnational diasporas (Cohen 1997). Cities have become "global" in a new way as large streams of immigrants retain active cultural ties to groups in other countries (Sassen 2002). For instance, South Asian communities in Canada are actively engaged with those in the U.K., Trinidad, South Africa, India, Pakistan and many other countries. Not only are half of Metropolitan Toronto's population of 5.5 million born outside of Canada, but an equal number of new Canadians live in surrounding municipalities (Toronto 2010; Statistics Canada 2006b). The last census shows that some of the fastest growing municipalities, such as Markham, have as many as two-thirds of their populations listed as visible minorities (Statistics Canada 2006a). Because these immigrants mostly arrived in a time of increasing world food trade, they found it easy to import traditional prepared foods and ingredients, as well as fresh ones, that suited their traditional and cultural preferences. This contrasts sharply with prior waves of immigration in which many new Canadians became farmers, while urban dwellers, both old and new, prepared and ate the crops and livestock grown mostly by surrounding farmers.

Emerging Potentials for Food Sovereignty

Renewal of food and farming depends on bringing people of all kinds — eaters, growers and everyone in between — into new and increasingly conscious relationships with each other and with land. Those relationships must first provide the conditions in which people can protect agricultural land and think creatively about all the ways and places they can grow food. Second, they must find a new policy hinge for understanding how to link growing food and eating — for example, a focus on health policy can reconnect land and food that have been disconnected from one another by the market as it has worked so far. Third, they must build on the potential of agri-food for green economic renewal. Fourth, they must use public education to promote food literacy and skills. Finally, a regional infrastructure to (re)connect growers and eaters after many years of disconnection must reach across the divide that has developed between rural and urban cultures. Fortunately, all of these changes are taking place. If these factors can be connected by conscious practices and policies, food sovereignty becomes imaginable.

Renewing Agriculture: The Greenbelt, Urban Agriculture, Rewarding Sustainable Farms

The government of Ontario introduced a pioneering policy for environmental protection in 2005. The Greenbelt, the largest in the world, is 1.8 million acres of provincially protected land covering a good portion of the Golden Horseshoe. It encompasses diverse natural landscapes and watersheds, hundreds of towns and villages and over seven thousand farms, mostly family or sole proprietors, which account for over 50 percent of the land (for more details see <greenbelt.ca/about-the-ontario-greenbelt>). This comprises some of Canada's most valuable agricultural land, and its farms produce fresh fruits and vegetables, dairy, beef, pork and poultry products, sheep and lambs, wine, mushrooms, maple syrup, flowers and plants. It includes the historically fertile Niagara region, now shifting from soft fruits to vineyards and greenhouses, and the Holland Marsh (Friends of the Greenbelt 2010). But there are many unprotected areas, like the borders of the Greenbelt, that are the focus of intense speculation and put pressure on the Greenbelt itself.

The Greenbelt, which must be renewed as a protected area in 2015, offers an opportunity for supporting farming and connections with consumers through reconstruction of infrastructure to create a regional food system based on sustainable small farms. However, the Greenbelt faces two major limits that need to be addressed. First, the Greenbelt legislation did not consider or include farmers in its creation. Thus, there was little legislation supporting farmers in the Greenbelt. For example, it did not include changes to policies, such as taxation (that currently discourages value-added on-farm food processing), to better support farmers within the Greenbelt. Moreover, it did not address the problem encountered by many who wish to enter farming of accessing good farmland, especially near the markets of the Golden Horseshoe. Consequently, there is now considerable opposition from an alliance of "developers" and farmers who wish to realize speculative gains from selling farmland. Second, the Greenbelt itself is full of unprotected "holes" as many areas surrounding the smaller and most rapidly growing municipalities of the Golden Horseshoe reserved land in their outskirts, including farmland, for future urban expansion. These "holes" are called the "white belt." The perimeters of these holes, together with the external boundaries of the Greenbelt, have led to serious speculative pressure at the many edges of the Greenbelt.

Urban and peri-urban agriculture are also growing. Yet urban-rural divisions have left a policy legacy that inhibits urban and peri-urban food production and sales. Creative civil society initiatives are pointing the way towards identifying regulatory barriers and seeking ways to resolve problems specific to crops and livestock in cities (Nasr et al. 2010). New links across jurisdictions have been created by two pioneering partnerships between the City of Toronto and the Toronto and Region Conservation Authority (TRCA): the Toronto Urban Farm at Black Creek Pioneer Village, near to one of the most marginal urban neighbourhoods in the Jane-Finch area; and the FarmStart McVean New Farmers Project which helps new Canadians experiment with adapting crops to the region, located in a conservation area near Toronto in the City of Brampton.[4] For example, one East Indian farmer at McVean Farm proudly described to me the two varieties of coriander, named after his children, which he has bred to suit both local conditions and his taste. Nearby plots on conservation authority land included new crops from Thailand, Ghana and other countries. Crossing jurisdictions also includes work by the Ontario Ministry of Aboriginal Affairs (OMAA 2003), which is helping farmers who have difficulty finding or affording land to farm.

Another initiative is the proposal by two visionary councillors from the Town of Markham for the creation of a "foodbelt." This proposal, which complemented Markham's "smart growth" policies for transportation, density and energy, envisioned a municipal limit to further encroachment on farmland in the "white belt" surrounding the town and a request to the Province of Ontario to include this land in the Greenbelt. It lost by one vote, but citizen engagement and public awareness rose through the efforts of these councillors, along with several food, farm and environmental organizations, both local and national (Suzuki Foundation 2010), as well as a coalition of academic experts. The conversation has shifted, and urban expansion onto farmland is no longer presumed to be "natural" (Robb 2010; Suzuki Foundation 2010; Gombu 2010).

From the rural side, a farmer-led movement called Alternative Land Use Services (ALUS) is advocating payment for environmental services. Existing farm policies strongly encourage single crops now called "commodities," in contrast to high-value crops more amenable to mixed and sustainable farming systems. Commodities are at the heart of the farm income crisis and of the political dilemma between good prices for farmers versus affordability for (low income) consumers. At current prices, many farmers either use methods that damage soil and water and emit greenhouse gases, or they engage in environmental practices at their own expense, at times even paying to introduce "environmental farm programs." If farmers could multiply their income streams by getting paid for ecological management including carbon sequestration (as a payment for a service, much as teachers or nurses are paid, rather than participating in a "carbon market"), they would not have to recover all their costs through the prices of their crops. This could create a shift of public resources away from single products to site-specific, experimental, knowledge-intensive farming. For example, Bryan Gilvesy, the leading advocate in Ontario, took a great economic risk when he shifted from tobacco to an agro-ecological way of farming that combines pasture-fed beef with wildlife habitat, native pollinators, carbon sequestration, natural insect control (bluebirds) and much more, all based on the reintroduction of native perennial grasses <www.yuranch.com>. Payment for environmental services could help jumpstart entrepreneurial initiatives, such as one being undertaken by members of the Holland Marsh Growers' Association (HMGA) who are experimenting with new crops such as baby bok choy and red carrots, in demand by Chinese and East Indian communities, respectively (Reinhart 2009).

Other services deserving payment include training apprentices, whether farmers' own children or other young farmers. At present, young farmers are being trained by a network of sustainable farms called the Collaborative Regional Alliance for Farmer Training (CRAFT <www.craftontario.ca>), and by non-governmental organizations (NGOs) such as Everdale Environmental Learning Centre (EELC <www.everdale.org>) and FarmStart <www.farmstart.ca>. FarmStart also runs a program called "FarmLINK" which "brings together new farmers who are looking for land or mentorship with farm owners who have land available or expertise to share" <farmstart.ca/programs/farmlink/>. Farmers are not paid for this public service, and NGOs are always scrambling for donors.

To "Connect City and Countryside through Food" is a priority of the visionary Toronto Food Strategy (TFS) to look beyond the borders of the city. The TFS notes that Toronto "has already begun to strengthen the regional foodshed through the adoption of a local food procurement policy"; it envisions expanding public procurement by schools and social services (Toronto Public Health 2010: 29). Beyond this, it advocates partnership with many civil society organizations, quasi-public agencies, like the Ontario Food Terminal, and provincial government agencies to "build links between local farmers and Toronto's diverse markets" and "develop a regional food strategy that addresses the needs of farmers and Toronto residents" (Toronto Public Health 2010: 29). Other TFS priorities include "food friendly neighbourhoods," "eliminate[ing] hunger," "empower[ing] residents with food skills and information," and "urg[ing] Federal and Provincial Governments to establish health-focused food policies" (Toronto Public Health 2010: 23–26). The Toronto Food Strategy can make such connections by linking many apparently separate problems, from diet-related health costs to municipal climate change strategies.

An Emerging Metric: Health

The Toronto Food Strategy represents a new level in envisioning multi-scale and cross-sector collaborations to change the food system. It is the culmination of patient work inside city government and with community groups, inside and increasingly outside of Toronto. TFS represents a breakthrough in public policy, democratic consultation and social awareness. It began with a process of community consultations, based on a draft report in spring 2010 that represented discussions between city and community partners about existing and future food initiatives. These conversations revealed themes including "affordability of healthy food, lack of access to quality food stores, the specific needs of newcomers adjusting to a new food system… concern about the lack of basic food skills and the unhealthy diets of children and youth, and the poor quality of food available through food banks… [as well as an expectation for] governments to play a role in facilitating solutions" (Toronto Public Health 2010: 4, 18). The discussions led to a revised document called *Cultivating Food Connections* which was presented by the Medical Officer of Health to the Toronto Board of Health. Subsequently, it was approved as official policy in June 2010. *Cultivating Food Connections* is at once visionary and provisional. It is the most recent document in a long-term project:

> [to] build a vision and inspire action toward a health-focused food system. A strategy is more than just a report or set of recommendations. It is the ongoing process of identifying, building and strengthening positive connections — between local government and residents, among City Divisions, within the community, and with the countryside. (Toronto Public Health 2010: 4)

This means that *Cultivating Food Connections* is the most recent step in "embedding food system initiatives in City Government." Making food a priority is not about creating one more thing for busy officials to do but "about being proactive and using food activities as a way to enhance efforts to meet Toronto's ongoing goals." The strategy recommends that city agencies work in "active partnership with residents, community organizations and businesses" (Toronto Public Health 2010: 19) to enable the deep changes in thinking and practice consistent with the goals of the food sovereignty movement.

The move towards a health-focused food system brings together human health, social justice and ecosystem health as priorities for public policy: its principles are "resilience, equity and sustainability" (Toronto Public Health 2010: 13). Public policy can affect incentives towards healthy food choices, availability of fresh foods in low-income neighbourhoods and access to good foods by vulnerable populations such as seniors and those with physical limitations. Public health policy starts with food, which can be a "strategic vehicle for meeting city goals" (Toronto Public Health 2010: 13). Instead of being divided into separate government departments, food solutions become synergistic ways to solve multiple problems, from waste management to depressed neighbourhoods to children's school performance.

A health-focused food system includes recognizing and supporting farmers as environmental managers and producers of quality foods that can reach consumers quickly. Healthy soils, water, and air, fewer carbon emissions and more carbon sequestration though sustainable techniques are all dependent on strong networks linking farmers to consumers: "a sustainable food system is also economically and socially viable over the long term, especially for local farmers" (Toronto Public Health 2010: 14). Building on the innovations of the Toronto Food Policy Council, which, from its foundation in the early 1990s, brought farm representatives into a City body and which pioneered in helping to create the Greater Toronto Area Agricultural Action Committee (GTA AAC) composed of farm and planning organizations throughout the region, *Cultivating Food Connections* sees an integrated food system as key to building a creative economy, not only in Toronto (Donald 2009), but also in the region as a whole.

Food Security: Economic Renewal and Jobs in a Creative Food Sector

Importantly, an integrated food system must include great sensitivity to the many changing cultures in the neighbourhoods of Toronto. One of the key recommendations of *Cultivating Food Connections* is to identify neighbourhood food access problems and solutions. These can build on existing initiatives, such as the Toronto Urban Aboriginal Framework (UAF), in which Toronto Public Health has collaborated with community organizations to develop special programs, such as the Peer Nutrition Program (PNP) for the Aboriginal community. These solutions include integrating initiatives in Toronto Community Housing, and from community gardens, bake ovens and community kitchens to fresh food markets — many organized by nonprofit organizations such as FoodShare Toronto, the Stop Community Food Centre and other smaller initiatives.

Social enterprises like these are joined by entrepreneurs committed to values of equity, diversity, or sustainability, as well as their own livelihoods. Arvinda's <arvindas.com> is a small business that is creating new links between farmers, cooks and cultural cuisines. Arvinda's Healthy Gourmet Indian Cooking School was started in 1993 by retired civil servant Arvinda Chauhan; she soon realized that time-pressed cooks needed some prepared foods, which she innovated. Then in 2005, her daughter Preena, while pursuing an advanced degree in environmental studies, got a government start-up grant to create a spice mix business. This has now expanded into a range of activities, including culinary tours of "little India" in Toronto and longer ones of big India, too. Preena has used her knowledge of business and environment to encourage Golden Horseshoe farmers to supply the ingredients needed for her products and for Arvinda's classes; she has also relied on her sense of social justice to find or create fair trade for those products which must be imported. Her brother Paresh left his early career in software development to join what is a new type of family business and social enterprise.

The link between economic vitality and culture is thus key. Public and non-profit initiatives support diverse artisanal businesses to produce, distribute, sell and serve food, hoping to capture a greater share of the $7 billion spent on food annually in the city. These are knowledge- and skill-intensive jobs, as are those of sustainable farmers and of the people who link them directly to customers and to a resilient ecosystem. The Food Strategy proposes to support these projects through a not-for-profit Food Business Incubator, funded in part by Toronto's agency for Economic Development and Culture. Next steps are planned, involving work with Business Improvement Associations and the Toronto Food Policy Council (TFPC), the Ontario Culinary Tourism Alliance (OCTA) and other partners to support culturally diverse, healthy and sustainable food. All of these initiatives have a green focus: they fit under one of the priorities of the TFS — "Make Food a Centerpiece of Toronto's New Green Economy." Regional food cultures are reviving in tandem with cultural renewal of agri-food in the region — and with new social justice movements.

Other initiatives are aiming to "scale up" and "join up" towards a tipping point. One is the astonishingly successful non-profit certifying organization for local sustainable foods called Local Food Plus <localfoodplus.ca> that, in just a short time, has built on institutional purchases to draw retail into support for local sustainable farmers and food artisans. For example, Local Food Plus was instrumental in the University of Toronto's decision to incorporate an increasing percentage of local and sustainably produced food in its food service contracts, beginning in 2006 (Friedmann 2007). It is now helping organizations to start up or build onto existing initiatives in other provinces across Canada. Chefs who have given long-standing support to local farmers have joined initiatives that combine equity with quality food: these range from Slow Food <slowfood.to> to the Ontario Culinary Tourism Alliance <ontarioculinary.com> to the welter of farmer markets with ever-expanding educational, economic and community roles. Older farmers' markets have long served as complex community hubs. The Evergreen Brickworks <ebw.evergreen.ca> is the newest example of this, connecting market initiatives with school gardens and potentially with an urban farm.

Finally, FoodShare is the oldest and most established of the non-profit food security organizations in Toronto <foodshare.ca>. FoodShare has over twenty years of experience in innovation in Toronto food systems. It began with the Hunger Hotline, which it still runs, to direct callers to food banks in their areas. It pioneered the Good Food Box, which delivers approximately five thousand boxes a month of fresh fruits and vegetables, sourced locally as much as possible, to groups of households. The Good Food Box is itself a community builder — people from all walks of life help to pack the boxes, which are delivered to neighbourhood or workplace hubs. It is a pioneer in social marketing — creating a universal program in which everyone wants to participate while targeting low income communities for drop-off locations. Debbie Fields, Director of FoodShare, says that "this is a dignified program because everyone pays for the box and is therefore a 'customer' rather than a 'client.'" Contributions cover the full cost of the food and some of the delivery, while staff costs and infrastructure such as trucks and warehouse space are supported by grants from the government, foundations and individuals. The Good Food Box has been copied and adapted widely. For example, it has created niche boxes for pregnant women, for organics (which tend to be more expensive) and for cultural cuisines.

FoodShare incubates and partners with many food organizations, as innovators take their experiences and experiments into new social ventures. A central partner, headed by Anan Lololi, is the Afri-Can Food Basket, whose mission statement states: "The Afri-Can FoodBasket is a non-profit community food security (CFS) movement that is committed to meeting the nutrition, health and employment needs of members of the African Canadian community, in particular, those who are economically and socially vulnerable" <www.africanfoodbasket.com>. The Afri-Can Food Basket encourages sustainable agriculture, local food access, youth development and food justice, all with festivals, music, cooking, markets and fun.

FoodShare has innovated practices such as training young people in cooking, catering and gardening — including beekeeping, composting, rooftop gardens, sprouts and more. It has pioneered a kitchen incubator used mainly by young entrepreneurs from immigrant communities to experiment with commercializing their culinary products. FoodShare is an inspiring social enterprise, combining non-profit with entrepreneurial activities, including income generation through its excellent catering service (which also provides training), its sale of seedlings and more. It has been a leading partner in student nutrition programs in public schools, trying to fill the gap shamefully left by federal and provincial governments that have no universal student meal program. FoodShare hosted and cosponsored its first food sovereignty conference in Ontario in fall 2009.

A New Coalition: Public Schools to Revive Food Knowledge and Communities

In 2010 FoodShare is moving many of its projects to a new level and focus by launching a comprehensive advocacy campaign called Recipe for Change <foodshare.ca/school-recipeforchange.htm>. The campaign aims to make food literacy and food practice required in the curriculum of public schools in Ontario from Junior Kindergarten to Grade Twelve. Building on a recent poll in which 85 percent of Canadians supported healthy food and snacks as a universal school program, FoodShare is gathering allies among government officials, farmers, teachers, health organizations, food movements, students and the general public to work in coalition to make food literacy — including practical skills from compost to cooking — part of a school curriculum: this program will help young people understand the food system and empower them to make healthy food choices. The campaign is shifting public focus from fear of "obesity" and other dysfunctions of the food system to a focus on knowledge, experience and community, based on healthy foodways. FoodShare director Debbie Field envisions the spread of food literacy programs throughout the schools, in the same way that computer literacy — and computers themselves — were introduced only fifteen years ago, starting with one model school that led the way.

At FoodShare's 2010 Annual General Meeting, a panel devoted to Recipe for Change reflected new links between farm and city. The panelists included a member of the Toronto District School Board, who reported on model school gardening and cooking programs in the city, such as the "foodprint" garden at James S. Bell public school. In this program, students do complex composting, using kitchen scraps and vermicompost, and cook their produce, as well as learn everything from carbon saving to writing haiku verses, all based on "respect, responsibility, and teamwork." Other panelists included a farmer and a chef. The Holland Marsh farmer is proud of the red carrots he grows, which are much in demand by East Indian cooks. He sees himself as both traditional, like his grandfather who began the farm and had to learn how to grow crops for the region, and innovative in the way that he uses direct marketing to cut costs and to allow both profit for himself and good prices for his customers. He interprets current, popular attitudes towards food as based on fear — a fear that comes from separation, distance and ignorance of food. He supports Recipe for Change as a means to help people understand the whole food system and to "learn to cook again." He sees government research into new crops, though still small in scale, as indicative of a positive change in policy,. At the other end of the food system chain, a local chef who has worked both in expensive restaurants and at the non-profit The Stop Community Food Centre has become a leading public educator and advocate, recently leading a culturally diverse group of chefs to present a deputation in favour of the Toronto Food Strategy to the Toronto Board of Health.

In addition to smaller innovations, including salad bars and gardens, the Recipe for Change initiative envisions a Good Food Café in every school, and institution of a curriculum in which all students are taught to cook, garden and compost throughout all the subject areas. This entails (re)introducing kitchens and changing curriculum, big challenges that nonetheless promise to attract allies. Programs for children, as well as health and synergistic solutions for multiple social and economic problems, link Recipe for Change to the Toronto Food Strategy and to regional initiatives that work to transform the food system of the Golden Horseshoe and beyond.

Rebuilding Infrastructure for a Regional Food System: Sustain Ontario and Menu 2020

The most recent initiative bringing food system change to a regional level is the report called *Menu 2020: Ten Good Food Ideas for Ontario* (Baker, Campsie and Rabinowicz 2010). It is the pinnacle of a remarkable multi-year collaborative process that reflects the best thinking about what to do about the food system right now in Ontario. When it was first released, a 2008 Metcalf report "Food Connects Us All" (Campsie 2008) made a splash in the food movement because it highlighted a call for considerable change, including the following recommendations:

(1) *"Wide-Ranging Policy Reform"*: in farm support, labelling, extension services to farmers, research that is appropriate for small-scale and sustainable farming, safety regulations fostering centralization of processing industries, payment for environmental services, and farmland conservation, as well as food access for people with low incomes, education about food and health, support for community food programs and school food, planning for urban agriculture and community gardens, planning for healthy street food vending and public procurement.

(2) *"Remaking the Middle"* of the food system which has become dangerously undone by oligopolistic food retailers. The report noted that "78 percent of the retail market is captured by just three large companies: Loblaws, Sobeys, and A&P/Dominion" (Campsie 2008: 31). Profits flow to outside shareholders rather than circulating within local economic networks. In particular, processors such as mills, abattoirs and canneries have largely disappeared, making it more difficult for small farmers to find markets.

(3) *"Building Self-Sufficiency,"* including support for moving food banks into community food security organizations that help people to grow food, cook, learn nutrition and work together, as well as access emergency food. Urban agriculture figured importantly, as well as community and school gardens.

(4) *"Bridging Divides"*: overcoming the social and cultural gap between farm folk and city folk. This includes Community Supported Agriculture (CSA) and farmers' markets, as well as dealing with frictions at the edges of farms and cities and the deep divide over "cheap food," which angers farmers, and "expensive

food," inaccessible to people with low incomes.

(5) *"Changing the Conversation"*: nutrition education, especially in schools, and food system education about local and seasonal foods, as well as the real cost of sustainably produced foods. (Campsie 2008)

Based on the report's comprehensive analysis, the Metcalf Foundation funded organizations dedicated to specific changes outlined in the report, notably the new certifying organization, Local Food Plus. It also funded a new organization to pursue all the goals of a regionally integrated, sustainable food system: Sustain Ontario, "a province-wide, cross-sectoral alliance that promotes healthy food and farming" <sustainontario.com/about> modelled on the U.K. organization Sustain.

The Metcalf Foundation then commissioned several research reports on specific aspects of making the changes outlined above, including rural entrepreneurship, fruit and vegetable processing, urban agriculture and community food centres. Many of these well-researched themes were integrated into *Menu 2020,* which "offers an integrated vision for farming and food that will contribute to health and economic viability along the food chain" <sustainontario.com>. *Menu 2020* produced ten "good food ideas" for Ontario.

These ideas are specific, accessible and practical: they encompass the experiences of food innovators, from farmers to food security activists, and provide guidelines for research and organizational development. The report has taken the inspired approach of documenting in each point a "gap" between health and agriculture and then proposing ways to "bridge" each gap. Thus, it has provided a guide to the next steps toward food sovereignty in the Golden Horseshoe, the Greenbelt and Ontario.

Box 10-1 Ten Good Food Ideas for Ontario

- Support producers of locally consumed fruit, vegetables and meats
- Make room for new farmers and alternative markets within the supply-managed system
- Harvest the whole value of ecological goods and services from agriculture
- Plant urban Ontario
- Implement a school food program, and embed food literacy in the curriculum
- Support community food centres
- Establish local food infrastructure through regional food clusters
- Expand public procurement of local, sustainably produced food
- Link good food with good health
- Plan for the future of farming and food

Source: Baker, Campsie and Rabinowicz 2010.

Growing a Sustainable Food System

I wrote some years ago that a sustainable food system would allow people to grow what is good for the earth, eat what is good to grow and design social and political institutions to make the first two of these possible (Friedmann 2003). The present food system does the reverse: farmers grow what dominant corporate buyers demand, eaters buy what is offered by the same corporate actors, and ecosystems and health suffer, as do social and political systems, both urban and rural. Food sovereignty has the enormous task of reversing these trends. In the Golden Horseshoe, farmers and farmland are disappearing, but the Greenbelt and many initiatives are working to renew farmers and save farmland. Eaters are unequal and unhealthy at younger ages and in increasing numbers. These conditions present a great challenge for change: the initiatives are aimed at creating those much-needed changes.

Most importantly, the gap between food growers, preservers, cooks, traders and eaters has grown very large in recent decades. An enormous gulf has arisen between farmers and changing urban populations in the three decades of globalization that have inspired the challenge of food sovereignty. In Ontario, where once most immigrants were farmers and most urbanites had close connections to rural life, today's global diasporas, global food markets and concentration of supermarket power have driven a great cultural and social wedge between the two (Winson 1992; Kneen 1989; Burch and Lawrence 2007). Thus, as a farmer-focused movement, food sovereignty faces special challenges in a large, urban, multicultural region such as the Golden Horseshoe. On one side, farmers have lost touch with the complex array of urban eaters; the most entrepreneurial among them are changing their crop mixes to reflect new tastes among culturally diverse, health-conscious consumers, while others remain locked in low-price "commodities" for the industrial food system. On the urban side, Carolyn Steel (2009a) reminds us that the present urban ignorance about where food comes from, and, by extension, about the natural basis of cities and the people who eat there, is almost unprecedented in human experience. Echoing Baker and her colleagues in *Menu 2020*, but speaking more philosophically, Steel goes on to say:

> The first thing we need to do is to stop seeing cities as inert objects and recognize them as organic entities, inextricably bound to the natural ecosystem.... What we urgently need is an alternative to utopia: a model that aims not at perfection but at something partial and attainable. My proposal is sitopia, from the ancient Greek words sitos (food) and topos (place). Sitopia, in essence, is a way of recognizing the central role that food plays in our lives and of harnessing its potential to shape the world in a better way. The good news is that sitopia already exists. Wherever food is valued and celebrated,

> from ordinary family dinners and food co-ops to international movements such as Slow Food and Transition Towns, there is growing recognition that, far from waning as an issue, food is set to become our greatest global challenge. The trick is to scale up such recognition to the point where it affects not just our daily habits, but our socio-economic structures, cross-cultural understanding, and value systems — our very conception of what it means to dwell on Earth. Food is the great connector. If we can learn to share it as a conceptual tool, we can use it to shape a better common future. (Steel 2009b)

The initiatives I have described here point in this direction — food sovereignty has become a framework shared by many who work toward such radical change. I outlined the specific challenges faced by cities and urban regions in achieving food sovereignty: I have also described how recent projects are relinking cities, food and farmers in a totally new context in Southern Ontario. The links among these initiatives and the trust that is incipient in the new networks suggest that a community of food practice have come into being (Friedmann 2007). If Margaret Wheatley and Deborah Frieze (2006) are correct, and I believe they are, then "suddenly and surprisingly a new system emerges at a greater level of scale…[which] possesses qualities and capacities that were unknown." We seem to be getting closer to this moment of great change.

Notes

1. Farm workers are also included in the category, "people of the land." This is often contradictory, as farmers, even small farmers, are often employers. It is especially problematic in Toronto farms and greenhouses, which employ temporary migrant workers under conditions unacceptable to citizens and immigrants (Sharma 2006). I won't deal with this issue in this chapter, but it is crucial to address for food sovereignty.
2. See Kloppenburg et al. (1996) and Peters et al. (2009) for discussions of foodsheds.
3. Vertical integration involves a firm owning and/or controlling several aspects of the supply chain; for example, production of inputs, growing food, processing, marketing and distribution.
4. The following websites provide more information <trca.on.ca/understand/near-urban-agriculture/toronto-urban-farm.dot and trca.on.ca/understand/near-urban-agriculture/farmstart-mcvean-new-farmers-project.dot>.

References

Baker, Lauren, Philippa Campsie and Katie Rabinowicz. 2010. *Menu 2020: Ten Good Food Ideas For Ontario.* Toronto: Metcalf Foundation. At <metcalffoundation.com/downloads/Metcalf_Food_Solutions_Menu_2020.pdf>.

Burch, David, and Geoffrey Lawrence (eds.). 2007. *Supermarkets and Agri-Food*

Supply Chains. Northampton, MA: Edward Elgar.

Campsie, Phillippa. 2008. *Food Connects Us All.* Toronto: Metcalf Foundation. At <metcalffoundation.com/downloads/Food%20Connects%20Us%20All.pdf>.

Carter-Whitney, Maureen, and Sally Miller. 2010. *Nurturing Fruit and Vegetable Processing in Ontario.* Toronto: Metcalf Foundation. At <metcalffoundation.com/downloads/Metcalf_Food_Solutions_Nurturing_Fruit_and_Vegetable_Processing_in_Ontario.pdf>.

Cohen, Marjorie. 1988. *Women's Work, Markets, and Economic Development in Nineteenth-century Ontario.* Toronto: University of Toronto Press.

Cohen, Robin. 1997. *Global Diasporas: An Introduction.* University of Washington Press.

Day-Farnsworth, Lindsey, Brent McCown, Michelle Miller and Anne Pfeiffer. 2009. "Scaling Up: Meeting the Demand for Local Food." University of Wisconsin. At <cias.wisc.edu/wp-content/uploads/2010/01/baldwin_web_final.pdf>.

Donald, Betsy. 2009. "From Kraft to Craft: Innovation and Creativity in Ontario's Food Economy." Martin Prosperity Institute Working Paper. Toronto: Rotman School of Management. At <martinprosperity.org/media/pdfs/From_Kraft_to_Craft-B_Donald.pdf>.

FoodShare Toronto. 2009. "Serving Up Food Sovereignty in Toronto: Cooking Up A Plan of Action Conference." October 29.

Fowke, Vernon. 1957. *National Policy and the Wheat Economy.* Toronto: University of Toronto Press.

Friedmann, Harriet. 2007. "Scaling Up: Bringing Public Institutions and Food Service Corporations into the Project for a Local, Sustainable Food System in Ontario." *Agriculture and Human Values* 24, 3.

___. 2003. "Eating in the Gardens of Gaia: Envisioning Polycultural Communities." In Jane Adams (ed.), *Fighting for the Farm: Rural America Transformed.* Philadelphia: University of Pennsylvania Press.

___. 1993. "International Political Economy of Food: A Global Crisis," *New Left Review* 197, Jan./Feb.

Friends of the Greenbelt Foundation. 2010. "Facts and Figures." At <greenbelt.ca/facts-figures>.

Gayler, Hugh J. 1994. *Niagara's Changing Landscapes.* Ottawa: Carleton University Press.

Gombu, Phinjo. 2010. "Markham's 'Foodbelt' Proposal on the Line." *The Star* April 27. At <thestar.com/news/gta/article/801396—markham-s-food-belt-proposal-on-the-line>.

IAASTD (International Assessment of Agricultural Knowledge, Science and Technology for Development). 2009. "Summary for Decision Makers of the North America and Europe (NAE) Report." At <agassessment.org/docs/IAASTD_NAE_SDM_JAN_2008.pdf>.

Kloppenburg, Jack Jr., John Hendrickson and G.W. Stevenson. 1996. "Coming into the Foodshed." *Agriculture and Human Values* 13, 3.

Kneen, Brewster. 1989. *From Land to Mouth: Understanding the Food System.* Toronto: NC Press.

McMurchy, John C. 1990. "A History of Agricultural Marketing Legislation in Ontario." Ontario Ministry of Agriculture, Food and Rural Affairs. At <omafra.

gov.on.ca/english/farmproducts/factsheets/history.htm>.

Menzies, Heather. 1994. *By the Labour of their Hands: The Story of Ontario Cheddar Cheese.* Kingston, ON: Quarry Press.

Nasr, Joseph, Rod MacRae and James Kuhns with Martin Danyluk, Penny Kaill-Vinish, Marc Michalak and Abra Snider. 2010. *Scaling Up Urban Agriculture in Toronto: Building the Infrastructure.* Toronto: Metcalf Foundation.

OMAFRA. 2005. "Greenhouse Pepper Growers Vote For Joining Marketing Plan: Vote Means Stronger Voice for Growers." At <omafra.gov.on.ca/english/infores/releases/2005/033005.html>.

Ontario Farmland Trust. 2010. "Farmland in Ontario — Are We Losing a Valuable Resource?" At <ontariofarmlandtrust.ca/sites/default/files/farmland%20loss%20factsheet%20updated.pdf>.

Ontario Ministry of Aboriginal Affairs. 2003. "Aboriginal Farm Co-operative Harvests Benefits of Unity." At <aboriginalaffairs.gov.on.ca/english/news/archives/news_030219b_1.asp>.

Peters, Christian J., Nelson L. Bills, Jennifer L. Wilkins and Gary W. Fick. 2009. "Foodshed Analysis and its Relevance to Sustainability." *Renewable Agriculture and Food Systems* 24, 1.

Reinhart, A. 2009. "Marsh Madness." *Globe and Mail* Oct. 10. At <theglobeandmail.com/news/national/marsh-madness/article1319792/>.

Robb, Jim. 2010. Presentation to Markham Council. At <markham.ca/markham/ccbs/indexfile/Agendas/2009/Council/cl091201/Jim%20Robb%20Presentation.pdf>.

Roberts, Wayne. 2008. *The No-nonsense Guide to World Food.* Toronto: Between the Lines.

Sassen, Saskia. 2002. *Global Networks, Linked Cities.* London: Routledge.

Sharma, Nandita. 2006. *Home Economics: Nationalism and the Making of 'Migrant Workers.'* Toronto: University of Toronto Press.

Statistics Canada. 2006a. "2006 Community Profiles: Markham." At <12.statcan.ca/census-recensement/2006/dp-pd/prof/92-591/details/Page.cfm?Lang=E&Geo1=CSD&Code1=3519036&Geo2=PR&Code2=35&Data=Count&SearchText=markham&SearchType=Begins&SearchPR=01&B1=All&Custom=>.

___. 2006b. "Immigrant Population by Place of Birth, by Census Metropolitan Area (2006 Census) (Ottawa–Gatineau, Kingston, Peterborough, Oshawa, Toronto)." At <www40.statcan.ca/l01/cst01/demo35c-eng.htm>.

___. 2006c. "Ontario's Farm Population: Changes Over a Lifetime." At <statcan.gc.ca/ca-ra2006/agpop/on-eng.htm>.

___. 2003. "Who's Minding Ontario's Farms?" At <statcan.gc.ca/ca-ra2001/first-premier/profiles/03ont-eng.htm>.

Steel, Carolyn. 2009a. *Hungry City: How Food Shapes Our Lives.* London: Vintage.

___. 2009b. "Sitopia: A New Model for Feeding the World's Expanding Cities." *Design Mind* 11. At <designmind.frogdesign.com/articles/the-substance-of-things-not-seen/sitopia.html>.

Suzuki Foundation. 2010. "David Suzuki on the Markham Foodbelt." At <youtube.com/watch?v=kgJufwKy_t0>.

Toronto. 2010. "Toronto's Racial Diversity." At <toronto.ca/toronto_facts/diversity.htm>.

Toronto Public Health. 2010. *Cultivating Food Connections: Toward a Healthy and*

Sustainable Food System for Toronto. At <wx.toronto.ca/inter/health/food.nsf/Resources/340ACEEDBF1B2D6085257738000B22F2/$file/Cultivating%20Food%20Connections%20report.pdf>.

Wheatley, Margaret, and Deborah Frieze. 2006. "Lifecycle of Emergence — Using Emergence to Take Social Innovation to Scale." *Evolutionary Nexus.* At <evolutionarynexus.org/node/620>.

Winson, Anthony. 1992. *The Intimate Commodity.* Toronto: Garamond.

Winne, Mark. 2008. *Closing the Food Gap: Resetting the Table in the Land of Plenty.* Boston: Beacon Press.

11. "SUPER, NATURAL"

The Potential for Food Sovereignty in British Columbia

Hannah Wittman and Herb Barbolet

"Super, Natural" British Columbia (B.C.) — this provincial slogan brings to mind images of towering mountains, lakes, acres of pine forests and stunning coastlines greet the visitor to Canada's westernmost province. Less visible to the outsider is B.C.'s equally distinctive agricultural diversity — from the market vegetable farms in the Lower Mainland to the expansive grain farms in the Peace River and the internationally recognized fruit orchards and wineries in the Okanagan. B.C. has the most diverse agricultural landscape in Canada, producing almost 250 land-based commodities and more than eighty species of fish, shellfish and marine plants harvested or raised in B.C. waters.[1]

B.C.'s Agricultural Land Reserve (ALR), an innovative farmland protection policy dating back to the 1970s, together with the rising number of small, organic farms and local community food initiatives, provide an important structural foundation for food sovereignty in the province. However, small-scale farmers and local production systems in B.C. are struggling to position themselves within what is increasingly a "neoliberal food regime" — that is, a regime that prioritizes export-oriented production and trade liberalization, international harmonization of regulatory practices and the deepening of transnational capital integration (Pechlaner and Otero 2008, 2010). Food regimes are enduring political and economic structures that shape how agricultural production systems are constructed, coordinated and maintained as elements of the global economy (Fairbairn 2010; McMichael 2009). Food regime analysis considers the role of changing forms of state regulation, the institutional norms of international food production and the role of trade relations between nations (Pechlaner and Otero 2008). Since neoliberal shifts in food regimes threaten local food security, environmental sustainability and local community development, they often trigger reactions and the creation of alternatives by civil society, which in turn can pressure governments to consider the needs of local production and consumption, pushing them to create more responsive regulatory frameworks. Thus, to better understand what is happening in B.C. around agriculture and food, it is also critical to examine the role of community groups and social movements, and how they resist agricultural concentration and "neo-regulation" in efforts to establish alternatives to the current neoliberal food regime.

We can begin to see the potential for food sovereignty in British Columbia through an analysis of the reality and contradictions of food production and policy in the province. The imposition of a neoliberal food regime poses a number of policy contradictions and structural constraints for developing and strengthening sustainable food systems across the province. There are several examples of the adverse local impacts of a neoliberal food regime, particularly in cases of farmland regulation, the transformation of B.C.'s meat processing regulations, and the conflict between wild and farmed salmon. In response to the challenges and contradictions posed by neoliberal regulation, there is increasing pushback from committed groups of civil society actors in British Columbia seeking to strengthen connections to local food systems.

The Potential for Food Sovereignty in B.C.

In British Columbia, farming is regionalized, with grains and oilseeds dominating in the North, beef ranching in the interior, dairy and orchards in the Fraser Valley and north Okanagan, and small fruits, vegetables, and poultry and egg production in the Fraser Valley. Using production and consumption data from 2001, a 2006 B.C. Ministry of Agriculture and Lands study calculated B.C.'s food self-reliance at the primary production level in order to provide a baseline for assessing the impacts of future changes in eating habits and population levels (BCMAL 2006). The study estimated that B.C. is 48 percent food self-reliant; in other words, under current levels of production, if all food produced in the province were consumed locally, B.C. farmers would be able to supply 48 percent of all foods consumed in B.C. This assessment shows that B.C.'s self-sufficiency level in food is one of the highest in Canada, providing a strong potential for the achievement of food sovereignty in the province.[2]

Since the mid 1980s, the amount of B.C. farmland in production has risen by almost 20 percent (Ostry and Morrison 2010). This rise in food production has been accompanied, however, by a significant shift in the composition of food crops, with more than a 300 percent increase in the production of specialty greenhouse vegetables and a shift towards fruits, especially blueberries, grown for export markets. A decline in the production of staple fruits and vegetables has been matched by increases in the production of wine grapes and the amount of land devoted to animal pasture and grain production. This has led to significant decreases in the availability of locally grown cereal grains, fruits and vegetables (See Table 11-1).

In B.C., about 0.5 hectare of farmland is needed to produce enough food to sustain one person for one year. To produce a 100 percent self-sufficient, healthy diet for the projected B.C. population in 2025, 2.78 million hectares

Table 11-1 Provincial Consumption and Production of Food, 1986 and 2006 and % Self Sufficient

	Provincial Consumption		Provincial Production		% Self-sufficient	
Tonnes	**1986**	**2006**	**1986**	**2006**	**1986**	**2006**
Total fruits	233,231	388,075	168,335	188,879	72%	49%
Potatoes	105,968	121,232	91,000	108,182	86%	89%
Field Vegetables	193,253	308,805	76,043	39,049	39%	13%
Cereals (human consumption)	141,050	245,746	376,200	132,600	267%	54%
Meat	204,967	276,257	131,688	259,245	64%	94%
Fluid Milk (kilolitres)	211,275	249,565	488,808	627,229	231%	251%
Eggs ('000 doz)	39,287	51,602	58,987	63,370	150%	123%

Source: Table reproduced from Ostry and Morrison (2010), compiled from Statistics Canada CANSIM Table 051-0001, 002-0019, 003-0011, 003-0020, 003-0035, 003-0036 and 2006 Census of Agriculture.

of B.C. agricultural land will need to be in active production, an increase of 300 percent over 2001 levels (BCMAL 2006). As Table 11-2 demonstrates, B.C. currently has a surplus of available farmland, but a shrinking number of farms and farmers at the provincial level. Between 1996 and 2006, B.C. experienced a 9.1 percent drop in the number of farms. Farms are also becoming increasingly capitalized, with the average capital value of farms more than doubling since 1996. The increase in this figure, comprising the total value of land and buildings, machinery, equipment, and livestock and

Table 11-2 Farmland in British Columbia

	1991	1996	2001	2006
Total Farm Land, Hectares	2,392,341	2,529,060	2,587,118	2,835,458
Crops	556,796	565,738	617,545	586,238
Pasture	241,004	240,236	233,044	245,793
Summerfallow	57,476	39,017	36,765	25,581
Unimproved	1,030,568	1,172,591	1,207,553	1,499,563
Average Capital Value/Farm	448,075	633,030	780,265	1,255,025
Number of Farms	19,225	21,835	20,290	19,844

Source: Statistics Canada 2006.

poultry, is partly due to a tripling of land and building values and a doubling of machinery and equipment values, as B.C. farms are becoming increasingly more mechanized and oriented toward rapidly growing export markets in blueberries, cranberries and greenhouse vegetables.

Rising land values due to urbanization and associated development pressures have also contributed to the capitalization of B.C. farms. British Columbia is highly urbanized, with 82 percent of the population living in cities and towns.[3] Within the rural population, 92 percent are not farmers, and the best farmland is concentrated at the periphery of rapidly urbanizing areas (Smith 1998). More than 80 percent of B.C.'s population is located in the South Coast and Okanagan regions, which comprise less than 3 percent of B.C.'s provincial land base[4] but produce almost 80 per cent of B.C.'s gross farm receipts (Campbell 2006; Smith 1998). The difficulty of protecting farmland for farming and food sovereignty in the face of a continually rising demand for development and "sprawl" in B.C.'s urban peripheries is a constant point of tension among policy planners, developers and farmers, and those in cities working towards building a more just and sustainable food system.

At the same time, growing interest in local and sustainable food, especially in the Lower Mainland and Vancouver Island regions of British Columbia, has fostered a rise in the number of small farms since the mid 1990s. By 2006, 77 percent of all farms in B.C. were less than ten acres, and 16 percent of B.C. agriculture is now classified as organic, the largest percentage in Canada (Morton 2008). Farmers' markets in the region are also growing rapidly, both in number and sales. For example, in 2009, several farmers' markets in the Fraser Valley outside Vancouver reported growth rates between 30 and 100 percent, and the number of farmers' markets in B.C. had risen to over 125 by 2009. A 2006 study by the University of Northern B.C. indicated that farmers' markets in B.C. contributed over $118 million to local economies (Connell et al. 2006). Coupled with rising demand for local and organic food, neighborhood associations and consumers have organized several innovative food production initiatives and are actively forming food policy councils in municipal and provincial forums. These community organizations view food issues as integrally related to climate, energy and health concerns: it is this context that the conversation about food sovereignty is taking place in the province.

Significantly though, several challenges to food sovereignty exist that limit the ability of B.C. farmers to meet this growing demand for local food. These include a contradictory, neoliberal policy environment that, on the one hand, provides some incentives to foster production for local markets through such programs as the Agricultural Land Reserve (ALR), the BuyBC Program and the B.C. Healthy Eating Initiative, among others, but that, on the other hand, undermines this ability through ALR land exclusions, the

Trade, Investment and Labour Mobility Agreement (TILMA) and restrictive meat inspection regulations.

Growing Forward: B.C.'s Agricultural Policy/Regulatory Environment

Under the neoliberal agricultural regime, and particularly the North American Free Trade Agreement (NAFTA), the interdependence between B.C. consumers and U.S. food suppliers has grown. While much of the food that B.C. consumers eat is grown in the United States and Mexico, B.C. farmers and processors are increasingly dependent on U.S. customers as B.C.'s biggest export market, followed by Japan and China (Alexander and McCrae 2002: 4; BCMAL 2010b). For example, exports of B.C. agricultural and fish products during the first 10 months of 2009 averaged $204 million per month (Schrier 2009). In addition to more than $2.4 billion per year of international exports, B.C. also exports $2.5 billion of agricultural products to other Canadian provinces (Burkinshaw 2010; BCMAL 2010a). At the same time, farmers are finding it difficult to make a living (see Chapter 2). In B.C., farmers lost a total of $117 million in net income in 2007, compared with a loss of $42 million in 2006 (Morton 2008).

Since 2003, agricultural policy in British Columbia has been delivered under a common policy framework agreed to by Canada's federal, provincial and territorial agriculture ministers. The current agreement, entitled Growing Forward, was signed on June 28, 2007, and covers the period from 2009 to 2013. The agreement supports an export market-driven vision for Canada's agriculture and agri-food sector. Based on an investment of $1.3 billion over five years, to be cost-shared on a 60:40 basis between the federal and provincial-territorial governments, the federal *Growing Forward* vision and agricultural policy framework provides for three common federal policy outcomes, to be implemented separately in each Canadian province (Agriculture and Agri-Food Canada 2008):

- *A Competitive and Innovative Sector:* To enable the sector to "maintain and expand its share in international and domestic markets," the policy recommends "modernizing regulatory systems and improving regulatory cooperation."
- *A Sector That Contributes to Society's Priorities*: To enable the sector to "meet and exceed standards and requirements [and mitigate risk], notably those related to food safety and the environment, while building profitability" the policy framework recommends "modernizing and implementing innovative regulations and standards... beyond what is enforced by legislation... [and] facilitating the development and implementation of full-chain tracking and tracing capabilities."

- *A Sector That Is Pro-Active in Managing Risks*: "To enable the sector to take pro-active steps to reduce the risk of disease outbreaks," the policy recommends the provision of "tools to mitigate financial risks to agriculture."

B.C.'s commitment to *Growing Forward*, to be implemented between 2009 and 2013, is limited to four programs: the Farm Business Advisory Services (FBAS) Program (consulting support for business and marketing strategies, and risk assessment); B.C. Food Safety Systems and Implementation Program for Producers; B.C. Food Safety Systems and Implementation Program for Processors; and the B.C. Enterprise Infrastructure Traceability (EIT) Program (including agri-environmental risk assessment) (BCMAL 2010a). All of these programs are designed to facilitate the large-scale export of B.C. agricultural products, while reducing the risk of food contamination. For all intents and purposes, the dual emphasis on being innovative and reducing export-related risk resulted in the development of programs that are not aligned with the priorities of B.C.'s majority small farms, which are oriented to local production and consumption.

In 2005, British Columbia set about developing a provincial agriculture plan. The British Columbia Agriculture Plan, released in 2008, emphasized "promoting B.C. food products, making the agriculture a leader in reducing climate change impacts, and reconnecting British Columbians with locally grown food," with Agriculture Minister Pat Bell arguing that "agriculture is everyone's business, and we need to ensure that the people who produce our food have access to the tools, people and technology they need to remain competitive" (BCMAL 2008a). The five key themes of the agriculture plan (See Box 11-1) would seem well positioned to support the foundation of food sovereignty in the province.

Laudatory as these goals may be, the B.C. Agricultural Plan emphasizes local food and the environment without addressing the inherent contradictions found in the current mainstream export-oriented agendas of the federal and provincial governments. For example, the BuyBC program was launched in 1993 by the provincial government to increase demand for locally produced food by enhancing consumer awareness of B.C. products, with over 1200 companies and associations using the BuyBC logo in their advertising and promotional materials for over 5,000 products.[5] However, the program struggled to maintain its funding from the B.C. Ministry of Agriculture. In 2003, as an alternative to cancelling the program altogether, the province handed over ownership and control of BuyBC to the B.C. Agriculture Council, a group representing agricultural industries in B.C., with no funding attached. The council added a user fee to the program. Consequently, there was very limited up-take from farmers, BuyBC stagnated, and for all intents

Box 11-1 B.C.'s 2008 Agriculture Plan

- Producing local food in a changing world — Promoting B.C. agriculture and food products to support B.C. producers in supplying fresh, healthy food directly to consumers; and developing a "food miles" program to create public awareness of the distance food products have been transported, and the effect on greenhouse gas emissions.
- Meeting environmental and climate challenges — Shifting farm practices to turn agricultural residues like plant material, animal and organic waste into renewable energy; and investing in environmental farm planning, to encourage producers to adopt more environmentally friendly ways of handling their livestock, fertilizer, farm buildings and engine emissions.
- Building innovative and profitable family farm businesses — Supporting the agriculture industry in addressing B.C.'s farm labour shortage; and supporting agriculture's diverse sectors in developing sector-specific strategic plans to work towards sustained profitability.
- Building First Nations agriculture capacity — Establishing a program to certify First Nations food products prior to the 2010 Olympics; and delivering a "local foods for healthy eating" program for First Nations, including community gardens.
- Bridging the urban/ agriculture divide — Increasing funding for agriculture in the classroom programs to reconnect children with the source of their food; and reviewing zoning by-laws and farm use by-laws to ensure the regulatory structure supports the sustainable growth of farming in B.C.

Source: BCMAL 2008a.

and purposes, it disappeared. In 2008 the B.C. Agriculture Plan called for the reinstatement of BuyBC: the subsequent B.C. budget earmarked $1 million over 4 years for its resuscitation. Comparatively, Ontario expanded their Buy Ontario plan by announcing a grant of $56 million over 4 years (OMAFRA 2008). In comparison, B.C. producers, wholesalers and retailers felt that the B.C. allocation to the BuyBC program was insufficient to accomplish its objectives. As of fall 2010, the program is still not operating.

The marketing initiatives encompassed in the BuyBC campaign may help increase demand, but, because BuyBC did not address the need for aggregation of products from a large numbers of small producers, nor the need for re-introducing significant processing capacity, they will not address commercial-scale supply issues. Nor do they indicate support for local food policy councils or community food initiative groups that are working on market-based initiatives to increase sustainable food production. The B.C. plan also fails to acknowledge problems of lack of income for a significant portion of the population that is unable to afford healthy, high quality food. The implementation of the plan (the little that has been actually funded to date) is also an indication of the underlying priorities that hinder, rather than support, the development of strong local food systems in B.C. Of the twenty-three strategies encompassed in B.C.'s 2008 Agriculture Plan, less than one-third has been allocated a budget. Of this one-third, approximately 75 percent was earmarked for a food-safety testing lab ($14.5 million) and biofuel production ($10 million) (BCMAL 2008b).

Both *Growing Forward* and recent provincial policy are situated within a broader shift towards regulatory harmonization. B.C.'s agriculture budget and priorities, now mirroring those of the federal government, respond to the exigencies of the increasingly globalized food regime which has been challenged by a series of massive food recalls, particularly in the United States meat and vegetable processing industries. In response to calls for "streamlining" and reducing government intervention in agriculture, the 2007 recommendations of the North American Competitiveness Council, (NACC), a key industry advisory group, include harmonizing regulatory policy in the food and agriculture sector (NACC 2007). In practice, this would require regulators to "reference international technical standards" and facilitate "North American economies of scale" by minimizing differences that would impede food trade as an integral part of a "safer and more reliable food supply" in North America (NACC 2007: 31). Conveniently ignoring the food recalls, the NACC argues that harmonizing and streamlining regulatory procedures that favour large-scale producers would reduce costs and improve competitiveness for fruit and vegetable growers, shippers and wholesalers (NACC 2007: 32). In response, since 2006, the federal government cut twenty million dollars from Agriculture and Agri-food Canada (AAFC) in the name of "efficiency." Despite some recent modest reinstatement of funding for food safety, general funding for advisory groups and to the Canadian Food Inspection Agency (CFIA) has been reduced (Government of Canada 2006).

Although important to increase awareness of local food availability and to provide secure markets for locally produced food, the B.C. government's focus on food marketing does not address the commercial-scale supply issues that are limiting the expansion of a local food system that could meet growing demand. These supply issues include the high cost of farmland, low financial returns for many farmers, shortages in farm labour, loss of processors, loss of infrastructure and conflicting policies and regulations — or what some producers call "regulatory roadblocks" (Thompson 2010). These roadblocks include Agricultural Land Reserve restrictions on the construction of on-farm housing and other buildings, the difficulties of achieving long-term tenure for farmers on provincially owned farmland (Wittman 2009), contradictory municipal and provincial zoning laws and conflicting environmental, health and safety regulations. In the following sections, through short case studies of B.C.'s land reserve policy, health regulation effects on the meat processing industry and salmon aquaculture, we explore three specific instances of such regulatory roadblocks. These case studies highlight the regulatory tensions between regional, provincial and national regulatory frameworks that present serious obstacles to the achievement of food sovereignty in B.C.

The Agricultural Land Reserve

The Agricultural Land Reserve (ALR) of British Columbia is a groundbreaking agricultural zoning program initiated in the 1970s by the New Democratic Party (NDP) government, when more than 11.4 million acres (5 percent of provincial land area and almost 80 percent of prime agricultural land) of public and private land was designated as farmland and prohibited from further subdivision, industrial or residential development. The best farmland in B.C., in fertile valleys along eastern Vancouver Island and in the Fraser River Valley, is under increased development pressure as non-ALR protected working farms are converted to residential housing, country estates and hobby farms, with an accompanying loss of market production. Thus, the ALR has been critical in protecting farmland in B.C., and has also contributed to limiting the range of urban sprawl.

However, property owners within the ALR can apply to have their property "excluded" by arguing that their land is inappropriate for agriculture or that the community would benefit from its exclusion. For example, the conversion of ALR land into sports fields has been a common rationale for removing restrictions on farmland development. This has opened up a significant loophole leading to subdivision and residential, commercial or industrial development. While the total land area within the ALR has remained, until recently, almost constant over the last three decades, the regional distribution of these lands has shifted drastically. Over 72 percent of the land removed from the ALR has been in the more populous regions of southern B.C., where fertile delta land has traditionally been used for high-value vegetable crop and animal production. Designated replacement acreages have been placed in B.C.'s Northern regions (see Figure 11-1) which are primarily used for grazing (Campbell 2006). Since almost all B.C. beef is exported to Alberta for feedlot finishing (and from there back to B.C. or to export markets), this represents a very clear shift from land-protection favouring local markets to that favouring export markets. South-to-North transfers of reserve agriculture land in the rapidly urbanizing regions of southern B.C. have ranged from 8 to 33 percent of ALR land, with an almost 67 percent approval rate for exclusions (ALC 2007).

While agricultural zoning in British Columbia has perhaps slowed conversion of agricultural land to other uses, government land-use planning is still perceived by many rural landowners as a threat to private property and as a hindrance to regional economic development. In addition to the process of applying for exclusion from the Agricultural Land Reserve, farmers with non-ALR status can also apply for exemption from other municipal agricultural zoning by-laws, which can vary with changing political regimes and socio-economic circumstances (Feitelson 1999; Merenlender et al. 2004).[6] Applications for exclusions continue, with a 30 percent increase between 2003 and 2004 (McNaney 2007). In addition, ALR land is not required to be in active agricultural production. As such, much ALR land is held speculatively or used for luxury rural living as country estates. For example, the Garden City Lands, a 136-acre field adjacent to downtown Richmond, B.C., have been vacant for almost a decade while local developers and the city of Richmond have pursued several unsuccessful applications to remove the land from the ALR. Active community support for keeping the land within the ALR has led to a variety of grassroots proposals for community gardens, agricultural demonstration sites and recuperation of native bog species.

Figure 11-1 B.C.'s Agricultural Land Reserve, 2010

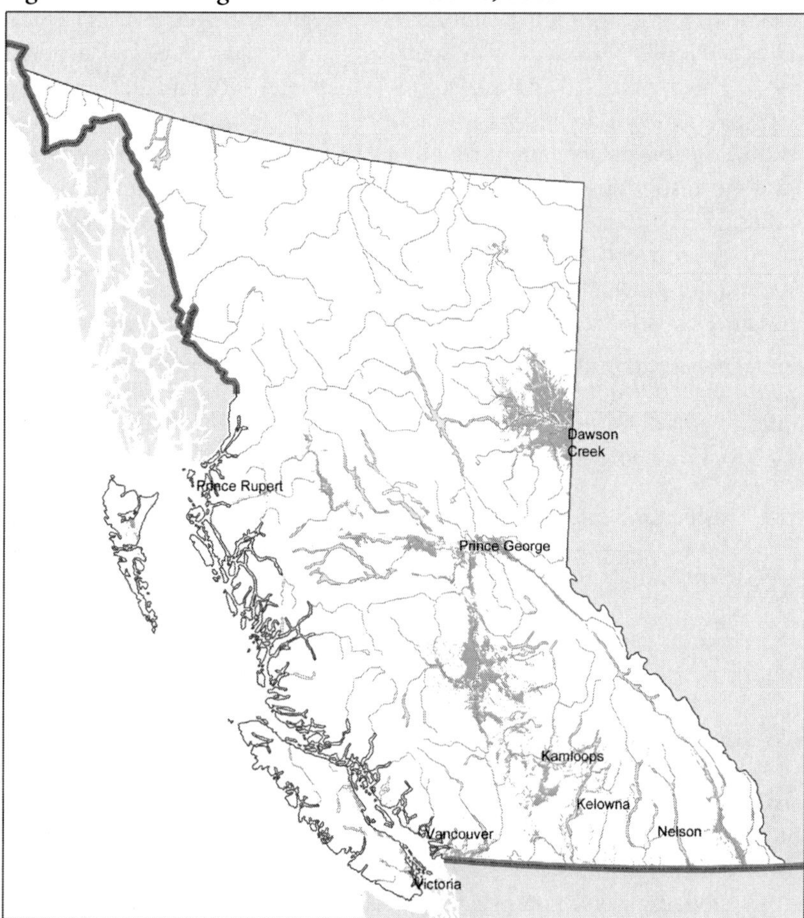

Source: British Columbia's Provincial Land Commission 2010.

Finally, in order to restrict residential development on farmland, ALR regulations prohibit the subdivision of ALR lands and restrict the construction of additional housing and buildings. Although additional housing for farm workers may be permitted on ALR land for "clearly demonstrated" farming purposes, including housing for apprentices, farm workers and additional farmers, in reality a history of abuse of the regulation and illegal subdivision has limited municipal approval of sub-housing development. This poses a challenge for the development of small-scale, organic farms, which are labour-intensive and have a corresponding need for more flexible housing arrangements. In practice this has led to the use of temporary, substandard housing for farm- workers and additional farmers, and has been identified as a serious barrier to young farmers seeking to farm in B.C. (Wittman 2009).

Despite continued political support of the ALR, differing development objectives at the municipal and provincial levels have led to a loss of farm services, increasing traffic and pollution in ALR regions, especially in the Fraser Valley and Lower Mainland. Land speculation has rapidly driven up farmland prices, which increased 76 percent in B.C. between 2001 and 2006, with the biggest increases occurring in the Fraser Valley and Okanagan (Penner 2008). Overall, the loss of farmland through ALR exclusion, government expropriation for transportation corridors (e.g., the Gateway Program, a massive road building and infrastructure project designed to reduce traffic congestion in Metro Vancouver), and the development of residential housing, country estates, hobby farms and other non-productive land uses has increased the operating costs for remaining farms in the region and created an increased opportunity for speculators to argue that farming is not economically viable. Additionally, although it is an illegal practice, farmland is sometimes used as a dumping ground for "waste" from urban development. According to the ALR Annual Report, South Coast Commission, 2006–2007,

> Vast amounts of soil are excavated and must be taken to disposal sites. Tipping fees are attractive to many landowners, with the result that much of the soil "fill" is spread over prime farmland without any authorization and with potential long-term impacts to the suitability of that land for producing food for our growing population.

B.C.'s Meat Inspection Regulations

Another example of a regulatory roadblock — one that has had major repercussions for the availability of locally produced and processed meat — was the modification of B.C.'s Meat Inspection Regulation (MIR) in 2004 under the *Food Safety Act*, following international outbreaks of bovine spongiform encephalopathy (BSE) and other food-borne pathogens in meat. The MIR changes, which came fully into effect in September 2007 after a several year "transition period," initiated a new licensing system governing meat producers and processors under a North American "harmonization" program for health and safety regulations (NACC 2007).

Although B.C.'s Health Authority had no evidence of food-borne illness related to local B.C. meat production (Johnson 2008), they feared a spread or repeat of contamination problems originating in large-scale slaughter facilities in the United States and other regions of Canada. As part of the harmonization process that transitions agricultural regulation from a local scale, based in Regional Health Authorities, to provincial and federal levels of licensing and inspection, the new B.C. Meat Inspection Regulation Policy enacted in 2007 required that all unlicensed (including on-farm) slaughter and processing facilities become licensed in order to sell meat for human consumption, and that all animals slaughtered in licensed abattoirs must be inspected before and after slaughter. The new regulations also included provisions related to environmental protection, waste disposal, animal health and welfare, as well as requirements to comply with workplace safety and labour regulations, and to subject local processing facilities to "rigorous government oversight" (PHSA 2009). Compliance with these regulations required high levels of capital investment and increased operating costs, such that, in 2004, only fourteen slaughter facilities were provincially licensed. Conversations with staff from the Ministry of Agriculture and Lands revealed that by 2010, only 37 licensed facilities existed across the province, from an estimated 400 that existed before the new regulation, each of which had served between 200 and 400 farms and ranches.

In keeping with the dominance of small family farms in the B.C. agricultural landscape, the average cattle herd in B.C. is fifty head and the average sheep flock is thirty to forty ewes. Although the poultry industries in B.C. are regulated under national supply-management systems, which limit production by assigning a quota to individual producers, the B.C. Chicken Marketing Board (BCCMB) and B.C. Turkey Marketing Board each have programs allowing producers to raise birds for their own consumption (200 chickens and/or fifty turkeys per calendar year), or for small-lot agriculture (3000 kg chicken and/or 300 turkeys) without owning quota. These micro-scale producers depend on a traditional custom processing, cut-and-wrap system that is flexible, and often mobile, to meet consumer demands for high-quality local meat and specialty services such as organic, halal or kosher processing.

One study of the impact of the new meat regulations on the North Okanagan Regional District demonstrated the crushing impact of these regulations on local meat production (Johnson 2008). In the North Okanagan, the three remaining large-scale licensed abattoirs do not undertake custom processing of poultry, limiting their intake to large-scale input from the supply-managed system. Five custom processing facilities, which processed

55,000-70,000 chickens and over 5,000 turkeys per year, have shut down as a result of the licensing changes, leaving over 800 poultry producers without access to a local slaughtering facility. Four of eight custom processors for red meat processing also closed.

Now, when they can get space in a facility, small producers face higher slaughter, transportation and waste disposal costs — all leading to lower profit margins, lost revenues, possibly lost farm status and reduced livestock production (Johnson 2008: 5). Those facilities attempting to become licensed also confront an extremely complicated and contradictory process involving up to eight major government agencies including the B.C. Centre for Disease Control (BCCDC), Canadian Food Inspection Agency (CFIA), B.C. Food Processor Association (BCFPA), and the B.C. Ministries of Agriculture and Lands (BCMAL), Environment, and Health. Each of these agencies pursue their own, evolving regulatory requirements. Producers often receive conflicting and/or delayed information from the various agencies, and the cost of compliance to upgrade facilities to meet the new standards ranges from $150,000 to $300,000 (Johnson 2008). Given that many custom processing facilities are small, family-owned enterprises that process a limited number of animals for local consumption, these costs are prohibitive.

Fish Farms — Allowing the Extinction of Local Salmon?

On the one hand, inadequacies in provincial land use restrictions and standardized health regulations have limited the flexibility and creativity of B.C.'s small farmers who are oriented to production for local food systems. On the other hand, government inattention to the social and environmental impact of large-scale and export-oriented commodity sectors has had devastating effects on local food systems. One key example of this can be found in the system of open-cage farmed Atlantic salmon on the B.C. coast, over 90 percent of which is controlled by three Norwegian companies. Farmed salmon has been B.C.'s largest agricultural export since 2005: the industry now employs almost 3000 workers, including many workers in First Nations communities. Although proponents of salmon aquaculture emphasize the benefits of job creation and export income, critics note that as wild salmon stocks fall, equal (or greater) numbers of jobs have been lost in artisanal fishing operations, wild fish packing and processing jobs, and tourism. For example, whale-watching operations in coastal B.C. have observed significant declines in orca whale and other populations that depend on wild salmon stocks for food, while recreational fishing operations that depend on tourism have also seen a decline in business.

A number of studies now provide evidence that fish farming in B.C. contributes to the erosion of wild salmon runs throughout the province, primarily via the infestations of sea lice, which are transferred to out-migrating wild juvenile salmon (Frazer 2009; Krkosek, Lewis et al. 2006). The decline of salmon runs has serious implications for Indigenous food sovereignty in the region (see Chapter 6). As a result, the Government of Norway, a major shareholder in the Cermaq corporation's salmon operations on the B.C. coast, has been criticized by some First Nations groups for failure to comply with the U.N. Declaration on the Rights of Indigenous Peoples. In a 2009 Press Release, Chief Robert Joseph, hereditary chief of the *Kwicksutaineuk Ah-kwa-mish* First Nation, stated:

> The demise of wild salmon... reflects the demise of our culture, way of life and spirituality. Since the advent of salmon farming in our territories we have seen an apocalyptic decline in the state of our wild salmon stocks in the Broughton Archipelago. And because Norway is the world leader in salmon farming and the Norwegian Government is the leading shareholder in Cermaq we are asking for their moral leadership to bring about best practices and to mitigate environmental degradation. (KAFN 2009)

Fish farm escapes are problematic as well. When fish farming was first introduced into B.C., assurances were made by both the aquaculture industry and the federal Department of Fisheries and Oceans (DFO) that Atlantic salmon cannot interbreed with Pacific salmon. The fact that they can, after all, interbreed, threatens biodiversity and the sustainability of the Pacific fish while also introducing them to diseases for which they have little in-bred resistance.

Despite these challenges to salmon aquaculture, including indicators of poor environmental health, limited levels of employment (fish farming's 3000 jobs are less than one percent of B.C.'s agricultural jobs), and lost revenues to local economies due to the export of aquaculture revenues, the B.C. provincial government and DFO continue to support present and future open-net salmon aquaculture.

Challenging Pro-industrial Agriculture and Food Bureaucracy from the Grassroots

Civil society organizations and social movements are working to strengthen local food systems in direct response to the structural policy contradictions of B.C.'s neoliberal food regime. For example, responding to producer resistance to the Meat Regulations, in the spring of 2010, the B.C. government introduced two additional licences, designed for small producers, to allow direct sales to consumers and secondary food establishments (restaurants and meat shops) in rural communities that do not have a fully licensed facility. The provincial government has also provided some money to the B.C. Small Scale Processors Association (BCSSPA) to help several abattoirs to come up to the standards set by the Meat Regulations. Growing social movement opposition to fish farms has led to delegations of B.C. fish farming activists meeting with the Norwegian Government (Frazer 2010) as well as to new labelling initiatives that allow restaurants and fish markets to certify their catch as sustainable. Good examples of sustainability labelling are B.C.'s Oceanwise sustainable seafood certification program, and a new Ecotrust Canada initiative for seafood traceability that will allow all seafood to be tracked back to the vessel on which it was caught (Ecotrust n.d.).

Food-based organizing in British Columbia has strong roots in the social history of cooperative movements for social and environmental justice. Farming and consumer cooperatives, dating back to the late nineteenth century, in the dairy and orchard sectors have been succeeded by organic grower and land cooperatives that link producers to consumers in diverse regional networks. In the 1970s and 1980s, food and sustainable farming were integral components of community organizing for social and environmental justice. For example, spurred by the "back to the land" movement, resistance to the Vietnam war and a growing search for alternatives to the industrial food system, the East End Food Cooperative (EEFC) in Vancouver opened in 1975, and is active today with over 4000 members (BCICS n.d.). Fraser Common Farm, a land cooperative, was founded in 1976 to link the country to the city: today it hosts Glorious Organics, a workers' cooperative that has been active since the mid 1980s in producing organic food for direct sales to consumers, restaurants and farmers' markets.

The growing range of civil society movements working for sustainable agriculture and healthy food systems continues to build upon a tradition of cooperation between the sustainable agriculture movement and the growing field of community nutrition. Despite the absence of federal and provincial leadership on food security, they continue to work for change. Shortly after the publication of his book *From Land to Mouth* in 1989 (Kneen 1989), Canadian author and food systems activist Brewster Kneen spoke with and inspired several community nutritionists in B.C. to develop a food policy for the province. The nutritionists were also inspired by the creation of Toronto's Food Policy Council (TFPC) in 1991. Around the same time, in 1993, the non-profit group FarmFolk/CityFolk was created to support sustainable community-based food systems, and began to work closely with Community Nutritionists, Oxfam and others to develop food-related programs and services across the province. This growing local food movement was further consolidated in October 1995 when a *Food Security: Action and Policy* Conference that brought together international, national and local policy analysts and food activists was convened in Vancouver.

By the early 2000s, food policy was firmly on the agenda of a wide range of community, farmer and consumer organizations, culminating in the creation of the Lower Mainland Food Coalition (LMFC) in 2002. The group defined a mandate, developed goals, agreed on a plan of action and prepared a background/briefing document entitled *Closer to Home: A Recipe for a Community-Based Food Organization* (LMFC 2003). This document addresses the key challenges of land preservation, hunger and food security, sustainable agriculture, economic and community development and human health. Importantly, the LMFC — whose core members include farmers, nutritionists, media personnel, researchers and citizens working on food issues in the community — also called for the development of Community-Based Food Organizations (CBFO) as vehicles to facilitate and advocate for:

- local procurement of food for institutions
- healthy school and hospital food
- Official Community Plans (OCPs) and by-laws that include food security and sustainable agriculture provisions
- contributions to public health legislation
- attracting small-scale food processors
- support for farmers' markets
- the development of a cooperatively-based, small business-oriented economic development model for food production and distribution.

The LMFC received support and funding from Health Canada, the Vancouver Agreement Food Task Team and the groundbreaking Growing Green Project, a two-year law, policy and regulatory reform project focused on sustainable food systems for southwestern British Columbia. Growing Green's goals were threefold: to develop practical recommendations for law, to reform policy and regulations in strategic areas and to strengthen the capacity of voluntary sector organizations to contribute to agri-food policy development. These developments in food advocacy led the Vancouver City Council to take several actions: they passed a motion to create a Food Policy Task Force in July 2003, created a Vancouver Food Policy Council in late 2004 and adopted the Vancouver Food Charter in February 2007. The charter proclaims Vancouver's commitment to "the development of a coordinated municipal food policy," and identifies several principles for a "just and sustainable food system": community economic development, supported by a reliance on locally based food systems; ecological health; social justice, focusing on food as a basic human right; and collaboration and participation through citizen engagement (City of Vancouver 2007). Finally, the city of Vancouver has engaged in a number of initiatives to assess urban food security in the municipality, including a comprehensive report that outlines the process of building a system for measuring food security in Vancouver (Joughin 2010).

These conversations and actions at the community and local policy levels are clear evidence of the growing awareness and importance of food sovereignty initiatives in B.C. Discussions of the theory and practice of food sovereignty as an alternative to the neoliberal food regime are emerging more explicitly, particularly in the gatherings of the B.C. Food Systems Network (BCFSN), which connects food policy activists from across the province with farmers, nutritionists and municipal and provincial policy makers in discussions around strengthening provincial food production and access to food. The BCFSN has also supported the Working Group on Indigenous Food Sovereignty (WGIFS — see Chapter 6).

Structural Obstacles to Food Sovereignty

British Columbia's geographic landscape provides a solid foundation for food sovereignty, with its wide variety of soil types and micro-climates providing for a diversity of foods that can be grown, fished, gathered and harvested within the bioregion. But, as we have demonstrated, a contradictory policy landscape presents a set of real challenges to implementing sustainable local food systems. A desire to support local food production, however expressed in policy, faces significant structural obstacles that effectively inhibit the expansion of local food systems. As the B.C. Healthy Living Alliance (BCHLA) concluded in *Healthy Eating Strategy* (2007), there is "no reliable system in place that makes B.C.-grown foods readily available to B.C. families" (20). While single programs that attempt to improve access to local foods at a reasonable cost do certainly exist, such as cooperative buying and "Good Food Box" initiatives, they face problems of limited supply of local food and program sustainability.

In many ways, producers and consumers in British Columbia find themselves in an evolving global agro-food order that has emphasized commodification and relocation of food production and consumption (Friedmann 1994; McMichael 2009). As Lockie and Goodman (2006: 102) argue, a "neoliberal rationality underlies a totalizing discourse of universal market rule that is reflected in attempts to impose uniform prescriptions for restructuring — based on economies of scale, specialization and entrepreneurialism — across otherwise diverse productive spaces." The British Columbia food production landscape can thus be characterized as a "post-productivist" countryside (Marsden 2003), where competing regulations and land use plans have begun to replace previous forms of food production and consumption. The result is a "contested countryside" (Marsden 1998), in which a growing interest in local food cultures and food sovereignty occurs within a context of neoliberalism that discounts the value and possibility of local production. The B.C. provincial government has followed the federal lead in supporting the agricultural policies of export-oriented production and "get big or get out" corporate concentration. The contradictions challenging the implementation of a food sovereignty paradigm in British Columbia are thus tied to the underlying principles of global agricultural restructuring, which include international harmonization of export-orientation principles and the standardization and homogenization of food products. Regulation and land-use policy, based on the notion of facilitating integration into export-oriented markets, has weakened the protection of agricultural land producing for local and regional consumption, and has instead supported marketing tools oriented towards expanding production of export-oriented crops like blueberries, cranberries and greenhouse vegetables. Failure to protect local fisheries from the environmental and social damages posed by farmed salmon is another example of an export orientation that has damaged not only traditional First Nations fisheries, but the future viability of wild salmon stocks along the entire B.C. coast. Finally, both the salmon and meat regulation cases demonstrate that provincial and federal governments are willing to ignore scientific evidence that the corporate concentration and deregulation of export-oriented food production harms local communities and environments.

Institutional insularity leads to contradictory agendas within the various levels of government in B.C. On the one hand, Canadian regulatory agencies are given mandates both to promote export-oriented agricultural programs and to regulate them (Royal Society of Canada 2001). Industry Canada, Health Canada and the Canadian Food Inspection Agency all play a role in both regulating and promoting cross-border meat and salmon aquaculture processing and export regulations, while other ministries, including Environment, Department of Fisheries and Oceans, and Agriculture and Lands, deal with other aspects of food production regulation and monitoring. But each of these institutions, as large bureaucracies, do not deal well with cross-sector communication, on the one hand, or with the diverse demands and strategies for food production emanating from the grassroots.

At the same time, local actors within the growing movement towards food sovereignty contest the ongoing imposition of limited, market rationalities by arguing that food is not a commodity. Extensive community-based research on food access and production in B.C. has shown that a wide range of foods oriented towards the diversity of local cultures, tastes and preferences cannot reliably be produced in an increasingly industrialized, mechanized and individualized system that severs existing connections between producers, consumers and the natural environment (BCHLA 2007; BCMAL 2007; Condon, Mullinix et al. 2010; Dietitians of Canada 2010; Gregory and Gregory 2010; Ostry and Morrison 2010). A sustainable local food system instead requires a variety of integrated policies that recognize the importance of multi-functionality and diversity of farm size and production strategies. It will involve enforcing regulations on preserving farmland, while at the same time creating flexible regulations on food safety and processing that allow a diversity of producers to sell food in their own regions.

Notes

1. We would like to thank Chris Bodner, Rachel Elfenbein and Melanie Sommerville for helpful comments on an earlier draft of this paper.
2. For an interesting comparison of future scenarios of sustainable agriculture and food self-reliance across Canada, see Van Bers and Robinson (1993).
3. This statistic is for 2006. See <http://www4.hrsdc.gc.ca/.3ndic.1t.4r@-eng.jsp?iid=34>.
4. Depending upon definitions, between 3 and 5 percent of B.C. land is considered arable.
5. <http://apps.bcac.bc.ca/buybc/index.html>.
6. In 2010, the provincial government embarked on a wide-ranging review of the Agricultural Land Commission, following several high-profile cases where commission members appeared to personally benefit from successful exclusion applications (c.f. ALC 2010).

References

Agriculture and Agri-Food Canada. 2008. *Growing Forward Agricultural Policy Framework*. Ottawa: Agriculture and Agri-Food Canada.

ALC (Agricultural Land Commission). 2010. "Agricultural Land Commission Review of Boundary Adjustment Subdivision within the City of Chilliwack." Burnaby, BC: Agricultural Land Commission of British Columbia.

____. 2007. "Agricultural Land Commission Annual Business Report. — 2006/2007." Burnaby, BC: Agricultural Land Commission of British Columbia.

Alexander, Lawrence, and Rod McCrae. 2002. "Agri-Food Foundation Paper." Vancouver: West Coast Environmental Law.

B.C. Healthy Living Alliance. 2007. *BC Healthy Living Alliance Healthy Eating Strategy*. Vancouver: BC: Healthy Living Alliance.

BCICS (British Columbia Institute for Cooperative Studies). n.d. "Stories of the BC Co-op Movement." Victoria: British Columbia Institute for Cooperative Studies. At <bcics.org/resources/galleria>.

BCMAL (BC Ministry of Agriculture and Lands). 2010a. "Growing Forward." Victoria: British Columbia Ministry of Agriculture and Lands. At <agf.gov.bc.ca/apf/GF_Programs_Mar31_2010.pdf>.

____. 2010b. "News Release: BC Agriculgure Exports Rise in 2010." Information Bulletin 2010AGRI0006-001603, Dec. 24, 2010. Victoria: British Columbia Ministry of Agriculture and Lands. At <www2.news.gov.bc.ca/news_releases_2009-2013/2010AGRI0006-001603.htm>.

____. 2008a. "News Release: BC Agriculture Plan Goes Local for Global Benefit." Abbotsford, BC: British Columbia Ministry of Agriculture and Lands. At <www2.news.gov.bc.ca/news_releases_2005-2009/2008AL0004-000208.htm>.

____. 2008b "Service Plan, Ministry of Agriculture and Lands, 2008 Budget." At <bc-budget.gov.bc.ca/2008/serviceplans.htm>.

____. 2007. "British Columbia Organic Industry Overview " Victoria: British Columbia Ministry of Agriculture and Lands.

____. 2006. "B.C.'s Food Self-Reliance: Can B.C.'s Farmers Feed Our Growing Population?" Victoria: BC Ministry of Agriculture and Lands.

Burkinshaw, Gregg. 2010. "Profile and Outlook for the BC Agrifood Industry." Vancouver: Business Council of British Columbia. At <bcbc.com/Documents/2020_201004_AgriFood.pdf>.

Campbell, Charles. 2006. "Forever Farmland: Reshaping the Agricultural Land Reserve for the 21st Century." Vancouver, BC: David Suzuki Foundation.

City of Vancouver. 2007. "Vancouver Food Charter." Vancouver, BC. At <vancouver.ca/commsvcs/socialplanning/initiatives/foodpolicy/policy/charter.htm>.

Condon, P.M., K. Mullinix, A. Fallick and M. Harcourt. 2010. "Agriculture on the Edge: Strategies to Abate Urban Encroachment onto Agricultural Lands by Promoting Viable Human-Scale Agriculture as an Integral Element of Urbanization." *International Journal of Agricultural Sustainability* 8, 1–2.

Connell, David J., Teresa Taggart, Kyle Hillman, and Adam Humphrey. 2006. "Economic and Community Impacts of Farmers Markets in British Columbia: Provincial Report." British Columbia Association of Farmers' Markets and School of Environmental Planning, University of Northern British Columbia, Prince George. At <unbc.ca/planning/localfood/>.

Dietitians of Canada. 2010. "Healthy Eating and Food Security: Promising Strategies for BC: A Discussion Paper." Vancouver: Dietitians of Canada. At <bchealthyliving.ca/healthy_eating_and_food_security_discussion_paper>.

Ecotrust Canada. n.d. "From the Pacific to your Plate." At <ecotrust.ca/fisheries/from-pacific-your-palate-0>.

Fairbairn, Madeleine. 2010. "Framing Resistance: International Food Regimes and the Roots of Food Sovereignty." In H. Wittman, A. Desmarais and N. Wiebe (eds.), *Food Sovereignty: Reconnecting Food, Nature and Community.* Halifax/Winnipeg: Fernwood Publishing.

Feitelson, E. 1999. "Social Norms, Rationales and Policies: Reframing Farmland Protection in Israel." *Journal of Rural Studies* 15, 4.

Frazer, L. Neil. 2010. "A Visit to Norway." Farmed and Dangerous. At <farmedanddangerous.org/uploads/File/blog_files/A_visit_to_Norway.pdf>.

____. 2009. "Sea-Cage Aquaculture, Sea Lice, and Declines of Wild Fish." *Conservation Biology* 23.

Friedmann, Harriet. 1994. "Distance and Durability: Shaky Foundations of the World Food Economy." In P. McMichael (ed.), *The Global Restructuring of Agro-food Systems.* Ithaca: Cornell University Press.

Government of Canada. 2006. "Canada's New Government Cuts Wasteful Programs, Refocuses Spending on Priorities, Achieves Major Debt Reduction as Promised." Ottawa. Report no. 2006-047, September 25.

Gregory, N., and R. Gregory. 2010. "A Values-Based Framework for Community Food Choices." *Environmental Values* 19, 1.

Johnson, Brigitt. 2008. "Impact of the Meat Inspection Regulation on Slaughter Capacity in the North Okanagan Regional District." North Okanagan Regional District: North Okanagan Food Action Coalition.

Joughin, Barbara. 2010. "How Food Secure Is Vancouver in a Changing World? 2010." Vancouver Food Policy Council/Fraser Basin Council/SPEC Vancouver.

KAFN. 2009. "Press Release: KAFN Urge Cermaq to Embrace the Spirit and Intent of the UN Declaration on the Rights of Indigenous Peoples." March 19. Kwicksutaineuk/Ah-Kwa-Mish First Nation. At <huffstrategy.com/MediaManager/release/

KAFN/31-12-69/KAFN-urge-Cermaq-to-embrace-the-spirit-and-intent-of-the-UN-Decla/1616.html>.

Kneen, B. 1989. *From Land to Mouth: Understanding the Food System*. Toronto: NC Press.

Krkosek, Martin, Mark A. Lewis, Alexandra Morton, L. Neil Frazer and John P. Volpe. 2006. "Epizootics of Wild Fish Induced by Farm Fish." *Proceedings of the National Academy of Sciences of the United States of America* 103, 42.

Lockie, Stewart, and Michael Goodman. 2006. "Neoliberalism and the Problem of Space: Competing Rationalities of Governance in Fair Trade and Mainstream Environmental Networks." *Research in Rural Sociology and Development* 12.

LMFC (Lower Mainland Food Council). 2003. *Closer to Home: A Recipe for a Community-Based Food Organization*. At <ffcf.bc.ca/gg_new2/PDF%20and%20linked%20documents/Closer%20To%20Home.pdf>.

Marsden, Terry. 2003. *The Condition of Rural Sustainability*. Assen, The Netherlands: Royal Van Orcum.

____. 1998. "New Rural Territories: Regulating Differentiated Rural Spaces." *Journal of Rural Studies* 14, 1.

McMichael, Philip. 2009. "A Food Regime Genealogy." *Journal of Peasant Studies* 36, 1.

McNaney, Kevin. 2007. "Holding the Line on Sprawl: Farmland Protection and Livable Communities in British Columbia." In W. Caldwell, S. Hilts and B. Wilton (eds.), *Farmland Preservation: Land for Future Generations*. Guelph, ON: Ontario Farmland Trust.

Merenlender, A.M., L. Huntsinger, G. Guthey and S.K. Fairfax. 2004. "Land Trusts and Conservation Easements: Who Is Conserving What for Whom?" *Conservation Biology* 18, 1.

Morton, Brian. 2008. "B.C. Farmers Earning Less: Profits Plummet as Fuel and Feed Costs Soar, Survey Finds." *Vancouver Sun* May 26.

NACC (North American Competitiveness Council). 2007. "Enhancing Competitiveness in Canada, Mexico and the United States: Private Sector Priorities for the Security and Prosperity Partnership of North America (SPP)." Ottawa, ON: Canadian Council of Chief Executives.

OMAFRA (Ontario Ministry of Agriculture, Food and Rural Affairs). 2008. "Ontario Expands 'Buy Ontario' Campaign." *Fruit and Vegetable Magazine* June 24.

Ostry, Aleck, and Kathryn Morrison. 2010. "A Health and Nutritional Evaluation of Changes in Agriculture in the Past Quarter Century in British Columbia: Implications for Food Security." *International Journal of Environmental Resources and Public Health* 7.

Pechlaner, Gabriela, and Gerardo Otero. 2010. "The Neoliberal Food Regime: Neoregulation and the New Division of Labor in North America." *Rural Sociology* 75, 2.

____. 2008. "The Third Food Regime: Neoliberal Globalism and Agricultural Biotechnology in North America." *Sociologia Ruralis* 48, 4.

Penner, Derrick. 2008. "Price of farmland soars." *The Vancouver Sun,* May 23.

PHSA (Provincial Health Services Authority). 2009. "Local Governments Key Partners in Local Meat Production." Victoria: British Columbia Provincial Health Services Authority. At <phsa.ca/NR/rdonlyres/0F878134-ABD7-4652-A30C-738297CE68D1/0/LocalGovernmentsKeyPartnersinLocalMeatProduction.pdf>.

Schrier, Dan. 2009. "Exports-May 2009." Victoria, BC: BC Stats. At <bcstats.gov.bc.ca/pubs/exp/exp0905.pdf>.

Smith, Barry E. 1998. "Planning for Agriculture: Resource Materials." Burnaby, BC: Provincial Agricultural Land Commission.

Statistics Canada. 2006. "Farm Data and Farm Operator Data Tables." 2006 *Census of Agriculture* At <statcan.ca/english/freepub/95-629-XIE/2007000/tables_menu.htm>.

Royal Society of Canada. 2001. "Elements of Precaution: Recommendations for the Regulation of Food Biotechnology in Canada." Ottawa: Health Canada; Canadian Food Inspection Agency; Environment Canada.

Thompson, Matt. 2010. "Making the Global Local: Exploring the Impacts of Global Overshoot, Peak Energy and Food Insecurity on British Columbia." M.A. thesis, School of Community and Regional Planning, University of British Columbia, Vancouver.

Van Bers, Caroline, and John Robinson. 1993. "Farming in 2031: A Scenario of Sustainable Agriculture in Canada." *Journal of Sustainable Agriculture* 4, 1.

Wittman, Hannah. 2009. "Community Farms in BC: Building Local Food Systems for Sustainable Communities." Vancouver: FarmFolk/CityFolk.

APPENDIX

Policy Recommendations for Developing an Inclusive Canadian Agricultural Policy

Participation of Farm Women

1. That AAFC, in conjunction with farm women's organizations and existing farm organizations with structures to promote women's participation and representation:
   - Require all input to agricultural policy development processes to identify and address gender issues and impacts.
   - Build a policy development process that, within four years, includes and responds equally and equitably to farm women's needs and vision for agricultural policy.
   - Ensure that all AAFC staff receive gender-sensitivity training and that training is updated regularly.
   - Provide funding to support the enactment of the federal plan by requiring that within four years, all farm organizations, commodity groups and businesses providing input to the development of agricultural policy develop and implement a strategy to achieve gender equality and equity in organizational structure and policy content. To qualify for funding support to achieve this goal, organizations will need to develop and enact strategies and policies that substantially increase women's participation and leadership in the organization.

Policy Development Process

2. That AAFC, with existing farm women's and farm organizations:
   - Undertake a community-based participatory process to develop an inclusive farmer-friendly agricultural policy development process.
   - Negotiate a realistic time line for developing agricultural policy, one that respects the seasonality of farming, the competing priorities that farmers must balance (e.g., off-farm employment) and the very limited finances farmers have to fund lobbying efforts on their behalf.
   - Provide farm and farm women's organizations with that time line.
   - Ensure that any changes in the time line are renegotiated at least six months in advance of the original time.

Farmer Participation in the Definition of Policy Goals

3. That AAFC, with existing farm women's and farm organizations:
    - Use community-based processes to define the goals and objectives that farmers and rural communities want a gendered Canadian food and agriculture policy to achieve.
    - Develop mechanisms to share these goals and objectives with other governments and government departments whose initiatives operate in or affect rural communities.
    - Engage in a grass-roots process to develop segregated marketing and distribution food chains.
    - Research, define and implement size-appropriate regulatory requirements.

Ensure Fair Compensation for Production and Labour

4. That AAFC, with existing farm women's and farm organizations:
    - Research and define market strategies by which farmers can be fairly compensated for legitimate production costs, receive a fair return on investment and earn an income equivalent to that of urban families.
    - Develop mechanisms by which identified farmer-friendly market strategies can be implemented and expanded.
    - Track the distribution of consumer dollars in food prices by developing criteria defining what constitutes "fair distribution" of profit among players in the food chain, establishing consequences for non-compliance, implementing the plan and monitoring compliance, and disseminating results with the general public.
    - Define and determine what constitutes a fair price for particular farm inputs and whether farm input prices are fair.
    - Determine and monitor compliance, and implement consequences for unfair pricing.

Redistribute Power and Control

5. That AAFC, in consultation with existing farm women's and farm organizations:
    - Identify and act upon opportunities to increase fairness in international trade. One way of doing that is to support strongly farmer-friendly production and marketing structures in international trade negotiations, and encourage the development of similar strategies in other countries.
    - In conjunction with existing national farmers' organizations, research and develop legislative and regulatory mechanisms to limit

vertical integration in food-related industries, thereby increasing competition.

- Support the participation of existing farm organizations and movements in having a legitimate place, voice and influence in international forums where agricultural policies are discussed and decided.

Environmental Stewardship

6. That AAFC in conjunction with existing farm women's and farm organizations:
   - Establish research funding for existing farm and farm women's organizations to partner with academic researchers to investigate the comparative quality of food produced under different farming systems; calculate the real costs and benefits of small-scale, organic and conventional agriculture; determine the value of farmers' environmental stewardship and responsible production practices; investigate methods by which farmers can be fairly compensated for environmental stewardship and responsible production practices; select the most appropriate remuneration strategy and develop an implementation plan for remunerating farmers for environmental stewardship; and enact and monitor the plan.
   - Co-fund a plan to remunerate farmers for environmental stewardship, together with other federal departments and provinces.

INDEX

ACKNOWLEDGEMENTS

This book is dedicated to all those in Canada who struggle for food sovereignty.

The book is the result of an exchange of ideas and ongoing debates that started in late 2008, when we gathered together at the University of Saskatchewan for a workshop on food sovereignty. The workshop, which brought together researchers, farmers and activists, was generously hosted by St. Andrews College and the National Farmers Union.

We wish to acknowledge and thank a number of people and institutions that helped make this endeavour possible. Financial support was provided by the Social Sciences and Humanities Research Council of Canada, Simon Fraser University and the University of Regina. Special thanks go to Martha Robbins for logistical support in organizing the workshop. We would also like to thank the graduate research assistants who lightened our workload and inspired us with their dedication to food justice: Chris Hergesheimer, Christina Bielek, Rachel Elfenbein and Jennifer Thomas at Simon Fraser University; Yolanda Hansen and Naomi Beingessner at the University of Regina and Terran Giacomini at the University of Guelph. Finally, many thanks to Wayne Antony for his interest, enthusiasm and support, and to the staff of Fernwood Publishing, particularly Beverley Rach, Eileen Young, Debbie Mathers and John van der Woude for seeing this collective project through to final production.